CW01649085

The Cast-Off Kids

By the author of *Four Waifs on our Doorstep*

The Cast-Off Kids

Trisha Merry

with Jacquie Buttriss

SIMON & SCHUSTER

London · New York · Sydney · Toronto · New Delhi

A CBS COMPANY

First published in Great Britain by Simon & Schuster UK Ltd, 2016
A CBS company

1 3 5 7 9 10 8 6 4 2

Simon & Schuster UK Ltd
1st Floor
222 Gray's Inn Road
London WC1X 8HB

www.simonandschuster.co.uk

Simon & Schuster Australia,
Sydney

Simon & Schuster India,
New Delhi

A CIP catalogue record for this book is available from the British Library

Paperback ISBN: 978-1-4711-6144-5
Ebook ISBN: 978-1-4711-3853-9

Typeset in the UK by Hewer Text UK Ltd, Edinburgh
Printed in the UK by CPI Group (UK) Ltd, Croydon, CR0 4YY

FSC www.fsc.org MIX Paper from responsible sources FSC® C020471

Simon & Schuster UK Ltd are committed to sourcing paper that is made from wood grown in sustainable forests and support the Forest Stewardship Council, the leading international forest certification organisation. Our books displaying the FSC logo are printed on FSC certified paper.

To my precious family and all of the foster children who made it possible, I want to dedicate this book to you.

Contents

1.	A Rocky Start	3
2.	Dalek!	15
3.	Bush-Baby	27
4.	Promises	37
5.	Skip-Boy	47
6.	A Steal a Day	56
7.	Fire, Fire!	65
8.	Disturbing the Doves	78
9.	A Terrible Shock	91
10.	Real Elephants	103
11.	Gone Missing	112
12.	The Milkman's Tale	122
13.	Fetch the Police!	135
14.	Piggy-Bank Raid	144
15.	Expelled	152
16.	Revenge	159
17.	Jekyll and Hyde	173
18.	Taking Ten to Bournemouth	184
19.	Psycho	198
20.	Sex on the Rockery	209
21.	The Porn Film Kids	217
22.	Down the Chute	228

23. Mystery Illness 236
24. The Awful Smell 243
25. Porch-Boy 251
26. Scarpered 261
27. A Man on a Mission 270
28. Cold Comfort 282
29. The Bombshell 290
30. Clinging On 301
31. Setting Fire to the Past 310
32. A New Memory Box 324
33. Finders Keepers? 333
Acknowledgements 343

1

A Rocky Start

'Can you take two new children this afternoon?' asked the voice on the phone.

I crooked the receiver to my shoulder and carried on bottle-feeding our newest foster-baby. 'How old are they?'

'They're sister and brother. A girl of two and a boy of one.'

'Oh,' I gulped. 'That will make it eight children under five.'

'If that's too much for you to manage, Mrs Merry . . .'

'No, no. That'll be fine.' I made a mental note to put an advert in the village shop for a part-time helper. 'Any idea what time they'll arrive?'

'About two o'clock. Their father will bring them along with the social worker.'

'Oh, that's unusual. Do you know why they're coming into care?'

'No, I'm afraid not. I'm just the messenger.'

A standard reply. I shrugged as I put the phone down – we weren't supposed to know anything, but it was always worth a try.

There wasn't much time to get everything prepared for these two newcomers, and my husband Mike was doing overtime at his engineering works that Saturday. So, after putting baby Katie down to sleep, I phoned Val, a very good friend, to come and keep an eye on the toddlers in the playroom for a couple of hours, while I made up a cot and a bed in our smallest bedroom. I often put newly arrived siblings together for their first night or two, to help them settle in.

'I bet you sometimes wish you'd stayed in your nine-to-five office job, don't you?' said Val, as we sorted out the children's lunchtime mayhem.

'No, never for a moment! I couldn't stand office work, so seeing that poster for childminders seemed like my perfect way out. Mind you, I didn't expect it to develop into fostering – that sort of crept up on us when the local authority needed more help!' I laughed. 'This is my perfect job. I just play all day long.'

'And cook and wash and change nappies and . . .' Val grinned.

'Well, I never think about all that,' I said. 'It all gets done.'

Val glanced at the clock. 'It's nearly two now, so you go and look out for the new children's arrival and I'll take care of all the others.'

It was a hot, late summer's day, so I opened all the windows wide to create a through-draught as I waited in the hall, wondering why it was the father who was bringing the children. What had happened to the mother? My imagination went into overdrive, as always. Maybe she was having another baby, or was ill, or had been in a car crash . . . or maybe she had died young. I hoped not. Would I have to be the one to tell the children? It often fell to me to break bad news, and it never got any easier.

Just after two, I heard a car pull up outside, so I watched out of the hall window. A young woman, presumably the social worker, got out accompanying a pale-faced little girl with straight blond hair in a short, angular cut. The woman plonked the toddler's feet on the pavement, where she stood still and put her thumb in her mouth; then she leant into the back of the car and this time picked up a baby, whom she carried towards the house. She called over her shoulder and the forlorn little girl trailed dutifully behind.

As I opened the front door and stood on the doorstep to welcome them in, a lanky young man emerged from the car. He looked no more than a teenager, with his baggy, black T-shirt and dark, shoulder-length hair that looked as if it hadn't seen a drop of shampoo for months. He hung well back behind them, carrying a battered sports bag, sauntering slowly, with his eyes down. Yet, despite his evident reluctance to be here, I remember thinking this young dad had a bit of a swagger about him.

The baby boy's head had a thin covering of straight ginger hair, and his neat little face was bright red as he wriggled about in the social worker's arms. It must have been nearly thirty degrees, and he was dressed in a polo-neck woollen jumper, with a nylon jacket on top, its elasticated sleeves gripping his wrists. Just seeing him dressed like that made me feel hot and prickly. No wonder he was agitated.

By contrast, the little girl was wearing a light, sleeveless summer dress and plastic sandals.

'Hello,' I welcomed them, with a wide smile and my warmest voice. 'Lovely to see you.'

The boy, so small he could only just have turned one, fidgeted to get down. Meanwhile, the girl stood still and fixed me with her sombre gaze. Not a flicker of a smile. On the surface, she seemed unusually self-contained for a child of two, particularly in this situation, though I don't suppose she knew what was happening. Underneath it all though, I detected her inner fear and distrust, like a stunned, day-old calf without its mother.

'This little fellow is Paul,' said the young woman. 'And this is Daisy,' she added, taking the little girl's hand and helping her up onto the front doorstep. 'I'm Judy, their social worker.'

'Come in, come in.' I stood back to let them through. 'You look hot. The playroom is full of children already, and they're all being well looked after, so come into the kitchen where it's cool.'

'I'll go and put the kettle on for us,' I said. 'Or would you prefer something cold? And what do the children like to drink?'

'I don't know,' said Judy, shaking her head. We both looked at the young dad, but he just pursed his lips together and shrugged.

I took a couple of beakers out of the cupboard, filled them with cold water and a splash of blackcurrant juice, screwed on the lids and handed them to the two little ones, who took them eagerly and drank several gulps each. Then I passed round the biscuit tin.

'Do you mind if I take off Paul's jumper?' I asked. 'He must be sweltering in that.' We all looked at the baby's face, bright red against his ginger hair. Neither of the adults replied, so I changed him into a T-shirt from the top of the ironing pile.

His cheeky smile was enough thanks, as he took out a drum from the toy-chest and started to bang it. After a few beats, Judy skilfully prised the drumstick away from him and took out a car for him to play with instead. 'Brrm, brrm,' she sounded, as she showed him how to move it.

He laughed and copied her, sending it clattering across the tiles, then speed-crawling after it.

'I wish I had that much energy!' I laughed. 'I bet he'll soon be running around.'

'Yes. He's just had his first birthday, so I'm sure he'll be mobile in no time.'

'He looks mobile enough already,' I grinned. 'Look how he's climbing up onto that chair.' It was true. Paul easily scaled the rungs onto one of the kitchen chairs, then stood up against the table and tried to pull himself up onto it. I dashed over to stop him falling off.

'Yes. He's quite a handful, isn't he?' Judy agreed.

I lifted him down onto the floor, with a few more cars to play with. 'I can see I'm going to have to keep a close watch on this scrambly daredevil,' I said, laughing at his impishness.

'Daisy was two in June,' added Judy. 'They're very different personalities. Daisy is much quieter.'

I turned to the silent young man with the sullen look, who seemed quite detached from us all. There was something creepy about him that put me on edge.

'And you're the children's dad?' I asked.

'Oh, sorry,' exclaimed Judy, looking flustered. 'I should have introduced you. Yes, this is Rocky.'

'I'm glad you're here, Rocky. I'm sure it will help the children to settle in.'

I wasn't sure, of course. If only he could be a bit more engaged with them – even play with them. But there seemed to be no warmth in this young dad. He was like a left-over spare part, that didn't fit.

'I can't stop long,' he muttered, as he leant down to unzip his sports bag. He opened out the sides and pushed it along the floor towards me. 'I've got their clothes in here and everything's clean,' he said in a cocky voice.

'Oh good.' I nodded with a smile. 'Did you wash them all yourself?' I was determined to get him talking a bit if I could. Judy gave me a disapproving look, but I ignored her.

'No,' he admitted, with a barely concealed grin, as if he found that idea funny. 'No, it wasn't me. Their grandmother did all their washing. They stayed with her for a few weeks every now and then, but she just couldn't manage them any longer. In between it was mostly me looking after them, off and on.' He paused. 'Their mum walked out after Paul was born, when Daisy was just turned one. So they don't remember her.'

At that moment, Paul stood up and tumbled awkwardly, so Judy went over to pick him up. I took advantage of her temporary preoccupation to probe for more information. It was the only way to find out anything, because I knew Social Services would never tell me.

'So you can't keep them yourself?' I asked.

'No. I'm a chef,' he explained, with an air of pride. 'Mostly in Swindon.' He paused. 'But I have to move around with work and stay in digs, so I can't have them with me . . . and there's nobody else.' For just a moment, his body drooped in on itself and he had a vulnerable look in his eyes. 'I don't know what else to do.'

'Yes, it must have been difficult,' I agreed. 'I hope you'll be able to visit the children when you can?'

'I'll try,' he half-agreed, hanging his head. 'But it won't be easy.'

'Well, just let me know when you want to come.' I turned to the social worker. 'Will that be all right?'

'Yes, fine. As long as he lets you know beforehand.'

I wrote down our phone number on a piece of paper, which he stuffed in the back pocket of his jeans. I wondered whether he would ever look at it again.

I took Daisy's hand and carried Paul as we went along to the playroom to join the rest of the children, with Judy right behind us and Rocky lagging further back.

'Let's have a look at the toys,' I said, as I sat on the floor with our newcomers, leaving Judy to go through the forms with Rocky.

I had a lovely group of children at that time. Sheena, aged three, came and took Daisy's hand to join her and four-year-old Chrissy, our eldest foster child, playing with some dolls. Paul crawled in a bee-line across the floor, heading straight for a red tractor. He picked it up and brandished it triumphantly, next to our other three boys, playing with a farm.

Both Daisy and Paul seemed happy enough for now, without even a glance towards their father. Children coming into care didn't often have a parent with them, but when they did, they tended to be clingy. Not these two. They seemed wary of him. And having been moved around so much, between family members, perhaps they had gained some resilience along the way.

Judy sat on the sofa next to Rocky, whose legs twitched up and down with impatience as she explained the forms to him and gave him a pen. Rocky didn't hesitate for a moment before signing his children away into our care. I did think that strange. I wanted to ask him more questions, but I knew the social worker would have stopped us. Foster parents weren't allowed to know anything back in the 1960s.

Once he'd signed the forms, Rocky was clearly keen to go, but he realised Judy wasn't yet ready to leave. He sat back and half-heartedly gazed out of the window as his children played, like a prisoner eager for his release. At one point, both Daisy and Paul came over to him, sitting on either side to show him their toys, but he failed to engage with them. I yearned for him to take an interest and give them cuddles, but no. They were just three separate souls in a line on the sofa, till the two children gave up and drifted away.

At that moment, I wouldn't have left a dog with Rocky.

'I need to get back,' he said to Judy. 'I'm working tonight.'

'OK,' said Judy, giving me an apologetic look.

'Come and say goodbye to your dad, kids,' I said, picking up Paul and taking Daisy's hand to walk across the hall to him. Rocky looked embarrassed and hesitated.

I thought for a moment that he was going to refuse. Maybe he thought any affection would be bad for his image.

'Bye-bye, Daddy,' said Daisy, as if trained for this scene, which I suppose she was.

That did it. He gave in, crouched down and gave them both a brief hug. They clung a little too long for his liking, so he carefully unentwined himself from them. 'See you soon, kids.' He turned and left. I took the children to the front doorstep to wave, as Rocky and the social worker drove away in the car, but he didn't even turn his head to look.

We all sat round the long wooden table in our kitchen for the children's teatime. I was coaxing Daisy and Paul to try dipping some fingers of toast into their eggs, when Mike arrived home from work.

'Hello, kids,' he said with a cheery grin, unfazed by the two new faces he didn't recognise. It was a running joke for us that Mike never knew when he left for work in the morning how many children he would come home to – who would have gone and who else would have come. He never turned a hair. He always loved our chaotic houseful of children, in which almost nothing was ever predictable.

He took off his jacket and sat himself down at the table, taking over baby Katie's bottle feed, while I went to get out a big tub of ice cream from the freezer to cool everyone down. Meanwhile, Paul sat in his high chair, throwing crusts at partially-sighted Brian, who valiantly felt around and managed to pick one up and throw it back, unexpectedly scoring a bullseye on Paul's nose. I waited for the wail, but Paul just giggled. It was clear that he felt quite at home already. As for Daisy, I could see she was much more reserved. She seemed to take an interest in the older ones' banter across the table, but she sat slightly apart, silent and still.

While Mike watched them finish their tea, I took Rocky's old sports bag upstairs to unpack before bedtime. It was full of clothes and scratchy, grey nappies (they would have to go); pyjamas and wash bags. Even a hairbrush. But no toys or books or cuddlies. Not one favourite thing.

So I found a couple of furry animals in my secret store – a rabbit with floppy ears for Daisy and a bright yellow teddy for Paul. I put them next to their pillows, for them to find at bedtime.

'Come on, kids,' I called downstairs, mainly for Mike's benefit, so that he could round them up and send them to me, while I ran a big, bubbly bath for them to play in. We washed them by turns – Mike doing the baby baths and me doing all the rest. I did the baths in shifts – first the girls and then the boys, with bubbles, bath toys and the mini sprayer for their hair. While I washed them, Mike dried and nappied the little ones and the older ones tried to dry themselves, with a little help from me.

The more children we had, the more chaotic bathtime became. It was like a production line. Everything was. Especially eating and bedtimes. But I loved it – I absolutely loved every moment of it. Fostering was a joy, although we definitely needed some help. It was time to put that ad in the village shop and cross my fingers for a fairy godmother to apply.

After baths, we had group bedtime stories, then off to their own beds. Daisy and Paul lapped it all up, Daisy quietly and Paul with more gusto. 'Night-night,' I said as I plonked a kiss on each of their foreheads and tucked them in, both holding their new cuddlies. I tiptoed out and listened in the night-light's dim glow. They didn't say a word and within minutes all I could hear was the heavy breathing of sleep.

'The two new ones seem like good kids,' said Mike over supper that evening.

'Yes, Daisy is quiet and rather subdued – I'll keep an eye on her. Paul is very different – he's already making his presence felt!'

'Yes, I noticed,' agreed Mike with a grin. 'Do you know anything about their circumstances?'

'They came with their young dad – very detached. The sort that would probably be a swaggery jack-the-lad with his friends, but he didn't want to be here. There was something shifty about him. I don't know whether he has a criminal record, but I wouldn't be surprised.'

'Do you think he would harm the children?'

'I don't know. Probably not, but I wouldn't leave him alone with them.'

I told Mike about their mother abandoning them, and how their grandma too couldn't keep them. 'And now their dad can't manage them either. They're like cast-offs.'

'Do you think he'll come and visit them?'

'He said he would when he can. But I'm not so sure.'

'Poor kids. I hope he doesn't let them down.'

2

Dalek!

Sunday was another warm day, but showery. We always tried to take all the children out somewhere together on Sundays, so after everyone had finished their breakfast Mike asked, 'Who wants to go and feed the ducks?'

'I do,' they all shouted out in unison.

'I'll hold the bread,' offered four-year-old Chrissy, the eldest.

'Can we have an ice cream?' pleaded Ronnie, a few months her junior.

'They don't sell ice creams at the duck pond!' Mike laughed.

'Good job too,' I added. 'You can have ice cream after lunch if you're good. Right, everyone get in a line. Let's put your welly-boots on first, so you can jump in the puddles, but we don't want anyone getting their feet muddy near the edge of the pond.'

'We might fall in!' Ronnie always hoped for something exciting to happen.

'I don't like it where the grass is squishy,' three-year-old Sheena made a face.

'That's where the ducks do their pooh.' Ronnie giggled.

Mike finished squeezing them into their boots while I tore up some slices of bread into paper bags, and gave them out to the older ones.

''Snot fair,' moaned little Peter, who used to be the shy one, but was getting braver now. He glared at the others. 'They got more than me.' A tear started to trickle down his chubby cheek.

I calmed him down and off we all went down the lane. Mike went off first with the walkers and I followed a few moments later with the big pram for baby Katie and toddlers Brian and Paul. We rounded the bend just in time to see two-year-old Peter fall headlong across the muddy grass.

'Yuk,' yelled Ronnie with delight.

Peter sat up and wailed. Chrissy tried to help him up, but fell over him instead.

By the time we got back home again, everyone was covered in mud. Oh what fun!

After lunch it had stopped raining and the sun was out again, so they all ran outside to play in the garden while I rocked baby Katie to sleep in the pram. Chrissy encouraged Daisy to join in with her and Sheena in the Wendy house, while Paul hooted and laughed as he was pulled all around the garden in a large cardboard box with a bit of rope threaded through by Ronnie. That kept both of them happy until the box gradually fell apart and Paul landed in a puddle.

* * *

First thing Monday morning, before the children were awake, I wrote out a quick advert to stick in the village shop's window.

Mother's helper wanted part-time.
Evenings and weekends.

I added our phone number and tucked it into my bag for later. Right now I needed to feed and change the little ones, get the others up and dressed, then set out the children's breakfasts and a cooked breakfast for Mike.

After only two nights, Daisy and Paul had settled in so well that no one would guess they were new. I was beginning to see their characters coming out now – very different from each other. Even at two, Daisy was a dainty, thoughtful and rather serious little girl who didn't like things to be untidy, but I could already see she had a will of her own and wasn't afraid to stick up for herself if she had to.

Paul, on the other hand, was as lively as a bag of monkeys – a happy-go-lucky little boy with an infectious laugh – nothing seemed to faze him.

Once they were all up, washed, dressed and fed, I put babies Katie and Paul top and tail in the pram, then Brian on the seat, as before. The other five had to hang on – one at each end of the pram handle, one on each side, holding on to the apron flap, and one in front, holding on to the hood. In this way, I took the lot of them down to the village. It was a slow process, and quite tricky down the bank at one point, but we made it without losing or injuring anyone – a bit of a nightmare.

As we reached the flat ground and passed the bus stop, Paul threw his teddy out of the pram, so I put the brake on. Two women, waiting for a bus, glanced at all the children, and the little ones in the pram, then gave each other a look.

As we started off again, the snootier of the two turned to her friend.

'These Catholics – they don't know what contraception is!'

I had to turn away to suppress my helpless laughter as I bustled us all off down the road. If only they knew!

The advert went into the village shop window. 'Do you think anyone will reply?' I asked Ron, the friendly shopkeeper.

'I know just the person,' he said with a wink. 'I'll give her a ring this afternoon.'

Next on my list was the chemist. The doorway to the chemist's shop had an old-fashioned bell contraption that the children loved. If they'd had their way, we'd have been in and out of that door at least six times.

There were quite a few people in the chemist's, including a nun, in black robes down to her feet and a white head-dress. I'd never seen a nun in the village before, so goodness knows where she came from. I checked afterwards, and nobody knew what she was doing there.

I held on to Brian's hand as his eyesight was very poor. He used to wear those round, wire-framed National Health glasses, with glass as thick as bottle-bottoms.

Even with his glasses on, he was always bumping into things. However, he could see solid colours and shapes, as long as they were straight in front of him. The chemist's wife was giving all the children a 'healthy' sweet each from her special jar, so I started picking the things we needed from the shelves.

Suddenly, Brian shouted at the top of his voice. 'Dalek!' He clutched my long skirt in terror. 'No, no . . . Dalek! Don't like Dalek!' He could hardly breathe, he was so frightened.

Meanwhile, the nun had turned round to see what the noise was about, and what she saw was this little toddler staring at her and shouting that unintelligible word. Understandably, she looked horrified, assuming that 'Dalek' might be a swear word. Or maybe she thought we were putting a curse on her!

I was torn between picking Brian up to comfort him, and calming down the offended nun, so I did both, giving Brian a cuddle, while at the same time apologising to the nun.

'I'm so sorry. He didn't mean to be rude. He's almost blind, that's the trouble. He probably just saw you as a black shape.' I paused. 'Do you mind if I just hold him in front of your face, so that he can see you are a real person?' I asked her. 'And then he will stop being frightened of you.'

'All right,' she agreed.

'Look Brian, here is the nice lady you thought was a dalek. Can you see her smiling?'

Fortunately, the nun took her cue and gave Brian a weak smile. 'Hello,' she said.

'Not dalek?' asked Brian, still clinging on to my clothes.

'No,' I reassured him. 'Not a dalek.' Brian relaxed his grip.

'What is this word "dalek"?' asked the nun.

So I then had to try to explain to someone who had probably never watched television in her life. 'Well, it's a kind of metal character on a TV programme. Not a person; more like an alien . . .' I was struggling for words to describe it.

'I don't really understand,' she interrupted my confusion, with a smile that said she was humouring me. 'But it's all right. No harm done.'

Phew, I thought. 'Thank you. I'm sorry we upset you.'

'Please don't worry.' She bowed her head and turned, her robes swishing past us as she walked out of the shop.

As soon as the door closed after her, everyone in the shop burst into laughter.

'Well,' chortled the chemist. 'That was a first on both counts. The first nun in my shop and the first dalek as well!'

I think we made his day.

After that, we carried on down the lane to register Daisy and Paul at the doctor's surgery, then back home again.

By the time we arrived back at the house, and I set to getting the children's tea ready, I was full of hope about the advert in the shop window. I remembered the shopkeeper's confidence that he knew just the person. What a difference it would make to have a helper, even if it was only an hour or two at tea, bath and bedtime. I wondered who this paragon might be.

* * *

Mike had the Tuesday afternoon off, so he took all the children out into the garden, including baby Katie, who was now six months old. She was still suffering the effects of her burn injuries, when her father had poured boiling water on her chest and arm a week after her birth. So Mike made sure she was protected from bright sunlight on her skin. Only the day before, we had heard that Katie's father would be tried the following week, and would probably be sent to prison for two or three years. That might sound long enough to some, but Katie would suffer the scars all her life.

So there she lay in my pram, under the shady apple trees, while all the other children played with the assortment of ride-on and pull-along toys that Mike had got out of the shed for them. It was good to see three-year-old Ronnie pushing little Paul, laughing like mad, on a toddler-trike, while four-year-old Chrissy and three-year-old Sheena encouraged Daisy to join them, rolling small logs to make a 'camp'.

As I was unloading the washing machine, the doorbell went. It was Fay, baby Katie's social worker, popping in as she passed by. We went out to look at Katie, fast asleep in her pram, under the trees.

As if on cue, Katie woke up and looked straight at us, then set off with her hungry cry, trying to eat her little fist.

'She looks well,' said Fay as I lifted her out of her pram and we turned to go back inside.

At the kitchen door, we met three little girls – four-year-old Chrissy leading Sheena and Daisy.

'What are you three up to?' I asked with a chuckle.

'We showed Daisy where we wash our muddy hands,' said Chrissy, holding hers up to show how clean they now were.

'Well done.'

'Come on,' Chrissy said to the other two, with a giggle. 'Let's go outside again.' They scampered down the steps, with Daisy, the smallest, bringing up the rear.

'That little one's a poppet.' Fay smiled.

'Yes,' I agreed. 'That's Daisy. She only arrived a couple of days ago, with her little brother.'

'Well, it looks as if she's made some new friends already.'

'Have you got time to stay for a cup of tea?'

'Not today, I'm afraid.'

I put Katie's bottle to warm, while I comforted her at my shoulder and set all the food out on the table for the children's tea – one-handed.

I knocked on the window for Mike to bring the children in and it was all go for the pair of us, washing hands, sitting everyone at the table or in their high-chairs with their bibs on, making sure they all had the right food and drinks in front of them. By now, Katie was reduced to a pitiful whimpering, desperate to be fed.

'You look like you could do with a hand,' Mike offered, as he took Katie and her bottle and sat down at the table to feed her.

'Quite a few hands,' I agreed. 'That's why I put an ad in the village shop yesterday. Now that we've got nine under-fives, maybe we need someone to help us out. What do you think?'

'Good idea,' he agreed. 'You're the boss.'

We spent the next couple of hours going through the bath and bedtime routines, more frazzled than ever with a six-month-old baby to fit into the schedule as well.

'Are babies more demanding these days?' asked Mike. 'Or are we getting older?'

'Speak for yourself!' I grinned, as we started to clear away the children's tea things, before cooking supper for ourselves.

Just then the phone rang. I looked at the clock. It was half past seven and we were both hungry. It rang again and again as I looked at Mike.

'Don't answer it,' he said.

'I better had. It might be important.'

'Yes, we might have won the pools,' he said. 'Except that we don't go in for them.' He shrugged and carried on clearing up, while I picked up the receiver on its umpteenth ring.

'Mrs Merry?' It was a young female voice, sounding a bit tentative.

'Yes.'

'My name is Lizzie and I'm phoning about your advert for a mother's helper.'

'Oh yes?' I was so tired by now that I'd quite forgotten. 'That was quick. I only put it in the shop window yesterday.'

'Yes, Ron came out and showed me it when I was walking

home from the bus stop.' She paused. 'That's how I knew your name.'

'Good. So are you interested in working a few hours for us?'

'Yes, but I'm only fifteen and still at school, just starting my last year, so I could only come from about half past four to half past seven each evening. And maybe some of the weekend too, if you like.'

'That's just what I need. Your age is no problem, as long as you like playing with noisy children! Come round and we'll have a chat.'

I liked the brightness in her voice, but I wanted to see her with the kids. If she survived that, she could do as many hours as she wanted.

She came the next afternoon. She was a lovely girl and great with the children, so I offered her the job, starting the next day.

She was thrilled. 'I can't wait.'

It was what they call a baptism of fire for her that first evening, with all the kids clamouring to have her feeding or washing them, brushing their hair, giving them cuddles . . . She went home exhausted.

'She was good,' said Mike. 'Do you think she'll come back?'

Lizzie did come back; she kept on coming and she soon settled into our routines and idiosyncrasies. She made such a difference to all our lives. She really got stuck in and got to know all the funny things about the children. They idolised her. She loved it all – mess, bubbles, noise, everything. She was particularly good at getting them ready for bed and calming them down as she read stories to the older ones and sang songs to the babies.

Two or three mornings after Lizzie started, one of the ladies in the village came and knocked on our door.

'Hello?' I said with a smile as I opened it.

'I need to have a word,' she said, keeping her voice to a whisper, and glancing over her shoulder before she continued. I expected the KGB to come round the corner any moment.

'It's about Lizzie Hopkins.'

'Yes . . . OK.' I tried to look suitably serious.

She leant towards me and spoke in little more than a whisper, as if we were conspirators. 'Are you aware that she lives in a council house?'

Somehow I managed to keep a straight face, though I was giggling uncontrollably inside. 'Oh no!' I replied, in a shocked voice. 'Really?'

'Don't worry,' she continued. 'You weren't to know.'

'Thank you for telling me,' I said.

She turned and walked off, nose in the air. I closed the door and at last I could let out the laughter.

I think she thought I was taking her seriously. She probably went away happy that I would be sacking Lizzie immediately. Aren't people funny? I'd seen her before and I knew she lived at our end of the village, which she obviously thought of as the 'posh' end.

Sonnington was a quaint old village, a community of two

halves. And this woman clearly didn't think we should mix with the other end.

But although we lived in a big house, which we needed for all our foster children, in the 'posh' part of the village, we didn't fit the required profile . . . what with all our 'unruly' kids (which they weren't at that stage; they were just normal, lively toddlers) and our unconventional ways. I think they thought I was a hippy, with all my flowing skirts and long curly hair, so that didn't help. But nonetheless, I suppose this snob-woman presumed that even I wouldn't want to employ someone from a council house! If it wasn't so laughable, it would have been outrageous.

'So are you going to give Lizzie the sack?' Mike grinned when I told him about my snooty visitor that evening.

'No way!' I exclaimed. 'The children adore her – she's their Mary Poppins, and ours too. Lizzie is an angel.'

'Yes, she's made our lives a lot easier.'

'And more fun too. I couldn't do it without her now.'

'You're right,' agreed Mike. 'She's worth more than a hundred of Sonnington's posh matrons.' He paused. 'But what if they try to frighten her off?'

'I don't think our Lizzie would frighten easily!' I smiled, hoping I was right.

3

Bush-Baby

One evening, all the children were asleep, Lizzie had gone home and we'd had our supper. Mike put the bins out and I made us a hot drink to take into the sitting room. Much as I loved playing with the kids all day, and even doing the chores for them, this last hour or two before bedtime was always a calm haven to cherish some down time – just the two of us.

I picked up my knitting, while Mike read the local evening paper.

'Oh dear!' he exclaimed, showing me the front page headline:

ABANDONED BABY ON
ASHBRIDGE COMMON

'Poor little scrap,' he murmured.

'But that's only two or three miles away,' I said. 'Read it out. What does it say?'

'Underneath the headline it says "*Newborn baby found under bush*".'

'Really? Was it alive?'

'I don't know. Let me find out. "*An elderly couple were walking their dog across the common, when he ran off. They called him, but he wouldn't come back, so they went after him. As they approached the far end of the common, where their dog had stopped and laid on the ground, they heard a baby's cry.*" '

'So it IS alive,' I said, letting out a sigh of relief.

'Yes.' He read on.

' "*As they reached their dog, he was lying down next to the baby, licking its face.*" Clever dog,' added Mike.

'So their dog found the baby? I suppose he was following his instincts – trying to warm the baby up.'

'Yes. I'm sure that's it.'

'So what did the couple do with the baby?' I asked, impatient as ever. Babies and toddlers were my favourite people. An abandoned newborn baby seemed like the worst kind of crime, to me. But there was also the niggling feeling that the mother must have been desperate to have no other choice but to abandon her baby. Maybe she was under age, or the baby's father was a rapist, or . . .

'It says, "*the baby had been hidden in a grassy hollow, under a leafy bush*". There's a photo of it.' He turned the paper round for me to see.

'Look at that sheltered spot,' I said, reassured. 'Whoever left the baby there must have wanted to hide it but also protect it. Maybe they were confused – perhaps they felt they had no choice, or maybe there were mental health issues . . . but at least the baby was sheltered from the worst of the weather.'

'Yes, except surely it would have died if those people's dog hadn't found it?'

'I suppose so. But this baby didn't die. He or she was meant to be found.'

'Surely they would have left it by a hospital or police station if they had wanted someone to take it in?'

'Are there any more details? Go on.'

Mike found his place again. 'It says: "*The baby was snugly wrapped in an adult's woollen cardigan, inside a pillow case. The couple who found the baby took it back to their car and drove it straight to the hospital.*"'

'Why do they keep calling the baby "it"?' I protested. 'This baby is not a thing – it's a little person. A she or a he. Don't they know?'

'Wait a minute. There's a bit more. Maybe it will tell us . . . "*The police held a press-conference this afternoon, to make a brief statement*",' he continued . . . 'You'll be glad to know it's not an it . . . it's a she – a baby girl. She was found under a laurel bush, so the nurses gave her the name Laurel.'

'Oh, that's a good name. Did the doctors check her over?'

'Yes, it says here that when they took away the cardigan, they found she had a head injury. So they're treating it.' Mike sighed. 'That's all it says about the baby. At the bottom of the article it just says the police have asked for the mother to come forward, in case she needs medical help.'

As I got into bed that night, I couldn't stop thinking about that poor little babe, wounded as soon as she was born. What could have happened? How? Who had placed her under the bush? Would the mother come forward? . . . so many questions going round in my head. And most of all, would she need to stay in hospital, or would they put her into care? Would they ask us to take her? I knew there were a few other carers in our area, but I hoped they would bring her to us.

It was now about two months since Daisy and Paul had arrived at our house, and they had both settled in very well. They never mentioned their dad, or asked when he would come to see them, which was unusual for newcomers.

But that Saturday morning, the morning after we'd read about little Laurel, Rocky rang and asked to visit the next day.

'I'll be there to pick them up at two o'clock,' he said. 'Get them ready and tell them I'm coming.' Never a please or thank you from Rocky. But that was just his brash manner. I knew he didn't mean to be rude. It worried me that he wanted to take them out, but the social worker had said that was OK, so we couldn't stop him.

The next day, after an early lunch, I picked out some clothes from my drawers of spares – a pretty pink dress with embroidered flowers and a full skirt for Daisy; a smart blue and red shirt and shorts outfit for Paul.

'I like this dress,' said Daisy with a smile, as she twirled round to look at herself in the mirror. 'Can I keep it?'

'Yes, of course you can.'

At about ten to two, Daisy and Paul sat themselves on the bottom of the stairs, facing the front door. They wanted to be there ready for their dad when he came. I brought a kitchen chair out to the hall and sat with them, to keep them company, while Lizzie fed the baby and Mike played sponge-ball cricket with the others in the garden.

The children were in quite a state of excitement. Daisy wore a permanent smile as she smoothed out the skirt of her dress. 'Pretty,' she said with a sigh. 'I hope Daddy like it.'

'I'm sure he will,' I reassured her.

We could hear the seconds of the hall clock ticking slowly by. Two o'clock came . . . and went. Five past two, ten past . . .

'When will Daddy come?' asked Daisy, while Paul was clambering up and down the first few steps in his impatience.

'He should be here soon.' I hoped he would, but I had the sinking feeling that he wouldn't. This had happened before, many times, with most of the children I'd fostered. Usually there was some kind of excuse. A phone call, perhaps to say they would be late. Or they would call later to say they'd been delayed or had to go somewhere, which probably meant they'd forgotten to come, or had better things to do. We soon got to know the ones with genuine excuses and those who couldn't be bothered. But the worst thing was when someone didn't even let us know. It was so hard on the children.

I tried to get Daisy and Paul singing nursery rhymes with me, but that didn't work. 'No sing,' pleaded Daisy. It must have been my voice that put them off. The clock seemed to be ticking faster now; quarter past, half past.

'Come on, kids,' I said, trying to sound cheerful and

sympathetic at the same time. 'I expect Daddy's been held up. Let's go out and play with the others. We'll hear the doorbell if it rings.' We used to have a loud outside ringer, with the garden being so long.

'Daddy not coming?' asked Daisy, close to tears, struggling to hold them back.

'Maybe, sweetheart, but I'm sure he will come if he can.'

She could not contain herself any longer. The tears started to flow down her cheeks and I sat with them on the stairs, one either side, with my arms round them. When Paul saw that Daisy was crying, that set him off as well. I dabbed at each of them in turn with my hankie.

'I want Daddy,' sobbed Daisy.

'Dada,' repeated Paul.

'I know,' I said, giving them cuddles.

It was time to take their minds off their dad and try to cheer them up. I had a special cache of new toys for this sort of situation. 'I know what we can do.'

'What?'

'Come on.' I picked up Paul and took Daisy's hand. 'Let's go upstairs. I've got some special toys hidden away. Do you want to come and see what they are? We could play with them if you like.'

'Yes.' Daisy sniffed and tried to wipe away her tears with her other hand. Part of her wanted to come, but her heart wasn't in it. She kept looking back, in case he came. Paul was different. I suppose, at that age, he might only have had a vague memory of his father, or none at all, but he was affected by Daisy's tearfulness.

I took them up to the old sailor's chest in our bedroom, opened it and pulled out some special toys. We played with them for a while, but I could tell that Daisy was still distracted. She kept looking out of the door.

I took them down to join the others, but she insisted on sitting on the stairs again, so Paul joined her.

'Daddy come soon?' asked Daisy.

'No, darling. Daddy won't come now.' A few more tears, but still she sat doggedly on the bottom step, while I took Paul to join the others. Mike looked a bit frazzled, but Lizzie was still playing, while feeding baby Katie. What would I do without her?

Even when tea was ready, it was quite a job to persuade Daisy to come to the table. She ate very little.

Afterwards she went straight back to her place on the stairs. But not for long. It was soon time for baths and bed. I think she would have stayed where she was, if she could, till she fell asleep, so I had to coax her to come up with us. 'Look, sweetheart. Daddy won't come now. It's too late – nearly bedtime.'

Next morning, when the phone rang during breakfast, I thought it might be Rocky, to make his excuses. Daisy obviously thought the same and followed me out to the hall. But when I picked up the receiver, I heard a woman's voice.

'Please could you hold on a moment?' I asked her, then turned to Daisy.

'It's not Daddy, sweetheart,' I said to her. 'It's a lady.'

'Not Daddy?' she looked forlorn.

'No, Daisy'. I shook my head to make it clear.

She plodded slowly back into the kitchen, where Lizzie was helping us that morning. I think it must have been half-term.

'Sorry about that,' I said to the woman on the phone.

'That's all right, Mrs Merry. It's Social Services here.'

'Oh yes?'

'Did you by any chance see an item on the local news a couple of days ago, about a baby found abandoned under a bush?'

'Yes, I did.'

'Well, her name is Laurel and we need a temporary placement for her while we try to find her family. Will that be possible, do you think?'

'Yes,' I said with a smile. I was glad they were letting us have her.

'More often than not, the mother does come forward. But this is an unusual case.'

'Yes, that's what I thought.' I paused. 'They said in the paper that she has a head injury. Is that something that would need treatment?'

'I believe it wasn't as bad as they feared; just superficial, with no fracture or anything. It's been stitched up and Laurel is making good progress. She's still in the hospital at the moment, but the place is surrounded by the press and we need to get her away from all that. Can you take her today?'

'Yes, we'd love to have her. Today will be fine.'

As I put the phone down and returned to the supervised mayhem in the kitchen, I had a brainwave. This would be just the thing to take Daisy's mind off her father's no-show. So I told all the children we would be having another new baby in the afternoon. Then I took Daisy aside.

'And Daisy, I'd like you to help me look after her when she comes. Will that be all right?' I smiled to encourage her.

She paused for a moment, then smiled back. 'Yes please.'

I prepared the cot for baby Laurel and piled up some soft, white nappies, ready for use. Then I took Daisy to choose a cuddly toy from my secret store. She chose a floppy dog and I lifted her up to place it lovingly into the cot.

When the social worker arrived with baby Laurel, Lizzie had all the other children outside in the garden, but Daisy was with me as I opened the door. The social worker handed Laurel over to me and I knelt down for Daisy to stroke the baby's downy hair.

'Soft,' she said, with a sense of wonder in her voice. Then she noticed the white dressing on one side of the baby's head and pointed at it in puzzlement, almost prodding it, but not quite. 'What that?'

'It's where baby Laurel hurt her head. Now it's getting better.'

Daisy nodded solemnly. 'Getting better, baby.'

The social worker handed me some paperwork, full of blank spaces, and left.

'Come on, Daise. Let's take baby Laurel into the sitting room and talk to her a bit, so that she can get used to our voices,' I said.

We sat on the sofa, laying the babe between us and told her who we were.

'I'm Trisha,' I said. 'I'm your mummy for a little while.'

'I Daisy, I your fwiend,' she said proudly.

4

Promises

Six months after Daisy and Paul joined us Rocky rang for only the second time, as if nothing had happened. 'I want to come and see the children.'

'What happened last time, Rocky? You said you were going to come and take them out. You asked me to tell them and get them ready, which I did.'

'Really?'

'Yes. They were all dressed up and ready, sitting on the stairs so they could see you come through the front door when you arrived. I sat with them. We waited . . . and we waited. But you didn't come and you didn't phone. What happened?'

'When was that? I can't remember. I expect I got caught up in something. Maybe I was working.'

'You could have let us know.'

He was silent. I imagined him shrugging his shoulders.

'Look, Rocky. You've got to try and come when you say you will.'

'OK. I'm coming on Sunday afternoon. Three o'clock.'

'Will you definitely come this time?'

'Yes, definitely.'

'Or let us know if you can't.'

'Yes. I swear I will come this time.'

'Good. Daisy and Paul will be really excited that you are coming. They'll sit on the stairs waiting for you in their best clothes, like last time . . .'

'Yes, I know. I'll be there.'

Sunday came, the children sat ready for him. We went through the same build-up as last time, choosing outfits and doing a time count-down.

Three o'clock came and went. They waited . . . and waited, but again he didn't turn up – and no apology or excuse either. Yet again I had to take Daisy and Paul upstairs to bed, crying and upset to be let down so badly.

There were a few more times after that when he phoned to visit over the following months.

'You promise faithfully you'll come this time?'

'Yes.'

But he never did. Gradually they got used to their dad being unreliable. But at least he rang occasionally . . . unlike their mother, who didn't figure in their lives at all. Even Daisy didn't remember her, and I think they almost started to forget about Rocky too. Well, I'm sure Paul did, but Daisy still occasionally mentioned him: 'Do you think Daddy would like this top?'

It was sad for her, and hard for them both to have to watch other children's parents coming to take them out. It was seeing Daisy's solemn silence that hurt me. I always found it difficult to watch a child, especially so young, having to harden gradually every time their mum or dad didn't turn up. If only parents realised. I used to think: *Oh, for goodness sake!*

The one thing that helped ease Daisy's disappointment in her dad, over this time, was her special status in helping me look after our bush-baby, Laurel. Every now and then, she would come and whisper in my ear, 'Baby Laurel hungry', even though she was sleeping soundly, or she would tell me it was 'nappy time'. Often, Laurel would wake only moments after, as if on Daisy's cue, which was very obliging of her.

I showed Daisy how to fold the nappies and let her practise. And sometimes Daisy would sit next to me on the sofa with her little legs stuck straight out, holding the bottle up like I'd shown her, to help feed little Laurel.

Laurel's head wound had healed up now and the stitches were already fading away. Everybody loved her. She was such an easy-going babe, flashing her smile at everyone who came near. But she seemed most content when Daisy was with her. And these were happy times for Daisy too, who was often reluctant to join in with the other children's games, but always happy to 'help' me.

Paul, by contrast, was growing into more of a lovable tyke every day, completely at ease in the only family he could remember.

We had a happy band of children at that time, who all got on well together, apart from the odd hiccups. Chrissy, our eldest, was the first to go to school. Up till that point, she had been a quiet, gentle child, her big blue eyes always smiling, as she helped the little ones with dressing or picked them up when they fell over.

But gradually, as Chrissy settled in at school, she became moody and occasionally tearful. Then her teacher asked me to come in and 'have a word' about her frequent outbursts. I could hardly believe this was the same child. It made me think.

'It occurred to me later,' I said to Mike that evening, 'that it's only since she started school that her birth-mother has come back into her life.'

'Oh yes.' He nodded. 'But shouldn't that be a good thing?'

'Not Chrissy's mum. Every time she has taken her out for the afternoon, Chrissy has had to spend the evening in the toilet. And when I ask Chrissy if she had a good time, she always says she just sat in the pub, eating crisps, nuts and raisins.'

Meanwhile, Katie was thriving and her burn scars were a little less livid now. She had developed dimples and an infectious giggle which charmed us all. Big friendly Ronnie was always the joker, while dancing-girl Sheena was the one who loved tidying up. Sheena and Daisy, just a year apart, shared a room and got on well, but they often played separately. Daisy didn't interact much with the others and tended to enjoy solitary activities, like looking at books, or doing colouring and puzzles.

The two brothers, glum Peter and short-sighted Brian, had been with us for nearly a year now. We were all protective of Brian, especially since the Dalek episode, and they were lovely, well-behaved boys, so we were sad to hear from their social worker that they would be going home in a few days' time. They had originally come to us because their single mother had to have a major cancer operation and had stayed on while she convalesced. Now she had been given the good news. The operation had taken away the cancer, so she wanted her boys back home again.

We had a goodbye party for them, and invited their mum.

'I can't thank you enough for all that you've done for the boys and me,' she said, as she left.

'We shall miss them,' I said. 'They're such good boys and we've had a lot of fun, especially the day Brian saw a dalek!' We had a laugh about that, as we had done when I'd first told her about it.

Finally, one day, about a year after Daisy and Paul had come to us, their dad turned up out of the blue, with no prior notice. But when I opened the door, Rocky was beyond tipsy – so unsteady on his feet that he had to hold on to the wooden upright of the porch. I could smell the alcohol, and I could see his eyes were not quite focussed.

'I've come to see Daisy and Paul,' he said, his voice slurred. 'I want . . .' he stumbled over the words. '. . . to take them out.'

'I'm sure they'd love to see you, Rocky, but you're not in any fit state. I'm sorry, but I can't let you come into the house like that. And I can't let you take the children out if you've been drinking.'

He looked surprised, and forlorn, but he didn't try to deny it. His head lolled and I suddenly felt sorry for him.

'Not without checking with Social Services anyway. Just stay there and I'll ring them. Let's see what they say.'

He made no fuss, just nodded.

I shut the front door, so that he wouldn't be able to hear me on the phone, and I explained to the woman on the other end. 'He's turned up smelling strongly of alcohol; a bit staggery and slurring his words,' I told her. 'He wants to take them out, but I don't think he's sober enough. What should I do?'

'No, don't let him take them out,' she agreed. 'Let me just see . . .' She paused, presumably looking up the case-notes. 'He has the right to see them when he wants, so it's up to you, Mrs Merry. How does he seem? Do you think he's drunk enough to be violent?'

'No-o-o, he still knows what he's doing, just about. And, from what I've seen of him, I don't think he would have the strength to be violent with anybody.'

'Is he too drunk to be with the children, for them to see him like that?'

'No, he's not that bad – a bit wobbly, but not quite falling-over drunk.'

'Well, you can let him in if you think he would behave himself, but it would probably be best if you have another adult in the house with you as well. Could you do that?'

'Yes, my husband is here, and my helper as well.'

So I went back to Rocky, still standing on our doorstep, leaning against the wooden upright. 'It's OK. They said you can come in, as long as you behave yourself.'

He nodded his head and lumbered through the front door. I took him along to the kitchen and made him a cup of coffee, thinking that might sober him up a bit.

'What's the matter, Rocky?' I asked.

'Nothing.' He sat there, with his head down, looking morose. He sipped some of his coffee and let the rest go cold. He obviously didn't feel like speaking, so I just sat with him for a while, watching him as I sewed on a button, waiting for him to recover a bit.

'Can I see the kids?' he suddenly asked.

'Yes, as long as you try to pay them some attention.' I paused. 'They haven't seen you for a long time.'

So we went to the playroom, where I could hear Paul's voice, rising above the rest. Mike was reading his paper as usual, almost oblivious to the children playing around his feet. Lizzie was cuddling baby Laurel, while keeping a watch on Katie, now a toddler pulling herself up, walking along the furniture and trying at the same time to join in the silly card game that Chrissy and Sheena were playing. Meanwhile, Daisy was concentrating hard on threading some wooden beads and Paul was aiming cars to try and knock over Ronnie's precarious tower. We had a couple of settees in there, so we sat down. As soon as Daisy saw him, her face lit up. 'Daddy!' She came and climbed onto the sofa next to him. He nodded his head but said nothing

'Hello, Daddy. Do you like my dress?' As it happened she did have a summer dress on, but it wasn't anything special, as we hadn't known he was coming.

'Yeah, very nice,' he mumbled, giving her a lop-sided smile. When Paul heard what Daisy said, he turned round to see his father. He ran across and pulled Rocky's hand to come down on the floor and play with the building bricks. He didn't so much get down, as slid onto the floor. 'Make a garage, Daddy,' Paul said, passing his dad a large rectangular piece. Rocky hesitated. He turned the brick over in his hand, then balanced it skew-wiff on top of another one, but he seemed a bit unsteady with nothing to lean on, so Mike had to help him get up to sit on the sofa again.

I went back to the kitchen to make sandwiches and cut vegetables into pieces for us all, then called the children to the kitchen table, with Rocky trailing behind. The kids all tucked in with their usual enthusiasm.

'Go on, Rocky. Help yourself. They're for you as well.'

He gave me a nod and put a couple of sandwiches on a plate, eating the middles and leaving the crusts.

'The crusts are the best bits,' I said, making sure the children all heard me. 'Nobody leaves their crusts in this house.'

He paused, then nodded again and ate the crusts.

I tried to encourage him to talk. 'Are you still working as a chef, Rocky?'

'Yes.' At least his slurred speech had worn off.

'Where are you working now?'

'In a pub.'

'In Swindon?'

'No.'

'Near here?'

'Just around and about.' He waved his hand in a vague semi-circle.

It was hard work trying to make conversation with him in this state. I strongly suspected he might have been drinking quite a bit lately. He seemed depressed as well as drunk.

'Are you all right?'

'Yes.'

'I mean, I hope you are looking after yourself.'

'I'm OK,' he said, then added: 'Thanks.'

He didn't seem the brash young man from a year ago. But that was probably what the drinking did to him. I just hoped it wasn't too much of a habit. The children looked up at him every now and then, but they didn't seem bothered that he paid them little attention. I suppose they were just glad that he had come at last, after all those months of not turning up and letting them down so often.

Rocky made no attempt to leave, and I didn't think he was in a fit state to go until the drink had worn off properly, so he had a couple of cups of tea through the afternoon. Mostly, he just sat silently, in a daze. Gradually he became more aware of the children, but he didn't interact with them, so they stopped trying to gain his attention. They were very forgiving of him. Daisy was a quiet, long-suffering sort of child, so she was just content to have him there, giving him the occasional smile, which he rarely returned. Paul, who hardly knew his dad, ignored him for most of the time.

At one point he came over and handed his dad a shiny model police-car. 'You can play with that, Daddy,' he said, and went back to his toys.

'Thank you,' said Rocky, when Paul was nearly out of earshot, turning it over and over in his hands.

It wasn't till the evening, after the children had gone to bed and he sat watching a television programme with us, that Rocky decided it might be time to go. He seemed more or less sober by then, so we thought he should be all right.

I don't think we saw Rocky again for a long time after that. And the children stopped asking about him. But I'm sure that Daisy in particular was disappointed in him, and must have felt abandoned . . . yet again.

5

Skip-Boy

Babies and toddlers were often short-term placements, during a mother's hospital stay for example. Very occasionally, there was a rejection of the baby by the birth parents due to what they considered to be an 'unacceptable' medical condition.

'Can you take a baby with hydrocephalus?' asked the social worker over the phone one morning. 'She was born a few weeks ago and has been in hospital ever since, but now she's ready to be discharged and the parents have chosen to give her up for adoption. Can we bring her to you this afternoon?'

I'd never heard of hydrocephalus, but since she was a baby in need of loving, I didn't hesitate. 'Of course,' I agreed . . . and then, as an afterthought, I asked: 'What is hydrocephalus?'

'Another name for it is water on the brain. She's been having treatment and she's stable now and as well as she can be. She has a shunt which will need to be checked regularly. When the hospital rang first thing this morning, wanting to discharge her, we immediately thought of you.'

'Thanks.'

'I mean that in a good way, of course. I know we don't usually discuss medical matters with foster parents, but in this case, you'll have full support, I can assure you, including instructions and advice for looking after her, and a direct line for medical help.'

'Oh good. I know it sounds stupid, but I'm rather squeamish.' That was an understatement. I even had to ask Mike to take a plaster off a grazed knee! 'I won't have to change dressings or tubes or anything like that, will I?'

'Er, well . . . do you have anybody else in the house who could do that if necessary?'

I breathed a sigh of relief. 'Yes, I have an amazing helper called Lizzie, and my husband too. Would there be any training for them, to know what to do?'

'Yes, I'm sure we can arrange that for them at the hospital. And you'll have a health visitor coming almost daily to make sure all is well.'

'Oh good,' I said again. Then I had a sudden thought: 'Just one thing . . .'

'Yes, I know what you're going to ask. There will be an additional allowance for this baby's medical needs.'

'No, that wasn't what I was going to say.' I was shocked that she would think that. 'Will the parents want to keep in contact?'

'Ah. No, apparently they've not been in to see her since she was taken into the baby care unit, straight after her birth. The only thing they've given her is a name – Gail.

We'll be putting her up for adoption, so you may have her for some time, until that happens.'

Baby Gail arrived that afternoon, her head swollen and misshapen, but otherwise a beautiful baby with big blue eyes, fine blond hair and an adorable smile. Despite her serious condition, she was one of the most contented babies I have ever had. Even when she was hungry, she cried softly. All the other children took to her immediately and she soaked up the attention.

Despite being so young, Lizzie was accepted for training at the hospital, along with Mike, and they quickly learnt to deal with the shunt and anything else that might happen. Lizzie did it most days. She was such a treasure. She took it all in her stride, coming in every morning before school to tend to Gail, and every evening to check her over, before helping with the tea, bath and bed routines.

Soon, Gail was trying to sit up, but we couldn't risk her sitting where she might fall and bang her swollen head, or damage her shunt, so I painted the wickerwork of an old Victorian bassinette we had, like a Moses basket on a stand, and padded it out with lots of cushions tied to the wickerwork all round. With her reins on, she could now sit up safely and watch the other children, while playing with her toys.

A few weeks after baby Gail arrived, I had a call to say that little Katie would soon be leaving us. She was now nearly two years old and into everything, leaving havoc in her wake, but we all loved her. Her father had now been convicted of assault and grievous bodily harm, pouring boiling water onto his own newborn daughter and scarring her for life. Katie's mother had testified against him, under police protection, and he would not be out of prison for a number of years.

Now that her ex-partner was out of circulation, Katie's mother was allowed to have her daughter back. She had visited as regularly as she could afford to, and was overjoyed to have Katie at home with her again, without further threat of harm. The local authority had even re-housed her and helped her change her name by deed poll to make sure.

We did miss Katie when she left, but we were very happy for her and her mother to be safely together at last.

A fortnight later, I had a phone call from my friend, who did a lot of the admin and reception work. She told me about a local school who had called the police to report their concerns about cruelty to a little boy, and they'd also called Social Services as they felt his home circumstances were unsafe.

'I can't tell you his name, of course, but when his teacher asked him why he was so tired and hungry, he told her his dad had thrown him into a skip and he had to stay there all night.'

'That's terrible,' I gasped, knowing how cold it had been. 'How old is this boy?'

'I think he's five.'

'So where is he now?'

'With Social Services I think. I'll let you know if I hear anything else.'

Poor lad, I thought as I put the phone down. Just then, Lizzie arrived and I forgot about it till later, when I told Mike what little I knew.

'He could have died,' I said, as an afterthought.

'Yes, it was cold enough, poor mite. Maybe they'll put him into care,' he suggested with a smile. 'We've got room for another, haven't we?'

Sure enough, first thing next morning, the phone rang. We had finally got another phone installed in the kitchen, so that I could keep an eye on the kids while I was talking.

'Good morning, Mrs Merry,' a male voice said. 'I'm Mark, a case-worker, calling from Social Services. I see from our records that you may have a space available for a neglected little boy we're trying to place on a temporary order. Would you be able to take him?'

'Yes,' I decided straight away, knowing who this probably was, but I couldn't let on. 'When do you want us to have him?'

'Today,' he said. 'The sooner the better. We had to put him in a home with teenagers last night, but that wasn't suitable for him. I could go and collect him and bring him to you within the next couple of hours. Shall we say eleven o'clock this morning?'

'That'll be fine.' As soon as I put the receiver down, I realised I hadn't asked his name, but I'd soon find out.

Luckily, it was a Saturday and Mike was home, so he took all the kids for a chaotic walk, while I cleared away the breakfast things and dashed upstairs to prepare a bed for this boy. I decided to put him in with three-and-a-half-year-old Paul and Ronnie, who was now nearly five, so the closest in age. I wondered whether the new boy would think it beneath him to have a cuddly by his pillow, but I guessed he would bring nothing of his own with him, so I chose him a stocky dog with a black patch around one eye.

As I stood on the front doorstep to welcome our new arrival, I was shocked to see how pale and thin he was. His eyes looked dull in their hollow sockets and his hair looked matted.

'This is AJ,' said the friendly looking social worker. 'He's five years old.'

'Hello AJ,' I said in my warmest voice. 'Come in and I'll find our special biscuit-tin. Do you like chocolate biscuits?'

'Yes,' said AJ with a nod and a wary expression, like a hurt animal. I noticed that somebody had found him a warm jumper, though it was a couple of sizes too big for him and the cuffs had been rolled over at least twice.

I took them into the kitchen first, to let the boy acclimatise, and made him a drink to have with his biscuit. 'Is AJ actually his name?' I asked.

'Sort of,' said Mark, the social worker. 'It's what he answers to. I checked and his full name is Anthony John, but he says nobody calls him Anthony – only AJ.'

'Would you like to go down to the playroom, AJ, and meet some of the other children?' I asked him.

'Yes, OK,' he said with a shrug of his bony shoulders. Even with his clothes on I could see how thin and puny he was. I hoped his carers last night had given him a good hot meal and a long night's sleep.

'I'm afraid we don't have any of his things, any clothes or anything,' explained Mark as we followed the hubbub coming from the children in the playroom.

'That's all right,' I assured him. 'We've got plenty of spares in AJ's size.'

Mark left us once he'd watched AJ settle down to playing with Ronnie and given us the rudimentary paperwork – mostly empty spaces.

The day seemed to pass well for AJ, who ate ravenously at lunchtime before Ronnie and Paul roped him into building a garage and lining up the cars. Then it was teatime and he demolished a big portion of sausages, mash and baked beans.

After tea, while the others 'helped' Mike and Lizzie to clear up the tea-things, I took AJ up to see his room.

'This is your bed,' I showed him.

He immediately picked up the dog. 'Is this mine?' he asked, with his first proper smile of the day, then threw the dog in the air and it landed in the middle of his eiderdown.

'Yes, you can give him a name if you like.'

'Buster,' he said. 'I always wanted a dog called Buster.'

'I'm going to get you some clothes of your own, too,' I said, as I showed him his side of the wardrobe and the two bottom drawers that would be his.

'Thank you.' He looked at me with a solemn gaze. 'Will I be staying here?'

'Yes, sweetheart. I hope you can stay here for quite a while.'

'Good,' he said, trying to hold back the tears. 'I like this bed.'

After bathtime I tucked him up in his cosy bed, clutching Buster. 'Sleep well.' I gave him a peck on the forehead, dimmed the nightlight and half-closed the door, so that I could listen.

'You'll like it here,' said Ronnie. 'We're going to be mates, you and me.'

'And me,' added Paul.

'OK,' agreed AJ. Then silence. He must have fallen straight off to sleep.

'Our new little lad, AJ, looks very underfed, doesn't he?' asked Mike later that evening.

'Yes, but he's already started to make up for that. He ate three fat sausages for his tea, so I'm sure he'll soon start filling out,' I said. 'I'm more concerned about his emotional neglect. I gave him a kiss on his forehead as I tucked him into bed tonight, and he seemed to flinch. I don't know whether he was surprised or dismayed. It was as if nobody had ever kissed him before. It's hard to imagine, isn't it? A mother not kissing her own child.'

'Yes. No wonder he looks so miserable.'

'The other thing . . .'

'What . . . ?'

'Have you noticed his movements? How uncoordinated he seems to be? Almost as if he has a mild case of cerebral palsy.'

'I noticed that he was a bit clumsy today with the building bricks, and there's something odd about his walk,' agreed Mike.

'He seems to get on well with Ronnie, doesn't he? I hope they'll be good friends for each other.'

'As long as Paul doesn't mind the competition.'

'Paul's not like that,' I said. 'He likes a rough and tumble with the boys and they're the only three at the moment.'

'AJ seems a good lad.'

'Never speak too soon,' I warned with a smile. 'He may turn out to have a lot of problems!'

'I don't think so. We'll get some love into him and he'll be fine.'

I hoped Mike would be right, but I wasn't so sure.

6

A Steal a Day

On Monday morning, I trundled the pram and all the children down to the village school as usual. I dropped Chrissy off at her classroom door, then the rest of us all went along to the school office to register AJ, so that he could be transferred to this school as well. A junior teacher came to take him down to Chrissy's class. I wondered how she would react, given her recent moodiness. No doubt we would soon find out.

At home time, we all returned to the school to collect them both. AJ came out first, with his distinctive walk, his knees almost knocking. In fact, seeing him in his school shorts, that's when it suddenly occurred to me . . . his legs weren't quite straight like the other children's. Could it be rickets? No, surely not . . . but maybe a mild form of it? That made some sense, knowing how underfed he had been.

As I waited for Chrissy to appear, their teacher came out to find me.

'Hello, Mrs Merry. I just wanted to come and tell you that AJ has settled in reasonably well today.' She paused, as if planning her words. 'He made an enthusiastic start. In fact, he reminds me of a puppy – all legs and eagerness!'

I laughed. 'That's a good description.'

'I put him at Chrissy's table at first, to help him feel at ease. But that didn't work at all, so I moved him across the room and he was much happier there. It's early days, but I think he's begun to make friends.'

It was a different story when he came out of school the next day.

'I'll come to the point, Mrs Merry,' said the teacher, with a stern yet also sympathetic face. 'We noticed a couple of things go missing yesterday, in the classroom,' she began. 'But they were only minor things that belonged to the school – a box of blackboard chalk and the ruler from my desk drawer. I assumed somebody had borrowed them and not put them back, which may still be the case of course.'

'Oh, right . . .' I said. I could sense there was more to come.

'But today, I found one of the other children crying at lunchtime, because her lunch-box had been raided and nearly everything was missing.'

'Maybe this child's parents left things out by accident,' I pointed out, with my fingers crossed.

'We thought of that,' she said. 'So we rang the child's mum at home and she said that nothing had been left behind. She was sure that she had packed everything in the box herself, and she listed what should have been there, but most of those things had gone.'

'Are you suggesting AJ was to blame?'

'I know AJ was to blame,' she replied. 'I checked his coat pockets and I found the crisp and chocolate bar wrappers in there. When I asked him about them, he said at first they were his. But when I asked him again in front of the other child, he seemed to crumble. He started to cry and then he apologised to her.'

'Did you ask him why he had taken her things?'

'Yes. He just said he was hungry. But then he added another thing, which I thought was quite strange. He said his dad made him do it.'

'Really? We'll have to look into this at home. I'm really sorry about his classmate's lunch. Did she have enough to eat?'

'Yes, we found her some replacements in the staff room,' said the teacher. 'But I'd appreciate it if you could please have a word with AJ tonight and see if you can get to the bottom of this. We don't want it happening again.'

'I will,' I assured her, then gathered my flock from off the climbing frame and left for home.

After tea, when Lizzie had taken the children off to the playroom and Mike was clearing away, I took AJ into the sitting room for a quiet chat. He seemed surprised to be singled out . . . and a little apprehensive.

'Your teacher, Mrs Hughes, told me about the missing lunch,' I began, and paused to see his reaction.

He said nothing, but shifted his bottom round on the sofa, looking away from me.

'What do you know about it?' I asked him directly,

turning him gently back towards me. He wriggled a bit, but looked lost for what to say.

'And Mrs Hughes said that she found the other girl's crisp and chocolate bar wrappers in your pocket.'

'Yes,' he said, hanging his head. 'But I don't know how they got there. Somebody must have put them there.'

'We could talk about this for a long time,' I said. 'But I don't want to take up all your playtime with the others, so why don't you just tell me the truth? Did you take those things out of the girl's lunch box?'

'No,' he insisted, turning his head away. 'I told you . . .'

'Yes, you did.'

Silence . . . and I let it last before saying anything.

'Why did you take them, AJ?'

'I was hungry.'

'You had lots of food in your lunchbox.'

'Everyone takes things,' he said, changing his tack.

'You told Mrs Hughes that your dad made you do it.'

'Yes,' was his sullen answer.

'What did you mean?'

'Well . . . my dad and my mum steal things . . .'

'OK.'

'And my dad makes me steal things too.'

'Really?'

'He said I have to steal something every day, so they can buy me food to eat.' AJ paused. 'I'm not very good at it.' He crumpled up and burst into tears, then wracking sobs, his bony shoulders heaving.

I put my arm round him and held him close for a while,

stroking his straggly hair. Gradually his sobbing subsided as he sat in a limp heap, cuddled up to me. I thought we'd said enough for now. But there was one thing I was puzzled about.

'I heard that someone found you in a skip on Friday. Is that true?'

'Yes.' He sniffed and I passed him a tissue to blow his nose.

'Tell me how that happened.'

'It was my dad. When he came home he wanted to see what I stole that day. But I couldn't, so he got angry. He took me outside and threw me in the skip.'

'Oh dear,' I sympathised. 'Was it empty or were there things in it?

'Nearly empty. Just some bits of wood and old carpet at the bottom. I tried to climb out, but I couldn't reach.'

'Did you call for help?'

'No. My dad beats me if I make a noise. It was dark and I was cold, so I made a little bed out of the bits of carpet and tried to sleep.'

I gave him another cuddle. 'You must have been very cold.'

'Yes.'

'Well you're here now.' I gave him a hug and sent him off to join the others for a short playtime before bed.

Later that evening, I told Mike what the teacher had said at school about AJ stealing, and what he himself had told me about his father and the skip.

'So has he stolen anything from us or the other children?' he asked.

'Not as far as I know. Not yet anyway.'

'Do you think he will?'

'Probably, yes.' I nodded. 'I think it's become the norm for him – something he has had to achieve every day, poor mite. It's turned most people's set of values entirely on its head. We can't expect him to suddenly shun everything he's known as being right and make his mind think of it as wrong. We may have a lengthy process ahead of us . . . if he stays that long.'

'Oh, that sounds too psychological for me.' Mike paused. 'I guess you're right. We'll have to watch him and help him understand . . . And maybe hide our valuables away where he can't find them.'

We sat in silence for a minute or two, neither of us wanting to voice how uncomfortable we felt about the way this situation was making us think.

'It's going to be an uphill climb,' Mike admitted. Do you think we're up to it?'

'I hope so.' I sighed. 'He needs us. We have to help him.'

The term ended without much further trouble, apart from AJ bringing home some of the decorations off the class Christmas tree, pinching a chocolate roll from another lunch-box and taking a Superman figure from a coat pocket in the cloakroom. We had to have words about those. There may have been other things too of course, but in all the end-of-term excitement I suppose they didn't come to light.

The run-up to Christmas at our house, from the beginning of December, was always a very busy time, with our huge tree to decorate in the hall, the paper chains to make and put up and the puddings to mix, with everyone having a stir and a wish.

'I wish I can have a red car to ride in,' said Paul.

'I wish someone would give me a Sindy doll,' added Sheena, with her stir.

'You don't just have to wish for presents,' I suggested.

Daisy took the wooden spoon, her face solemn with thought. As she began to stir, she looked at me and said: 'I want to learn to knit.'

'But you're not even five yet,' said Chrissy.

'I don't need to be five. I can learn,' replied Daisy, pouting stubbornly.

'Does anyone else want to make a wish?'

Chrissy shot her hand in the air. 'Yes, me please.'

They all took a turn and then finally AJ stepped forward. He looked down into the bowl as he began to stir. 'I wish I could stay here,' he said. The room was silent.

I stepped forward and put my arm round him. 'That's a lovely wish, AJ. I hope you can stay as long as you want.'

On Christmas Eve, all the children were hyper with excitement.

By the time they were all in bed asleep, and we'd tiptoed round and snuck little gifts and fillers into everyone's stockings, we were ready for an early night. Mike and I fell into a deep sleep, but it wasn't to last.

Paul burst into our room at one o'clock in the morning.

'Father Christmas forgot me,' he wailed. I'd never heard Paul cry quite like this before. He could be wild and troublesome sometimes, out of sheer exuberance, but mostly he was a ball of lightning with a sunny smile. But it was Christmas Eve and he really thought he had been left out. I took him by the hand, back into his bedroom, which he shared with Ronnie and AJ. I was sure we had left his stocking stuffed full of goodies, just like all the others, but it was completely flat and empty on the end of his bed.

'Maybe Father Christmas has put your presents somewhere else,' I suggested, wiping his tears away. 'Come with me now and you can choose something for you to keep from the secret treasure-chest in my bedroom.'

'OK,' he whimpered, taking my hand.

In the morning, in all the excitement of everyone up before dawn, laughing and smiling as they emptied their stockings out on their beds, Paul was able to do the same. I'd gone back and quietly searched their room, without waking a soul, but I didn't have to look far – I wasn't surprised to find Paul's missing gifts stuffed under the end of AJ's bed.

No wonder AJ looked so amazed to see Paul enjoying his stocking gifts.

'Pop your slippers on and keep your feet warm,' I said to all three boys, but I watched AJ as he knelt down to find his slippers, which I'd kicked under the bed. He stayed down there just a couple of seconds too long, surveying the empty space, and as he stood up again, his eyes widened and his face turned pale.

'Happy Christmas, AJ,' I said with a grin.

He gave me a sideways look, but said nothing. He didn't need to. I knew what he was thinking. I believe he may have guessed what I was thinking too.

Santa was kind to all the children that Christmas and they all played happily together with their new toys. As we approached New Year, we had two spaces in our house. I wondered who we'd have next to fill them.

7

Fire! Fire!

Daisy and Paul had now been with us two and a half years and they hadn't seen their father since the day he'd been drunk. I wasn't sure they even remembered him anymore. Six-year-old Chrissy and five-year-olds Sheena and Ronnie were all still with us. More recently, gangly six-year-old AJ had arrived and joined in with their games, especially with Ronnie – I don't know which of them was clumsier and they always came in muddy, whatever the weather.

Our little bush-baby, Laurel, was a toddler now, at eighteen months old, running around and trying to catch up with the older ones. She was a spunky little thing and rarely without a smile or a giggle. Her thick hair now completely hid the scar from her head injury the day she'd been found. No mother or relative had ever come forward, despite all the publicity, so the police had closed the case and she was now officially up for adoption.

It was six months since newborn baby Gail had joined us and despite her swollen head, caused by the hydrocephalus, having to be protected so much, she was a gentle and contented child, who loved watching the activities going on all around her.

We had a slide and a climbing frame with a net in the garden at Sonnington, and various outdoor toys and games. But what I loved watching best was when they were making things up, making wonderful fun out of very little. Some logs, some string, some old car and tractor tyres, some of which we hung from the trees; old boxes, cardboard tubes for sword-fights, old sheets and sticks to make tents with. They had three acres to run around and play in and all the fruit trees to climb, so they weren't hard work when they were outside.

Come rain or shine, the bigger ones would all be out there whenever they could. And on hot days one of the things they loved best was a good water-fight. They loved spraying each other with a couple of hoses, while the little ones ran and splashed about, screaming with excitement.

The older ones were very caring with the younger children. Most days somebody came running in to tell me 'Laurel's fallen over', or 'the baby's just been sick'. All the kids competed to rush in and do the telling when there was the slightest incident, which they had exaggerated into a major disaster by the time they got to me.

A few days into the new year we were joined by another eighteen-month-old toddler. Alfie was very shy at first and clung on to the cuddly elephant he had brought with him. He took it everywhere and could rarely be persuaded to let it go – even at bathtime. We had to pretend to wash 'Ellie' too.

A few days after Alfie came, we had a call from Social Services and welcomed four-year-old Gilroy, whose mother was something to behold. She told me she had saved Gilroy from a vicious beating from his father,

'He's a brute; he is always attacking us,' she explained. 'Only I couldn't watch him murder my boy.' She shot a quick glance at her sturdy son, who glared back at her.

There doesn't seem much love lost there, I thought. But at least she had protected Gilroy from serious injury, or worse.

'I ran down to the chippy and rang for the police,' she said. 'Fat lot of good they did. Just cautioned the sod. So I had to call Social Services to take Gilroy into care.' She paused. 'It's a good job we only had one child.' She raised her voice. 'And he's nothing but a pain.' I glanced at Gilroy, who looked away, hiding his anguish.

As soon as his mother had left, Gilroy's mood switched to anger as he ran out to join the gang, though I don't think they were too keen on the way he muscled in straight away. I watched him as he went from one child to another, pushing and bullying his way round the garden, until he came to little Alfie, cowering away from him. Gilroy grabbed his elephant and pushed the toddler into a muddy puddle. Then he threw poor Alfie's elephant over the fence. Alfie wailed loudly and the other kids came to his aid. Luckily it had landed on the top of a bush, so our tallest child, Ronnie, piled up some wooden crates, climbed up and just managed to reach it with his long arms. Gilroy kicked Ronnie's leg and ran off surprisingly fast. Luckily, good-natured Ronnie just ignored Gilroy after that, protecting the others as much as he could.

That boy was in a permanent strop from the day he arrived. I could see that his traumatic background and difficult mother would haunt him, and probably us as well, for a long time. Gilroy was the bull in our china shop and shook everyone up. His main pleasure seemed to be to hurt others. But he did gradually settle in and even relaxed a little as he wormed his way into our affections with his jokes and his dramatic exaggerations. Indeed, despite his young age, he dominated almost every situation, always on the lookout for ways to make things worse or unduly alarm people.

So when he rushed in to update me on any minor mishap, it was a major scoop and he made the most of it. 'Ronnie's fallen over. He's hit his head and the blood's pouring out. His eyes look funny. Do you think he's dead?'

I rushed out to find a tiny scratch and a bemused child. 'I only skidded on a wet patch.'

There was never a dull moment at our house, although the neighbours might take a different view of it all.

With our two new arrivals, Alfie and Gilroy, we re-arranged the bedrooms. First we took Paul out of Ronnie and AJ's room and paired him up in a separate room with Gilroy. Paul and Gilroy were the same age, and if any of our children could cope with Gilroy, it was boisterous Paul, who could always hold his own, though I knew it wasn't going to be easy. Luckily Paul seemed to take this change in his stride.

Meanwhile, Alfie shared Laurel's room, being the same age, eighteen months, and both still sleeping in cots. This turned out to be an excellent pairing.

Just when we thought we were straight, we were asked to take in a tiny newborn baby on an emergency placement. We were already full, officially, with ten children, but this was an exception because of the circumstances. During the birth, the mother had some kind of medical trauma and was now in intensive care. So we took in this little babe, just a few hours old. She didn't even have a name yet. We got all the children together in the kitchen to see her for the first time. They all had a 'gentle' stroke of her dark hair, as soft as down, and her little fistfuls of fingers fascinated every one of them, even Gilroy for just a moment.

'This is our emergency baby,' I said.

'What's her name?' asked Chrissy.

'She hasn't got a name yet.'

'Mergey baby!' Alfie blurted out, practising the sound of what he thought I'd said. 'Mergey baby'.

So that's what we called her from then on.

Paul was due to start at pre-school that week, so we enrolled Gilroy as well and they went bounding in on their first morning, scattering everything and everybody. They loved it from the start, but I don't think the other children and staff loved them. I had quite a frosty reception when I arrived to fetch them at the end of that first morning, and it went downhill from there. They caused such mayhem that, only two days later, they were both expelled – Paul for a week and Gilroy permanently.

'We have to think of the other children, Mrs Merry. They were all frightened and some of them were hurt. All the parents were complaining.'

It was a cold winter that year, and we lived in a large draughty house in Sonnington, with no central heating. So we kept a coal fire going all the time through the winter. Mike used to back it up with slack at night, before he went to bed. Then when I got up, early in the morning, I used to go down and give it a couple of pokes to get it going again and put the fireguard back in place when I'd finished, before heating up the bottles for baby Gail and Mergey. When they were ready, I went back upstairs to give them both their first feed of the day. After I'd winded them, changed them and put them back in their cots to play, I went down and made Mike some breakfast. I saw him off to work before going back up to get myself dressed, before anyone else needed me.

On this particular day, as I went out onto the landing again, I noticed an acrid smell, as if something was burning. I remember standing there, torn between going to pick up a crying toddler, or going down to check the fire. But I knew I didn't have any choice.

The smell was much stronger in the hall, and it was definitely coming from the sitting room, so I turned the door handle and pushed it open, at which point the fire gave a huge *WHOOSH* and blazed fiercely as it roared up the chimney. I slammed the door shut again and ran back into the hall, where I picked up the phone to dial 999 . . . just as the front door opened. We must have left it on the latch without realising. There, in the open doorway, stood a tall fireman, all kitted up, complete with his helmet, and sporting a sooty smear down one side of his face. I couldn't believe it. This was surreal. Beyond him, I glimpsed three more firemen on the path outside. I felt quite stupid, standing there with the phone in my hand and my mouth wide open.

'But I haven't even rung you yet!' I exclaimed.

'No need to now,' he said with a grin. 'We're already here. We just finished checking a false fire alarm that went off across the village when we saw the flames shooting out of your chimney. Boy did it go! So we came straight round.'

He tramped his big boots across the hall and into the sitting room. 'Ah yes.' The others all followed him in and they all stood in the room, watching the fire burn.

'Shouldn't you be rushing around with hoses and all sorts?' I asked.

'There's nothing we can do at the moment,' he explained with a reassuring smile. 'Except watch the fire, keep it safe and make sure it doesn't blaze outwards.'

'OK. So, is there anything you want me to do, or shall I just get on?'

'Are you the only one in the house?' asked the man in charge.

'Oh no, no, no.'

'Is there anybody in the rooms above?'

'Yes.'

'Well, the bricks will be getting very hot. You'll need to go and get whoever it is to come down, just in case.'

So up I went, picked up the first baby, Gail, from her cot and carried her downstairs, then stood like a fool in the hall, wondering what to do with her while I went back for the next one. 'Can you take her?' I asked, and passed baby Gail into his arms.

'Please be careful not to knock her head,' I said.

He looked rather incongruous, standing there in full fire-fighting gear, cradling a baby. 'What about your neighbours?' he suggested. 'Could they help?'

'Oh yes.' So we both went round to knock on their door. Luckily she was already up and about, but somewhat surprised when she saw me standing there with a fireman at half past eight in the morning.

'Mrs Clark,' I began. 'We've got a chimney fire blazing away in our house and I need to get the kids out.'

'Here you are,' said the chief fireman with a cheery smile as he plonked Gail into her reticent arms.

'Could you look after her for a few minutes, and be careful not to knock her head, while I go back for the next one?' I said.

'Oh, OK,' she agreed, holding baby Gail rather awkwardly, while giving the fireman a smile.

Of course, I realised, she and her husband had never had any children . . . but no time to worry about that. We rushed back into my house, where I went up and brought down the next one, Mergey, and handed her to the fireman, who looked rather bemused to see another, even smaller baby.

Up I went again, and this time came down with toddlers Laurel in one arm and Alfie and his elephant in the other.

Now the fireman looked at me in disbelief, as I turned to go up for the fourth time.

'How many kids have you got up there?

'Only seven more.'

His mouth dropped open.

'I'd better go and get them. I'll go round and wake them all up and most of them will be able to clamber or walk down the stairs with me this time.'

'I'll come up and help you carry some of them down, just to make sure they don't touch any of the walls.' He looked worried now. 'The bricks get burning hot and they could start an internal fire.'

Now he tells me!

Once the children were all safely round next door, with two of the firemen and Mrs Clark minding them, I phoned Mike and he came back from work. He went straight round and rescued the children, by now all desperately hungry and climbing the walls . . . along with Mrs Clark herself, I should think.

So back they all came, with great curiosity.

'Will the house burn down?' asked Gilroy. 'I hope so.' He sniggered. 'Our bedrooms will be burnt to ashes.'

'Don't be silly,' admonished Chrissy. 'You always exaggerate!'

'Ooh,' said Daisy when they went through the hall to the playroom. She held her nose. 'I don't like the smell.'

'No, sweetheart,' I reassured her. 'It will go soon.'

'What's that you've got in your hand?' asked Mike, prising the sparkly object from AJ's fist.

'I found it on the floor,' said AJ. Mike and I exchanged glances, knowing that was unlikely.

'It's a ring,' I exclaimed. 'You do not take things from other people's houses. I'll have to take you round later to give it back to Mrs Clark and say you're sorry.'

Mike fed, dressed and entertained them all for the rest of the morning, with a bit of help from me, in between making our visitors mugs of tea and coffee, and getting them to help me pull all the upstairs furniture away from the walls.

The firemen were still there at lunchtime, so I rustled up some plates of sandwiches, which they wolfed down like gannets. Paul and Ronnie came into the kitchen while they were sat there, eating.

'Can I try your helmet on?' Ronnie asked one of them.

'Me too!' clamoured Paul. 'I want to be a fireman.'

One of the men put his helmet on Paul's head and it fell right down over his eyes. He walked round bumping into things, which made everyone laugh, including him.

The firemen finally left at about two, when they were sure the fire was out and it was safe for us all to get back to normal.

'It was so funny,' I told Mike that evening. 'You should have seen that fireman's face when I kept on bringing babies and children down.'

'Did you tell them why we have so many children?'

'Oh no. I forgot to mention it.'

A few weeks after the chimney fire, Mrs Clark moved out of her house.

'Did you know she was going?' Mike asked me.

'No, she never said a thing.'

'Do you think it was something to do with us?' he grinned.

I laughed.

'I wonder who we'll have as neighbours next,' he said.

'Well,' I sighed. 'Whoever it is, I hope they like children!'

The following morning, a shiny black Rover car pulled into the drive next door. I held my breath and craned my neck as I stood with a baby in each arm, looking out of an upstairs window to try and catch sight of the new people, but I couldn't see much. A middle-aged couple, the man with grey hair and the woman wearing a head-scarf, walked swiftly to the front door and closed it behind them. There was nobody else with them.

About ten minutes later, while I sat on the window-seat, feeding Mergey, a huge lorry arrived with a classy name written on the side and three men in green overalls climbed out. Whoever these new people are, I thought, they certainly aren't doing this move on a shoestring.

Throughout the day there were comings and goings next door, but I was too busy with the kids' food, laundry and playtimes to look.

Lizzie had finished her studies now and was applying for full-time jobs, so she was able to come and help out with the children for more hours during the week, which was a brilliant support. She made such a difference and I hated to think of how I would manage when she had to leave, which probably wouldn't be long.

Early that evening, while Lizzie was supervising the children's teatime, I nipped next door with a casserole I'd cooked up for the new people.

The door opened and a rather serious-looking woman gave me a curious look.

'Hello?' she said in her cut-glass accent. 'Can I help you?'

'I'm Trisha and I live next door.' I smiled. 'Welcome to Sonnington.' I held out the dish. 'I thought you might like a chicken casserole, to save you cooking on your first night. You must be exhausted.'

'Quite tired, yes.' She nodded, with only a hint of a smile. 'Very thoughtful of you, my dear.' She took the casserole from me and put it down on the tiled floor of her porch. 'Which side are you from?' she asked, looking at the houses on either side of hers.

'That one,' I said, pointing.

'Oh,' she said. 'The one with the untidy orchard?' It wasn't the best start to a neighbourly relationship.

'Yes, that's right.' I nodded. 'We have a lot of children, and they love playing in the orchard.'

'Oh, I hope they won't be too noisy.'

'I don't expect so. They're just normal children, and the orchard is a long way back from the houses.'

'Well, thank you, Mrs . . .'

'Merry, Trisha Merry, and my husband is called Mike.'

'I hope you'll excuse me if I get back to unpacking boxes, Mrs Merry?'

'Yes, of course. Do you want any help?'

'No, thank you,' she replied, a little too abruptly, then picked up the casserole dish and held it out a little way in front of her, as if it were infectious. 'Most kind of you. Goodbye.'

'I hope you'll like living here,' I said as I turned to go.

'Well, that depends,' was her parting shot.

8

Disturbing the Doves

Paul was the stoic of the family, even at a very young age. Quite the little toughie. If he cut himself or grazed his knee, he never made a sound, no matter how much it hurt. He would sit with his lips wavering but clamped together, without complaint.

One morning, when all the children were playing outside, I called them into the kitchen for a drink and a piece of fruit. They came running in as usual, all except for Paul. Oh well, I thought, perhaps he doesn't want to stop what he's doing; though I couldn't remember him turning down a drink or a snack before.

I looked out of the window, down the garden and I couldn't see him, but I saw one of the giant tractor tyres swinging, so I assumed he'd just finished playing with that and had gone off to one of the camps, beyond the large shed.

The children ran off out again, and I thought no more about it. But when I called them in for lunch a couple of hours later, and Paul still didn't appear, I started to get worried. Really worried. He was only three and a half. The garden was surrounded and the gate at the side was bolted, so he couldn't have escaped. What on earth had happened to him?

'Has anyone seen Paul?' I asked all the other kids.

There were blank faces and shaking heads all around the table, so I walked over to the window again. It was an eerie sight to see that same tractor tyre swinging, turning and twisting all on its own. None of the other tyres were moving. It wasn't even windy. What could be causing it? And where was Paul?

'I'm just popping down the garden to see if I can find him,' I said to the children.

'Can we come with you?' asked Ronnie.

'Yes, if you want to.'

So all the boots went on again and off we all trooped, with me in the lead, hurrying towards the swinging tractor tyre.

'Paul,' I called as I approached it. 'Where are you?'

I heard a muffled sound, but couldn't make out what it was.

'Paul?' I called again, just as I reached the tyre and tried to stop it moving. I held on to it and, as it slowed down, I was able to see something move inside.

'I can't get out,' the muffled voice wailed. 'Help! I stuck.'

I reached in and tried to get my hands round him. He felt all hot and sticky, but he was stuck so deep under the heavy rubber lips of the tyre, which had closed in over him, that it was very difficult to lift him; and the tyre kept moving away from me.

'Ronnie, Chrissy, AJ – the tyre keeps slipping away from me. Can you all go round to the other side and push it towards me to stop it?' They were the only three tall enough to do this, so I hoped it would help.

Thank goodness it did. They held the tyre steady, and I was finally able, with all my strength, to lever poor Paul out of the bottom of his dark rubber prison. As I pulled him free, all the children shouted and cheered, then somebody clapped and the others all joined in.

'I couldn't get out,' said Paul. 'I stuck,' he announced to the other children, as if it was a badge of courage. He was so hot and sweaty that his ginger hair was plastered to his head and his face was bright red.

'Poor Pauly,' I said, lifting the wet wisps of his hair to get some air to his skin, then I pulled off his stripey jumper and put him down on the ground to walk around in his vest and shorts. 'That will cool you down.'

'I shouted,' he said, biting his lips to make sure he didn't cry. 'I shouted and shouted.'

'I'm sorry, sweetheart. I never heard you. But we got you out in the end.'

He just gave a solemn nod then ran indoors with the others, as if nothing had happened.

I never noticed any noise from the garden. I suppose there was so much space outside that the sound didn't reach the house. Or maybe I was just used to it. And the kids' behaviour (apart from Gilroy's) was never bad at home, because they were all outside running off their energy, so they only came in for food or sleep through the warmer months. And in the winter we had our big playroom, with masses to do. As far as I was concerned, the kids were a joy.

I used to think up new playthings we could make. One day I bought lots of saucepans and lids in a jumble sale for them to clatter and bang. Then the children helped me put rice or dried peas or even nuts and bolts inside empty plastic containers, stuck together for them to shake.

I joined in with them one afternoon, to make an impromptu orchestra. There we all were, banging and shaking things, playing in this band and making 'music' when Mike came home.

'Bloody hell, Trish!' he shouted as he came round the corner of the house. 'Can't you hear the noise?'

I stopped and listened to the others . . . and he was right. I had to admit, it was an awful racket. So perhaps we were a bit noisy sometimes.

Not long after our new neighbours moved in, the husband threw back a ball over the fence, and then another. And half an hour later, the wife came round to our front door with a third.

'I'm sorry, Mrs Merry,' she began. 'But would you mind please making sure your children stop throwing balls into our garden. They break off the delicate petals and new buds of our roses.'

'Well, I'll have a word with them,' I agreed. 'I'll tell the kids to throw them the other way.'

She looked quite shocked.

'I mean towards the end of the garden,' I explained.

'Oh.' She gave a little nod, and off she went.

Two or three days later, she came round and knocked on the door again.

'Mrs Merry. Some of your children are looking through our fence.'

'Yes . . . ?'

'Erm, we like it private. That's why the fence is there.'

'Right.' I was trying not to laugh. 'But it's a woven fence, so even the littlest ones can see through it.'

'Well, they should know not to look.'

'I'll have a word with the children about it,'

'Thank you.' She turned and strode away. What a moaner! It was true that I had seen them all lined up along the fence one day, peeking through, with little Laurel's bottom sticking out. In fact, she looked so funny that I went in for the camera and took a photo of her, and another one of all of them. I think I've still got those photos somewhere.

A few days later, a couple of men came into next door's garden and replaced the fence with a higher one that had stronger overlapping wooden slats.

'They won't be able to see through that,' she told me when she saw me.

Well, that was what she thought. In fact, the kids soon discovered the knots in the wood and started poking them out to look through. So it was all a lot of fuss and expense for nothing.

One morning, we decided to tidy up the orchard and

have a bonfire but next door had their washing on the line, so I went round to see her.

'I've just come to let you know that we're going to light a bonfire shortly, so you might want to take your washing in.'

'It's immaterial to us,' she said in her snootiest voice, '*what* you do in your garden.'

'Well, we could have lit it, but I thought it was only fair to come and let you know, so that your nice clean washing doesn't get covered in sooty smuts.'

She gave me a look. Then, without saying another word, she shut the door in my face. I couldn't believe it. As I walked back . . . I knew it was petty, but I thought *sod you*, and I blew a raspberry in the direction of her house. That made me feel better!

I went back to our garden and, as I struck the match, I caught sight of her closing an upstairs window and staring daggers at me. I lit the kindling and watched it go, sending black smoke up from a couple of tattered tyres in the middle. I was glad that she rushed out and took her washing in, before the smuts blew over that way.

But what I didn't realise was that, while I'd popped next door, Paul had picked up a plastic ride-on tractor and somehow thrown it up onto the top of the bonfire heap. I didn't notice it until he shouted, pointing at it, with the flames curling up between its wheels.

'Tractor's gone! My tractor's gone!'

'Too late to rescue it now,' I told him. 'Why did you throw it up there?'

'King of the Castle!' he shouted out.

Isn't it funny how children's minds work – doing things on impulse with a real purpose in their minds, but without any idea that there might be consequences.

It wasn't so funny how Gilroy's mind worked, except on this one occasion. I just caught sight of him doing a moony to the lady next door as she stared out of her window at us. She raised her hands in horror, then immediately drew the curtains across from both sides. Gilroy grinned from ear to ear . . . and, turning away from him to hide it, so did I.

As if the kids weren't rowdy enough, we had all sorts of animals too when we were at Sonnington. We had dog kennels and rabbit hutches spaced out between the trees. The dogs occasionally barked during the day, especially when the children were playing with them, and once or twice I heard the cats wail in the night. But I suppose the kids made the most commotion.

Our relationship with our neighbours was on a downward slope and they found fault with everything. The funniest complaint was the day she came round and Mike answered the door. I'm glad it was him and not me.

'Hello,' he greeted her cheerily. 'What can I do for—'

'This noise is going too far,' she interrupted him. 'Could you please stop your children screaming in the orchard?'

'Well, I'll try. But they're just happy kids, using up their energy and having fun.'

'That's not fun,' she said. 'They're doing it on purpose to annoy us.'

'Oh, I don't think so . . .'

'Well, I am asking you to stop them,' she insisted. 'We've got a pair of doves that are trying to mate, and your children are disturbing them.'

'Well' replied Mike. 'I find that surprising. It's never bothered us!'

Ronnie, Chrissy and Sheena were old-timers at school, and AJ had settled in well.

'It's much better than my old school,' he announced one day. 'We can have breaktime snacks at this school.' AJ hadn't forgotten what hunger felt like, so food was always the most important thing for him. We still had the occasional problem of petty thefts in school, and I was always being called in to help sort it out, with all my brood in tow.

It happened at home too, but usually only minor things that we managed to restore to their owners quite easily. AJ couldn't get rid of his need to steal. I suppose it was still too ingrained.

One day, when I checked his bedside table for any stolen loot, I was shocked to find a bracelet I thought I'd lost a couple of weeks before. I'd asked all the children if anyone had seen it, but they'd all said no. I looked everywhere that I thought I might have put it or dropped it, but had to give up in the end. I just thought it was gone.

I don't know why, but I really didn't expect to find it in AJ's bedside drawer. I'd have to have a talk with him that evening.

When the children got back from school, I gave them all drinks and sent the rest of them out to play. 'AJ, you stay with me,' I said. 'I want to talk to you about something.'

He looked a bit uncomfortable, but came and sat at the kitchen table with me.

'I've found something I want you to see,' I began, taking the bracelet out of my pocket. 'This is my favourite bracelet,' I said. 'The one I couldn't find and nobody knew where it was. Remember?'

'Yes,' he shifted uneasily on the chair.

'Do you know where I found it?'

'No,' he replied in a small voice.

'In the drawer of your bedside table.'

'Oh,' he paused, and then tried to cover his tracks. 'I didn't know it was there.'

'Well, that can only mean one thing,' I continued. 'It means that you must have taken it and put it in there to keep.'

He cast his eyes downward and his shoulders drooped. I waited for him to say something, but he didn't.

'Did you used to steal things from your mum?' I asked.

'No, she'd beat me if I did,' he mumbled.

'So why do you steal from me?'

'Because you don't beat people . . . and you're not my mum.'

'But while you're here with us, I'm your stand-in mum.'

He looked up at me. 'No. You're much too nice to be a mum.'

* * *

Daisy had really enjoyed school from the start. She loved learning and she was soon reading proper books. She did make a few friends there, but nobody special.

When Paul started school that year, it was a different story altogether. I think they found him a handful. He couldn't sit still – he had to be on the go. He was as boisterous and mischievous as Daisy was quiet and demure. It wasn't long before the school started to call me in to sort out one minor misdemeanour or another. He never did anything malicious though . . . except for just the once that I can remember.

He was in the Reception class when I had a phone call to go up to the school to speak to Miss Butcher, the headmistress, about Paul. That hadn't happened before, so I felt a bit apprehensive as I got the little ones ready, then off we went to the old Victorian village school.

We all trooped into Miss Butcher's study and sat down.

She looked incredulous. 'Are all these children yours, Mrs Merry?'

'Yes, I am fostering them all.'

'Oh, I see,' she said with what looked suspiciously like a sneer.

I got some small toys out of my bag to keep the toddlers occupied on the carpet and turned to the headmistress.

'What's all this about?' I asked. 'Is it something Paul has done?'

'Yes, Mrs Merry. I'm afraid there's been an incident.'

Just then, an assistant brought Paul in to join us and he sat on the chair next to me.

'What happened?' I asked him.

He didn't answer.

'It seems that Paul went into the toilets and another boy came in,' explained Miss Butcher. 'Apparently he said something to Paul, who didn't like it, so he pushed this boy's head down into the toilet and pulled the chain.'

'Oh dear,' I said, putting on my serious face. I turned to Paul. 'Is that right, Paul?'

'Yes,' he said quietly. 'But it was his fault. He was rude.'

'Well, if he said something that upsets you,' I told him, 'you must go and tell a teacher.'

'Yes, that's right, Paul,' agreed Miss Butcher, looking relieved that I'd said the right thing.

'What did the boy say to you?' I asked, but he refused to say anything. He just sat there looking uncomfortable, with his lips tightly closed.

'I'm afraid I have to ask you to take Paul home with you for the rest of the day, Mrs Merry. I'm sure you understand. It's as much for the other children as it is for him. We cannot tolerate this kind of behaviour.'

'No, I do understand, and I quite agree.' I turned to Paul again. 'You must not do that sort of thing. You could have hurt the boy. You could have killed him. He might have drowned.' I knew I was exaggerating, but I thought it was the best way to make sure he never did it again.

'Sorry,' mumbled Paul, keeping his head down.

After that, most of the times he got into trouble at school were for minor playground incidents. Yes, he was lively, but very lovable too. As for Daisy, her reports were glowing and her school work always neat and tidy.

What a shame their dad showed so little interest in his children's achievements. We didn't even have an address I could send her reports to.

It was Daisy who was more aware of her father's long absences. He would ring up now and then to say he was coming, but he only turned up about one time out of six. However, instead of sitting and crying about it like she used to when she was younger, Daisy just used to say, 'Oh, he won't come.' And she'd go off and read her book or do a puzzle.

For the past few months a lovely young couple had been making regular visits to us, getting to know baby Gail, the one with hydrocephalus. Now one year old, her parents had signed her away at birth, so she was up for adoption and this childless couple had passed through all the hoops and been accepted as adoptive parents. It didn't seem to faze them at all to see the shape of her head, to protect it when playing with her, to treat her like any other child, yet special to them. She soon took to them very well and laughed a lot when she was with them.

Finally, it was time for them to take her home with them, and we gathered all the kids to come and see them off. There were a few tears that day. I noticed Daisy with her arm around little Laurel as they waved. The bond between them was still clear to see, after all the times Daisy had helped me to look after Laurel when she first came. She knew that

Laurel had no parents either, so she must have realised that Laurel too might be whisked away from her, never to be seen again. She was right of course – it could happen; but not quite yet.

'If only some of the other kids could be adopted too,' said Mike that evening, with a glint in his eye. 'What about Gilroy?'

But of course, while Gilroy was a cast-off, like most of the kids we had at that time, and his father was in prison, he still had a mother – even though we hadn't seen her since the day he came.

9

A Terrible Shock

It was four months since we had stirred the Christmas pudding and Daisy had made her wish to learn to knit. So, one drizzly spring morning, I started to teach her. She watched closely, then I helped her get started, one stitch at a time. We'd just finished the first row when the phone rang.

'We have a young baby for you,' said the support worker. 'A little girl called Michelle, just a few weeks old, but very tiny. Can you take her this morning, in about an hour?'

'Yes,' I agreed. 'You said she's very tiny . . . ?'

'She's coming to you from the hospital. She has difficulty swallowing, so she is being fed every two hours.'

'If it's a medical problem, how will I know what to do if she gets worse?'

'We'll give you an information sheet, provided by the hospital, with an emergency number on it, in case of . . .' She paused.

'An emergency?' I asked.

'Yes, that's right.'

It sounded a bit worrying, especially as they never told us the whole story.

It was a weekend and Lizzie was with us that morning, so I gathered up the knitting things, only briefly noticing that there was a knitting needle missing. Where could it be? But I didn't have time to look.

We quickly prepared for baby Michelle's arrival and she was with us within the hour. The social worker had brought a ready made-up bottle, just in case, since we had such short notice. We took in this tiny mite, so light in my arms, and I laid her down in our carrycot. All the children were keen to see her. Chrissie stroked her fine, downy hair, while Paul gently put his finger in her hand.

'She squeezed me,' he said with pride.

They all came to touch her pale skin and watch her taking tiny breaths.

'Gently, Gilroy,' I had to remind him, as he was about to plunge his heavy hand into the carrycot. 'Do it like this.' I showed him, and for once he copied my lead and barely touched the sleeping babe. I wondered how long that would last.

Alfie was so taken with her that he put his cuddly elephant in next to her. 'There you are baby,' . . . and then he had second thoughts and took it out again. 'MY elephant,' he said, hugging it to his chest.

'Don't worry, Alfie,' I said. 'We'll find baby Michelle another cuddly that she can keep.'

Mike took over in the playroom, while Lizzie came with

me to give Michelle her feed. She took it very slowly, with a lot of breathy sounds. She seemed to have difficulty sucking, choking up almost as much as she managed to swallow. When I took the bottle out, I peeked inside her mouth. It looked as if some of her palate was missing, so presumably that was the problem. I suddenly felt faint and had to sit down before I fell. Lizzie took charge while I collected myself together. Why was I still so squeamish, after all these years?

I knew that lots of people have cleft palates and grow up fine, so I tried not to think about it. I changed her nappy and put her down in her carrycot to sleep. I decided to have her in our bedroom to start with, away from over-enthusiastic attentions.

Over the next thirty-six hours she was a quiet baby. I fed her little and often, giving her lots of cuddles, and she seemed to settle in fine the first night, then a similar pattern for the next day and night. She woke me once during the second night and had her bottle, then I laid her back down to sleep.

The third night, I woke up early, as usual, when the house was still dark and quiet, apart from Mike's snoring!

I had a quick peek in the cot, where she lay very still, just as I'd left her, then went down to prepare her bottle. When I came back into the bedroom, I put the bottle down and leant over the cot to pick her up. For barely a second, I remember a sense of foreboding. Then I realised she was too still. I couldn't see any sign of the cover over her little chest rising and falling. I hesitated, then did what I knew I had to do. I reached my hand down to hers. It was cold, and her skin was tinged with blue.

I flinched and screamed. Mike shot out of bed in a moment and came to my side.

'The baby is cold,' I wailed. I could hear myself making this wounded animal sound. 'Please God. She can't be dead! She CAN'T be dead!' I shrieked.

Mike held me and turned me away from Michelle's lifeless body.

I don't remember much about the hours that followed. I know Mike called an ambulance straight away, and while we waited, several of the children came running into our bedroom, having been woken by my screams. Mike took them downstairs and the ambulance came within ten minutes, though it seemed like hours. I do remember sitting on the edge of our bed as I watched an ambulance man gently lift Michelle out of her cot.

'Is she . . . ?' I couldn't bring myself to say the word.

'He nodded, sadly. 'Yes, I'm afraid so.'

I followed him downstairs and out to the ambulance. 'Can't you do something for her? I pleaded hysterically. Can't you resuscitate her?'

'I'm afraid not,' he said in a gentle voice. 'I'm sorry, Mrs Merry, but it's too late. I think she must have died an hour or two ago. The damage was done. I'm afraid we can't help her now.'

I went back into the house. I knew I had to carry on somehow, for the other children. But how could we tell them?

'Mr and Mrs Merry,' said the main ambulance man, coming to find us. 'I'm sorry to have to ask you, but I'm afraid we need you both to come and identify the baby's body, before we can take her away to the hospital.'

So we went back into the ambulance. It was a horrendous task. I can only remember seeing her tiny, naked, blue-tinged body lying in the middle of the white-sheeted stretcher, as if she were a porcelain doll. I shall never forget that image.

As Mike led me back inside, I was in a trance. I could barely think, let alone string a sentence together.

Mike must have thanked the ambulance crew and off they went.

I had never heard of cot death. I don't think people knew about it in those days. I'm usually such a positive, practical person, but I just couldn't pull myself out of the distress I felt over that little baby's death in my care. Nothing like this had ever happened before. It must have been my fault. I knew that would haunt me, but there was no time to dwell on it now.

The first thing we had to do, as the other children were waking up and feeling the tension, was to break the news to all of them, as gently as possible.

I was on my own in the sitting room, trying to take it all in, while Mike got the children up and dressed upstairs. In came six-year-old Daisy, in her pink pyjamas and sat next to me on the sofa.

'I saw the ambulance come this morning,' she told me, almost in a whisper. She shared a bedroom with Chrissy and Sheena, at the front of the house, so all the activity must have disturbed her. 'I looked out of the window and watched them take the baby out.'

'Yes, sweetheart.' I drew her towards me and put my arm round her. Daisy wasn't a cuddly child normally, but she seemed to appreciate being close. I think she felt afraid. 'The ambulance people came to try and make her better,' I said.

'Did they take her away?' Her bottom lip quivered.

'Yes, sweetheart. They took her back to the hospital.' She didn't ask the most important question. Perhaps it didn't occur to her, and I didn't tell her. It would be better to break it gradually to the older children, all together.

So Mike and I gathered them round the kitchen table for breakfast and told them what I had already told Daisy. There were a few tears, and some questions. We knew we had to answer them carefully, without being dishonest.

'Did she cry?' asked Chrissy.

'No. She didn't make a sound.'

'What is it?' asked Sheena.

'We don't know yet. I expect the doctors will do some tests and let us know.'

Most of the children were very quiet as they took this in.

'Poor little Michelle,' said Paul, with uncharacteristic sensitivity.

'Will she get better?' asked Ronnie, always looking for something more.

'I expect she's dead,' added Gilroy. 'They're probably burying her already.'

This was clearly getting out of control. I had to steel myself. 'Baby Michelle is now at the hospital and the doctors are trying to find out what made her ill. Let's not worry too much about her now. She is in the safest place. We'll see what we can find out during the day and I expect we will be able to tell you more when you get back after school.'

There were sighs and tears around the table, but most of the children nodded silently, shrugging off their concerns as they went off to brush their teeth and get ready to leave.

I was glad it was a school day, so I would only have the three younger ones at home with me, and they weren't old enough to understand what had happened. I needed time to try to come to terms with this tragic death myself. I could think about what to say to them all later.

After school, we broke the news more fully, together, Lizzie, Mike and I, so we could give all the children lots of hugs and reassurance.

We told them simply what had happened, that she had been unwell when she came to us and had died peacefully in her sleep, and her little body was as perfect as when she arrived three days before.

'Can anybody die in their sleep?' asked Ronnie, the eldest, with an anxious look.

The others all listened intently for my answer.

'Not unless you are very old. Otherwise people only die if they are already very ill.' Now I know that may not be strictly true, but I had to try and prevent them all worrying that they might die that way, so I felt that was the best answer I could give them.

As I went to bed that night, another wave of shock hit me. I couldn't stop shaking at first, and then I must have fallen asleep. I think I slept through half the next day too.

Sometime in the afternoon, somebody hand-delivered a letter. I found the envelope on the front door mat at teatime. The envelope was handwritten and addressed to me, so I opened it tentatively and read the two pages. Was it my imagination that the blurred ink was tear-stained?

It was only as I read it through the second time that I realised it was from baby Michelle's birth mother. That stopped me in my tracks. I had not given her a thought until I read her letter. It was a beautiful letter, in which she apologised again and again for having put me in such a dreadful position of responsibility for their sick child, and said how guilty she felt for my having had to face such a terrible situation.

I read the whole letter through three times, trying to take it all in through my own tears. At the end she said she would like to meet me, if I was willing, and gave me her telephone number. She told me she had taken a few days off work – compassionate leave they called it.

I mulled it over for an hour or two, thinking how much they must blame me for what happened. Perhaps that was why she wanted to see me. She might accuse me of causing Michelle's death. But as I read it through for the fourth time, later that evening, it seemed to be quite the contrary – she was blaming herself, and that wasn't right. So I rang her and invited her round for coffee the next morning.

When she came, I saw that she was a few years older than me, very gentle and well spoken. We sat down in my kitchen and she told me her story. She had a lovely husband and an older child. She and her husband were both successful professionals and she had planned to have a nanny or an au pair to come and look after the new baby while she was out at work. But when Michelle was born, though full term, she looked so small and frail, and needed to stay in hospital to have special care, so they decided to give her away to someone who could look after her better than they felt they could.

'Michelle died the first time just after she was born,' said Ellen. 'She had a heart condition as well as a cleft palate.'

'Oh, I didn't know that.' I was quite shocked. This was serious. *Why had no one told us? We should have known*.

'They immediately resuscitated her.' Ellen's eyes welled up. 'I know it sounds criminal to say so, but I wish now that they hadn't.'

I drew in a breath and she noticed my reaction.

'You think that's wrong, don't you? I suppose I would too if it was the other way round. How can a mother feel her baby would be better off dead? But it's not like that.'

'No, I'm sure you had Michelle's best interests at heart,' I soothed her.

'But it's true,' she said. 'Perhaps it would have been better for all of us if she hadn't been resuscitated at birth. She could have died a calm death, in dignity, without them causing all the pain and heartache you have suffered as a result.' She paused, the tears running down her cheeks. 'I feel so guilty that I didn't keep her from the start, but I didn't think we'd be able to cope. And now I feel even guiltier that I passed on the responsibility to you. And the tragic discovery of her dead body in the morning . . . I can barely imagine how terrible that must have been for you. I'm so sorry.'

We wept together. 'Yes, it was a horrendous shock,' I agreed, reaching my hand out to touch her arm. 'But that wasn't your fault. Please don't blame yourself. It must be more my fault than yours.'

'Why?'

'Because I should have noticed how poorly she was when I fed her in the middle of the night . . . but I didn't. And I must have done something wrong. It must be my fault. I blame myself.'

'You mustn't do that,' she sprang to my defence. 'I'm here for us to share our grief, and for me to support you through these difficult days.'

'Thank you,' I sniffed. 'And I want to support you too.'

'Society can be so unforgiving, can't it?' she said. 'But I'm not worried what other people might think of me. I know what I did wrong – I made that bad decision to wash my hands of my own baby and pass her and all her problems on to you. I knew she wouldn't live long – they told me that at the hospital, just after they'd revived her. So it was very wrong of me to pass her on to you, knowing the inevitability that you would be hurt.' She paused again to try and compose herself.

I was doing the same. Ellen was devastated, for them, for Michelle and for us. She was a lovely woman, intelligent and understanding.

'Well, my husband and I have talked about this together, and we want you to know that we don't attach any blame to you at all. Quite the contrary. We want to thank you for caring so much and so well for our little Michelle. We know that you gave her those two days of happiness and love. We should have been the ones to do that, but you and Mike did it for us, and we will be eternally grateful to you both for that.'

'Thank you. I appreciate that. But you must not let yourselves take on the guilt. As parents or foster-parents, all any of us can do is to do our best at the time.'

Because of Michelle's sudden death, the hospital had to do a post-mortem on her to establish the cause, which took several days.

Finally the day of the funeral came. We hadn't wanted to go, but Ellen insisted, so we had a support worker come in to help Lizzie look after the little ones while we were out and the older ones were at school.

The funeral itself was in a little church by the side of the road. Mike and I sat near the back. There was a hush for a few minutes, then the door opened and everyone turned to look, as the undertaker walked in, carrying a tiny white coffin, chest-high in his hands.

I froze. Seeing that coffin and knowing that baby Michelle's lifeless body was inside it was something I will never forget. At that moment, if I could have run a million miles away, I would have done. I don't remember the rest of the service at all.

We drove back home in silence, each with our own thoughts. It had been a difficult, sombre day, but now we had to move on. Ellen rang us a couple of days later to invite us to the interment of Michelle's ashes, but we decided not to go. It would be a family affair, and we weren't family.

'But you were the only family she knew,' said Ellen.

We dived straight back into our usual routines and carried on as before, but the inner turmoil and guilt never left me; not for a very long time. I could not think about looking after such a young baby ever again, and I refused even to pick one up for ages. I rang Social Services and told them I could only take six months upwards. That was my new rule. Somehow, just saying it gave me comfort. I could not go through all that again.

10

Real Elephants

Laurel, our abandoned baby, found under a bush, was now two and a half. But unlike Gail, the toddler with hydrocepahalus, who had been adopted the previous year, nobody had even mentioned the possibility of adoption for Laurel. So when her social worker came round one day, I asked her what was happening about it.

'Yes, we've been hoping to put Laurel up for adoption,' she said. 'But the fact she has no legal parents or relatives makes it much harder to process the paperwork. I believe a child can only be put up for adoption if his or her parents or closest relatives sign their consent to it. In Laurel's case, she has no known relatives, so I think we first have to make her a ward of court and then go through the court to gain consent for each stage of the adoption process, if Social Services decide to go that way. I'm sure they would if they could, because that way they wouldn't have to pay towards her keep.'

'Wasn't she made a ward of court when she was found?' I asked.

'Apparently not. Probably because of the police investigations to try and find her mother or any relatives. They went on for quite some time, so it wouldn't be possible to go for Ward of Court until the police signed off her case.'

'But I thought they'd done that by now?'

'To be honest, Trisha, I don't know. They don't tell me things like that. I'm just Laurel's social worker, after all.' I detected a hint of irony in her answer,

'And I'm only her foster mother,' I added. We both smiled.

'I'll see what I can find out,' she said. 'I'll let you know.'

Daisy and Paul had been with us for four years and we loved them to bits. Most of our foster children were now at school, so that gave me a bit of respite during the day, with only three little ones at home, although that was sometimes more time-consuming, without the older ones to keep them entertained. I did miss Lizzie, but she'd gone off to university now, as I knew she might. However, she came home quite often and always loved to help when I needed her most, during the school holidays.

Daisy loved school and did have a few friends there, but she was never invited round to tea or to play with any of them. Nor did she ever bring anyone back home. If I suggested it she went quiet. I suppose she was inclined to keep herself to herself, finding her own space, which was difficult in our house. But now she could read anything and loved reading longer books, when she wasn't drawing or knitting. Somebody gave her a Spirograph for her birthday, and she loved making patterns with it, which she coloured in beautifully.

Based on their characters and likes, it was hard to think of Daisy and Paul as siblings. He was always the action man, in the thick of things, cheeky and mischievous, sometimes a bit pushy. He was occasionally invited somewhere for tea . . . but never a second time. The trouble was, he grew very sturdy and didn't realise the impact of his own strength.

At about this time, we had a succession of emergency and short-stay placements. Most of them hardly stayed long enough for us to get to know them.

Then after a lull of a few weeks, there was another call from Social Services.

'Can you take a little one?' asked the woman on the phone.

'No,' I said. 'I told you I couldn't have any more young babies.'

'Yes, I know, Mrs Merry, but Mandy is not a baby. She is nearly two years old and her family live nearby. Her father is particularly keen to have her near enough to visit regularly, so please, do you think you could reconsider? It would be a perfect placement for this child.'

So I agreed and, as I put the phone down, I wondered about Mandy's mother. Why had she not been mentioned in the same sentence as her father? Maybe something had gone wrong there?

So Mandy came to join us. She was a lovely-looking child with dark wavy hair and rich brown eyes, but quite stubborn, and even at not quite two I could see she was a bright little button – I could almost hear her thinking. It looked like this child was going to be challenging in her own way, but I've always relished a challenge. I knew at once that I was going to enjoy having her to stay and watching her blossom. It's the psychology of children that fascinates me – the way they learn and the way they think. Mandy was going to be one to watch.

I always patrolled round the children's rooms at night before going to bed myself. On the night Mandy came, everywhere was quiet, but I looked into each room, paying particular attention to the little ones, Alfie, Laurel and Mandy. They were all fast asleep, so next I went into the older girls' room, where all was fine, then last the boys. AJ and Ronnie were sleeping soundly too, though I had to tuck AJ's legs back under the straightened duvet before going next door to Paul and Gilroy's room. They were in bunk beds, with Gilroy at the top, so I had to stand on the end of Paul's bed to check Gilroy . . . and I was shocked at what I saw. One hand was sticking out and in his fist was the missing knitting needle. I'd forgotten all about it. Although he was soundly asleep, he clutched it so tight that I had a job to extricate it from his hand. Fortunately he didn't stir, but even in sleep he had a malicious look on his face. I wondered what he was intending to do with it.

There was a clue a couple of mornings later, when Paul had a very lucky escape. Gilroy took the safety rails off the bunk-beds, then started bouncing up and down, harder and harder, until his top bunk gave away. Gilroy and his bed came crashing down on Paul's . . . and missed him by seconds. Paul had a very lucky break that day, having got out of bed to go to the toilet, unnoticed by Gilroy. When I heard the rumpus, I rushed up to their room, arriving only a second after the crash, just in time to see the triumphant look on Gilroy's face when he thought he had killed Paul, then his disappointment when Paul sauntered back into the room, very much alive and well.

Having not experienced the danger, Paul was quite amused. But the whole incident had unnerved me so much that I had to go out and buy two single beds for immediate delivery, so that we could split the boys up straight away.

The time had come to consider a move. We loved our house in Sonnington, loved the garden, loved the orchard . . . but we didn't love the neighbours. We didn't like the cliquey people who lived around us, and murmured to each other whenever I walked past them pushing the pram. They never took to us, with our rag-bag of children, and could never bring themselves to see how lovable they were.

Then there was the school. Sometimes when I was called to go and sort out one of the children's misdemeanours – mostly Gilroy's, but quite often AJ's or Paul's as well – it might be break-time and I would have to take the little ones with me to cross the playground. I was sad to see that my kids were usually playing in one corner, apart from the other children. I spoke to the headmistress about it.

'Whenever I come to the school,' I explained to her, 'I see all the other children keeping away from mine. Did someone tell them to do that?'

'Certainly not, Mrs Merry,' she said in her snooty voice. 'We believe in inclusion here. We treat everyone as equal.'

'Well, somebody needs to make sure,' I said. 'Because some children seem to be more equal than others . . . and there's no inclusion here for my foster-children, as far as I can see.'

We decided it was time to sell the house and move somewhere we might be more welcome and where there were more activities and clubs for the older children to join.

We didn't have to look for long before we found a huge Victorian semi in just the right place, a few miles away, on the edge of town, near a park. A semi probably wasn't ideal and I dreaded what these neighbours would be like; especially what they would think of having all of us moving in, with just a party wall between us. But it was a good house, well built, and it went back a long way. It had a big family kitchen and a room we could convert into a playroom for the kids. There were plenty of bedrooms too – enough to have Gilroy in his own room, away from Paul and the others. We wouldn't have three acres at this house, but the garden was larger than average, so it would be fine. The move couldn't come soon enough.

One weekend we were all sat around the breakfast table, wondering where to take the children for their Sunday outing.

'Where would you like to go today, kids?' asked Mike.

They were not short of ideas: 'The park . . .', 'the conker-tree woods . . .', 'the library' (Daisy's suggestion), 'a boxing match' (Gilroy's), 'the cinema . . .'.

'I like animals,' said Sheena.

'So do I,' shouted Paul. 'I love animals.'

'Now that's a good idea!' Mike grinned. 'We could all go to the zoo.' He turned to look at one child in particular. 'What about you, Alfie? Would you like to go and see some real elephants?'

Alfie looked confused. He looked down at Ellie, his cuddly elephant that he still took everywhere with him, tucked under his arm.

'Are real elephants like Ellie?' he asked, stroking her grey body and cream tusks.

'Yes, but bigger. We could go and visit her relations in the zoo. Would you like that?'

Alfie whispered to Ellie. 'Do you want to see your 'lations?' Then he listened. 'Ellie says yes. And I want to go too.'

He got up and did a little stamping sort of a dance. 'I can't wait!' and everyone laughed to see how thrilled he was.

So we cleared away the breakfast things and off we went to squeeze everyone into our big estate car, and Ellie as well, of course.

We were all in high spirits, especially Alfie, and the others hyped him up even further. Mike was the worst.

'Oh, you're going to see the elephants,' he sang in his deep voice, watching his driving mirror to see Alfie's face light up.

As we all piled out of the car, Alfie clutched Ellie to his chest and took hold of Mike's hand as we paid to go in – very expensive, but it was worth it for Alfie alone. I'm not keen on zoos myself – never have been – but I was looking forward to seeing this great encounter. Real elephants at last. Alfie would be so thrilled.

I was pushing the big pram with the toddlers in, while the older ones forged ahead with Mike. We followed the signposts and soon we approached the entrance to the elephant enclosure. Mike and the children waited outside, with Alfie jumping up and down in anticipation, while I caught up with them and we all went through together. When we reached the end of the path, we stood alongside the enclosure and looked.

'Where are they?' shrieked Alfie in his high-pitched voice, looking straight ahead. 'Where are they?'

'They're here,' said Mike, pointing forwards.

Alfie looked confused. 'Where?'

'There they are.' Mike pointed again, gradually taking his finger upwards.

Alfie followed Mike's finger as he gazed up and up and up . . . He gasped, then stiffened, as if struck by lightning, and then he ran. He was gone – disappeared. He was petrified, poor boy. Somebody must have been opening the gate and he just ran straight through and as far away as he could.

'You'll have to go after him,' I said in panic. 'I'll keep the kids here. You go and find him.'

So Mike went off in pursuit of the boy who loved elephants . . . as long as they weren't real. Finally he tracked him down, at the ticket office, cuddling Ellie as the tears poured down his face.

On the way back in the car, everyone was rather subdued, Alfie most of all.

'Were the real elephants too big, Alfie?' asked Daisy, in her kindest voice. She was always good with children in distress, whatever their ages.

'Yes,' he gulped.

'But we told you they were big,' said Mike.

'And I showed you pictures of how big they are,' I added. 'Do you remember, in that book? There was a boy in one of the pictures and they were much taller than the boy.'

'Yes,' he said. 'But I liked them in the pictures . . .'

We could tell he was on the verge of more tears, so none of us said anything else. But we all remembered that day. Especially Alfie, who never looked at the elephant book again, although his love for Ellie remained as strong as ever.

11

Gone Missing

The day came and we moved into our new house. The children went out to explore the garden, while we started unpacking the boxes.

I remember saying to Mike: 'I'm not speaking to the neighbours. I am NOT going to speak to the neighbours.' That was my one big worry.

Just as we finished unpacking in the kitchen, the doorbell went. I wondered who it could be as I walked with trepidation around the pile of boxes in the hall. I opened the door . . . and there stood a smiling couple, probably in their sixties.

'Hello,' said the woman, with a warm voice. 'I'm Edie . . .'

'And I'm Frank. We're your next-door neighbours.'

'Oh, hello,' I smiled back. 'It's good to meet you both.' They seemed genuine, but I couldn't help being wary. They obviously hadn't seen the children yet.

'We've made you a pot of tea,' continued Edie. 'And some biscuits.'

'We'll pop it through the hedge at the back,' added Frank.

'Oh right. Thank you.' I must have looked confused.

'We used to do that with the people before you,' explained Frank. 'We made a gap to pass things through.'

'Oh, I see.' I smiled. 'What a good idea.' Well, I hoped it was.

'And we can hear the children . . .'

Oh no, I thought. *Here we go!*

'Yes, we've made them all a drink too, and we'll pass all the drinks and biscuits through the gap for you.'

'That's very kind,' I said, breathing a sigh of relief. They seemed like a lovely couple. I just hoped they would still be smiling after a day or two of our kids' noise in the garden!

So I went right through the house and out of the back door, onto the crazy paving, and over to the boundary with our adjoining house. It looked as if the hedge had been trimmed down low for the first three or four feet away from the house. So that made the gap.

Mike came out to see what was going on.

'Call the kids,' I said to him, just as Edie came out with a tea-tray for us and handed it through to me. Then Frank passed through a huge jug of lemonade for the kids, a motley collection of plastic cups and a full tin of biscuits.

'Thank you so much,' I said. 'What a lovely welcome.'

'Come on, kids!' yelled Mike. 'Drinks and biscuits.'

They all came running over, the bigger ones dishevelled from climbing the trees and everyone excited to be somewhere new. Daisy brought up the rear, walking sedately, holding little Laurel's hand.

'Don't forget to say thank you,' I said to the kids.

'Thank you,' they all chorused as they stuffed the biscuits into their mouths.

'There are plenty left,' said Edie. 'Keep the tin and finish them if you like.'

'That's very kind. Thank you.' In fact, I could hardly believe it, after the last neighbours we'd had. Especially that woman with the doves! I just hoped this neighbourliness would last.

All went well to begin with. Then one afternoon, when the kids had been having a lovely time in the garden, making new camps and playing with the garden toys, I went out to call them in. 'Tea in five minutes,' I called out. 'Tidy all the toys away in the shed.'

'OK.' They knew that all the toys had to go in there before they could come in, so I left them to it.

Two minutes later I went out again. Brilliant, I thought. Everything was tidy. 'That was quick,' I told them. 'Well done. Now come in and wash your hands.'

They rushed in and had a quick hand-wash, then sat down round the kitchen table to have their tea.

Just then, the doorbell rang. I opened it.

'Trisha,' said Edie, standing on the doorstep with an anxious expression. 'Now there's nothing to worry about – no problem, and I don't want you shouting at the children or anything . . .'

My brain went into overdrive. I thought: *God, what could they possibly have done?*

'It's just that they've thrown all the toys over . . .'

'Oh, no!' I exclaimed.

'. . . onto Frank's vegetable patch.'

'I'm so sorry,' I gasped. 'I told them to put the toys away in the shed!'

'Yes, I heard you.' She gave me a wry smile. 'But they must have decided it would be quicker if they just threw them over the hedge!'

'Oh dear . . .'

'Don't worry.' She seemed quite amused about it all.

What a relief that she wasn't angry. But maybe Frank would be. 'Right,' I said. 'I'll bring the kids round straight away to apologise and collect the toys.'

I went back to the kitchen and made them all come with me, all ten of them, from eight-year-old Chrissy, right down to two-year-old Laurel, who had to run to keep up with us. 'Now you've all got to pick the toys up and say you're sorry,' I instructed them sternly.

As I rang Edie's doorbell, they all stood there, heads down, chins on chests. They knew I was cross with them for upsetting our lovely neighbours like that. They knew they were in the wrong.

Just like our house, Edie and Frank's went back a long way, so when Edie let us in, we all trooped through the hall, through the dining room, through the kitchen, through the glazed conservatory that had once been a wash-house and out into the garden. As we went out I could see Frank standing among the neat rows of his flourishing vegetable garden, right next to our hedge. I could also see our garden toys strewn all over the vegetables, any old how. A broken bean pole hung at a crooked angle, with a skipping rope dangling among the beans. One of the trikes had landed precariously on top of a water butt, and everything else was scattered across the plot. I felt awful.

'Oh no,' I said to Edie. 'I hope they haven't ruined Frank's cabbages or knocked over his tomato plants, or—'

'It's all right,' she reassured me. 'Frank will be able to sort them all out.'

We stood in the open doorway as the children picked up the toys, some more carefully than others. 'Sorry, Frank . . . sorry, Frank,' they each said in turn. 'Sorry, Frank . . .'

'Oh, don't worry,' he said. 'Don't worry.'

Just then I heard a giggle from Edie, standing next to me. We looked at each other and both broke into fits of laughter. What a lovely couple they were.

They continued to put up with everything our kids threw at them, almost literally. Frank was always throwing balls back, or cardboard tubes, or arrows with rubber suckers on the ends, or even stray shoes that flew off when the children kicked.

But Edie and Frank were never ruffled by anything our kids did. They were the best neighbours ever, and the kids loved them as much as we did.

We felt we'd really landed on our feet . . . for now, anyway.

At about this time, there was a bit of trouble in Daisy's class at school. I can't remember what it was about, but I found out later that Daisy had been in the wrong place when it had happened, and was one of the suspects who'd had to go and see the headteacher and be questioned about it.

I remember that coming out of school that afternoon she had her head down and didn't say a word. When we got home, the children ran upstairs to change into their play clothes and went down to the playroom while I started to make their tea. It wasn't until I called them all to wash their hands and come to the table that I realised Daisy was missing.

'Does anybody know where Daisy is?' I asked.

But no one had seen her since we'd all arrived home. So, I put everything to keep warm while the kids and I searched the house. 'Daisy, Daisy, where are you?' they yelled.

I began to feel quite anxious. She wasn't in her bedroom, nor in the upstairs bathroom. We looked everywhere, inside and out, but we couldn't find her.

I felt the panic rising inside me. What if she had run away . . . or someone had taken her? I was horrified as I started to imagine things. I had no idea how long she'd been gone. But I knew I had to be practical, so I tried to think back. Was I sure she had come into the house with the rest of us? *Yes*, I thought, but then I began to doubt myself.

I knew what I had to do.

'Hello, John,' I said to Daisy's social worker on the phone. 'I don't want to alarm you, but we can't find Daisy. I'm pretty sure she came in with us when we got back from school. But the kids and I have searched the whole house and we can't find her anywhere.'

'I'll be right there,' he said. 'Better give the police a call, just to alert them, in case something has happened.'

So I dialled 999 and explained the situation, giving a description of Daisy, just in case.

As soon as John arrived, followed by a policewoman a couple of minutes later, we started a new and more methodical search of the whole house. First downstairs and then on the first floor and finally the attic rooms. As we worked our way along the corridor where most of the children's bedrooms were, John stopped.

'What's this?' he asked.

'Oh, that's just the airing cupboard,' I said.

'Have you looked in here?'

'No. But it's tiny inside.'

John opened the door, and there was Daisy, blinking her eyes in the brightness of the light, standing in front of the linen-stacked shelves. She must have been in there on her own, in the dark, for at least three hours by then.

'What are you doing in there, Daise?' I asked her.

'Hiding,' she said with a sniffle.

Then I saw the tear-stains down her cheeks. She must have been crying silently and we hadn't known. I felt dreadful. I stepped forward and gave her a long hug. She didn't hug me back – just hung her arms limply by her sides. But I knew she needed this. 'I don't know what you're hiding from, sweetheart, but you don't need to hide from me, from any of us. Nothing can be so bad that you need to hide from me.' I stroked her short, blond hair.

She caught sight of the policewoman and started crying afresh.

'It's OK, Daisy,' said John. The policewoman has come to help us find you and to see that you're all right. But you're not in any trouble with the police, or anyone at all.'

She stopped sobbing and said, 'Thank you,' in a weak voice.

John and the policewoman left, and I shooed all the others off to the playroom for a few minutes, so that I could talk to Daisy.

'So why were you hiding, sweetheart?' I asked her.

'I had to go and see the headteacher,' she said, the tears streaming down her face again. 'But I didn't do it.' She looked so anxious, as if afraid I would think badly of her. Just the fact that she'd even been suspected of something was enough for her.

'I'm sure you didn't, Daise. You're always so good at doing the right things. So there's no need to worry about it.' I hugged her again, and this time she half-hugged me back.

'You must be hungry,' I said. 'Go and wash your hands and I'll call the others to come back to the kitchen. Then you can all have your tea. Afterwards, Mike will look after everyone else and you can come and sit with me in the sitting room and tell me all about it. Will that be all right?'

'Yes,' she said. 'But you won't be cross with me?'

'No, sweetheart. I promise I won't be cross with you. I'm sure that whatever it was, it must have been a misunderstanding . . . and we can put that right.'

Poor Daisy. She was so eager to please, so conscientious, that I knew she couldn't have been the one who had done whatever it was. And when I went up to the school the next day with her, I was right. To her great relief, the culprit had been found out and owned up, so it all turned out fine in the end.

As foster parents, we had some flexibility about the children, especially if it was a full care order, but the one and only stipulation that had been made when Daisy and Paul came into our care was how Daisy wore her hair. Nothing about their education, their accommodation, food, religion or any other major concerns; just that we were not to change Daisy's hair.

When she first arrived, her thick blond hair had been cut in a short, angular style – so severe it was almost geometric and, in my opinion, not at all suitable for a young child.

'Why can't I have pretty hair?' she asked me one day. 'Can I grow it longer, like Sheena's?'

'I wish I could say yes, Daisy. But when you first came here, your mummy sent a message to say that you must always keep the same hairstyle you had when you arrived.'

'I don't have a mummy,' she said, with a sad face.

'You did have a mummy, but you don't remember her. She left when you were one.'

'She's never been to see me, so she won't know if I grow it longer,' she reasoned, pleading with me.

'Well . . .'

'Please.' She saw I was wavering. 'Just a bit longer?'

Who would ever know? I thought. So we allowed it to grow down to her shoulders. She loved being able to swing her head and make her hair move through the air.

But the next time John, their social worker, came, he noticed the difference.

'You are aware that Daisy's mother wanted her hair to be kept the same?'

'Yes, I know, but Daisy was so desperate to grow it a bit, like the other girls at school; so I thought it wouldn't do any harm. She's so thrilled with it.'

'I'm afraid it will have to be cut,' he insisted.

So I had to take her to the hairdressers and cut it back to how it was. She was distraught, and I was livid – exasperated that a mother who never visited or took any interest in her child, not even one birthday card, should exert such control over her, presumably until she became an adult. The poor child only wanted to be like her friends.

12

The Milkman's Tale

Late one morning I was doing some ironing in the kitchen, when the doorbell rang. I assumed it must be Edie or Frank, but no. When I opened the door, it was the milkman standing there.

'Hello, Mrs Merry.'

'Hello. I left a note out for you,' I said.

'Yes, I found it.' He waved it at me.

'You're running later than usual aren't you? I hope nothing's wrong?'

'Not with me, no. But there was quite a palaver at one of the old terraced houses in Fisher Street this morning. I wondered if you'd heard anything, you being a foster carer and all?'

'No . . . why? What happened?'

'You're not putting the kettle on, are you? ' he asked me, taking his cap off to wipe his brow. I could tell that behind his smile he was feeling distressed and wanted somebody to talk to.

I nodded. 'Come on in. You can tell me all about it.'

We sat down at the table with our mugs of coffee and he took a few sips before telling me his tale.

'Well, I deliver to most of the houses in Fisher Street, so I was doing my round and stopped my float outside number nineteen, trying to decide whether to leave any milk there. It's a single woman with three small children who lives there, and she hasn't paid her bill for three weeks now. It's supposed to be weekly, like everyone else. I would have missed her out till she paid up . . . but I knew the little ones would need their milk.' He paused and I nodded.

'So, I went and knocked on the door to ask for my payment, but there was no answer, as usual. I was just turning to go and get a couple of pints to leave on the doorstep to tide them over when I heard a baby crying loudly inside. Then I noticed the old net curtain in the front window twitching, and a little face appearing. Very pale and thin.'

'Oh,' I gasped. 'One of the children?'

'Yes, the eldest – a girl. She couldn't have been more than five or six. She tapped the window and said something, but I couldn't hear. So she pressed her face to the window and shouted, "Can we have some milk for the baby?" I said, "No," in a loud voice. "Not until I talk to your mummy. Can you please go and get her for me? I need to speak to her." She shook her head. "Mummy's not here," she shouted. "Well, she's got to be there with you." She shook her head sadly. "No, she's not." I felt sorry for her.'

'Hmm,' I said. 'That sounds bad. What did you do?'

'I asked her if she could open the front door and she said "No." So I said "What about the back door?" and she said "I'll try." So I went down to the end of the terrace and round to the passage along the backs. I counted down to the right house and opened the gate. It was a glazed door, so I could see the little girl standing on a chair, fiddling with the key in the lock. Finally she managed to turn it.'

'Thank goodness. Were the children all right?'

'Just about,' he said. 'But the baby was desperately hungry. I could see that his sisters had been trying to feed him with a bottle of water, but obviously that didn't stop him crying with hunger. So I went out the front way to the float and brought in a couple of pints. We boiled a small panful up on the stove. Then I let it cool for a bit.'

'Where was their mother? Why wasn't she there?' I was imagining all sorts of things. Perhaps she'd fallen ill, or had collapsed and died upstairs . . .

'I asked the girl and she frowned, as if she wasn't sure whether she was allowed to say anything. "I think you'd better tell me," I said. "So that I can help you." Then she told me her mummy had gone out to a party. Apparently, she often did that, and she usually came back in the morning. I asked her "Was it last night that she went out?" "No. I don't think so. I can't remember," she said. I could see she was worried. I asked if it was the day before, and she said she didn't know.'

'So, what did you do?' I asked him.

'Well, first of all I wanted to make sure the baby could have some milk. She told me he was nearly a year old, although he looked smaller. So I knew he'd be OK with ordinary milk. I chatted with her a bit, sitting with her sister on the mismatched kitchen chairs. Then, when the milk was just right, I poured some into the bottle and started to feed the baby.

'"I can feed him if you like," she said, so I passed him over to her and went to phone the police. They were there in five minutes. They spoke to one of the neighbours, who didn't seem very happy about the situation.'

'I should think not! So what happened to them? Did they track down the mother?'

'No. They said they would sort her out later. First they had to take the children into care. So they put them into the squad car and off they went.'

'What a morning!' I sighed. 'No wonder you're so late finishing your round.'

'Yes, I left you till last, because I thought you might know something.'

'Not yet,' I smiled. 'There are other foster carers in Ashbridge too, I'm sure. So I might never find out.'

'Oh.' He looked disappointed.

'Give me your phone number,' I told him. 'And I'll let you know if anything happens.'

'Thanks. I'd like to know they're all right.'

An hour later, as I watched my kids tucking into their lunch, I couldn't help but think back to what the poor worried milkman had told me.

During the past week we'd had two departures. A short-stay toddler had gone back to his mother, and our longest-stay child, nine-year-old Chrissy, had to leave as well. After so many years with us, it was a real wrench to see her go. Her parents had finally got divorced and Social Services decided she should go and live with her mother. We had to break the news to her and when we told her she burst into tears.

'I don't want to go,' she wailed. 'I want to stay here. This is my home.'

'I know, sweetheart.' I put my arm around her shaking shoulders. 'We don't want you to go either. But it's not our decision.'

'Do I have to go?'

'Yes, I'm afraid so.'

'Why?' She looked from Mike to me with her beautiful, big blue eyes, silently pleading with us. 'It's not fair.'

'I wish we could keep you with us . . .' I soothed her. 'But we're not allowed.'

'You're part of our family,' added Mike. 'And we'll always think of you that way.'

The tears coursed down Chrissy's forlorn face. 'But I can't go. How will I manage? Mum's always at the pub.'

'Well, she probably won't be if you're living with her.' I didn't really believe that, but I hoped it all the same.

She was desperate to stay with us, but as her foster-parents we were powerless. It was very difficult for her, and for us and the other children too, especially Sheena and Daisy, who were the closest to her in age.

The hardest thing was that I felt strongly it was the wrong decision, but they didn't consult us. As always, Social Services were a law unto themselves. It would be cheaper for them to send Chrissy back to live with her mother, so that was it. As we watched her go, I knew we might never see her again.

It was mid-afternoon when the phone rang. 'Can you take an emergency placement – a family of three children?'

I thought, *here goes . . . the children the milkman told me about; it must be*. But they included a baby so I just wanted to check, as I was sticking to my rule of no babies under six months. 'How old are they?'

'Two girls of five and three, plus a nearly one-year-old boy.'

Yes, I thought, definitely the same family. It had to be. 'When do you want them to come?'

'Now?'

I sighed. I'd have a job to get everything ready in half a day, let alone less than an hour. And it would be a squash with eleven children, but I knew we could cope. 'OK,' I agreed.

Well, what a sight they were when they arrived! I had the door open and watched the social worker walk the two girls up the drive, while carrying the little one. The girls were dressed in what I can only describe as drab, jumble-sale clothes, that didn't fit them properly, and plastic sandals on their feet. The toddler had just a nappy and an open cardigan on, so big it was down to his knees, with no vest or anything else, plus a pair of black wellington boots, at least two sizes too large for him. The social worker put him down and, after two or three wobbly steps in those boots, he clearly decided he'd had enough for one day. So he did his own little sit-down protest on our gravel, bawling his head off and refusing to stand up. The social worker had to pick him up again, boots and all, to bring him to our door.

The two girls looked pale, their skin almost grey, and their bodies far too thin. They looked as if they hadn't been out in the sunlight for weeks, nor been anywhere near a bath. They were probably malnourished too, judging by their dull hair and slow movements. The boy, on the other hand, had a lusty cry, but I wouldn't have put him at more than seven or eight months old, to look at.

'Hi kids!' Mike grinned. He always said the same when he came in from work, no matter whether any were missing or new ones had come.

'What are their names?' he asked me quietly, against the noisy background, as we sat down with a cup of tea at one end of the table.

'Noreen, Linda and . . . Oh no!'

'What?'

'I've forgotten his name already. I'll have to look it up on the social worker's form. Apparently, they left the family home in such a hurry that nobody noticed he hadn't got anything on his feet, so they picked up a pair of wellingtons for him to wear. You should have seen him in them – they were far too big. The kids are all calling him Baby Boots.'

After their baths and bedtime stories for the younger ones, I settled the new family down to sleep that evening, all in the same room to start with. Later on, if they were still with us, they'd join the others.

We spent the next few days feeding the three of them up and sending them out to play in the garden. They hung back the first morning, but Daisy and Sheena encouraged the two girls to join in their games with Mandy and Laurel. Meanwhile, Paul took charge of Baby Boots and put him in a cardboard box with a rope round it and hauled him round the garden; just like when Ronnie had pulled him around in a similar box himself on his first day, I remembered with a smile.

Because of these three's emergency placement, we now had two more than a full house. In order of age, we had AJ, Ronnie, Sheena, Daisy, Paul, Gilroy, Noreen, Alfie, Mandy, Linda, Laurel and Baby Boots. We had a spare cot, but the bed space for Noreen and Linda could have been a problem, so we made it into a game.

Every night I tied a sheet to the bunk-beds to make a 'tent' down to the floor, and put a sleeping bag in it. Then I'd get all the children together and say, 'Now, who's been the very, very best-behaved child today?'

They would all be pushing themselves forward.

'I have.'

'Me.'

'No, ME!'

Each night I picked a different one. 'Yes, you have been brilliant today, so you can sleep in the tent tonight.'

The girl or boy I chose always looked so proud and their excitement was infectious. They all tried their hardest to be good, and they all had to have a turn. It worked a treat.

You'd think I'd given them a trip to Disneyland, with a hundred gold coins to spend!

So that was the beds sorted out. However, the only trouble was getting them all into our old estate car, which was now impossible, so we sold it and bought a large van, which was like a minibus, except without the windows; and it only had the three front seats. So we put lots of carpet offcuts and cushions into the back, along with some soft plastic toys for the kids to play with on long journeys. They were fairly good at making up their own games, too.

Baby Boots was a lot of fun. He had such a contagious giggle and was always excited about something or other. We all loved him, but we never called him his real name. I can't even remember what it was.

'Isn't he bootiful?' said Ronnie soon after he arrived, and we all laughed.

Daisy was usually the quiet one, often rather detached. But she really took to Baby Boots and wheeled him around the garden in our old pram. She used to cut toast into fingers for him at breakfast time and she often came and watched me change his nappies, amusing him with a mobile or some other toy while he was lying there. We'd had a lot of babies to stay but, apart from baby Gail, the one with hydrocephalus, and abandoned newborn Laurel, I don't remember Daisy paying any of them as much attention as she gave to Baby Boots.

It was quite a shock when the family's social worker, Ray, rang me a few weeks later to say they would be leaving us.

'Why?'

'Because they're going back to their mum.'

'But I thought the police were taking her to court?' I had learnt that from the milkman, whom I rang every now and then to update him on how they were doing. He even visited them one day at the end of his round. Noreen seemed pleased to see him, but the others didn't really know who he was.

'Surely the mother's not fit to look after them?' I asked.

'Well, you know I can't tell you much,' said Ray. 'They did take her to court, and there was such a good case against her from the police that everyone thought it would be an open and shut case. But . . .' I could tell he was being careful with his words. 'Let's just say that she had an excellent barrister and he got her off, so the judge agreed the children can go back to her.'

'Oh dear.' I sighed. 'I hope they'll be all right.'

'As you know, I can't comment.' His voice might have seemed calm to most people, but I'd known Ray a long time and I could sense the anger underneath his neutral tone. 'But I'll remain their social worker for a while at least.'

'Good,' I said. 'That's something.'

'I'll come and collect them at ten tomorrow morning.'

So, after two months, we said our sad goodbyes to Noreen, Linda and Baby Boots. We all missed them terribly – Daisy most of all. Nobody could replace Baby Boots.

We presumed that would be the end of it. But no . . .

A few weeks later I had a call from Social Services. A rule had recently been implemented that foster carers could not exceed their set number of children, no matter what the circumstances. 'The three children who left you recently are coming back into care,' said the voice on the phone. 'According to our records, you have nine children now. Is that correct?'

'Yes, that's right. But it would be no more of a squash to have the three of them back again than it was last time, and we managed very well then.'

'Yes, but as you know, we have new rules and your maximum is ten, so that means you can't have more than ten at a time.'

'But we have the space and we'd love to have them back,' I pleaded. 'I'm sure it would be less unsettling and better for them.'

'I can't comment on that, I'm afraid. We just have to follow the regulations. But you could have one of them. That would be a help.'

'Who would it be a help to?' I asked with indignation. 'It wouldn't help the children. They need to stay together, to support each other.'

'That may not be possible, Mrs Merry. So which one could you take?'

I refused to say. How could I take only one of them? And how could I choose? If they had to come back into care, they should be able to come back to us. We would love to have them. But if they couldn't all come, I didn't want to be the person who split them up.

'I can't have just one of them,' I said, 'and leave the others out in the cold.'

'Oh, that's going rather too far, Mrs Merry,' said the snippy voice on the other end.

'Well, it's how I feel. And if I can't have them all, I'd rather they've the chance of staying together somewhere else.'

So that was that. I felt sad for them, but there was nothing I could do.

'Let it go, Trish,' said Mike that evening, when I told him about it. 'You know you have to let them go.'

'Yes, but I can't help wishing.'

'I know, but rules are rules, so put it behind you. I'm sure they'll be all right with a new foster-carer for a while. After all, if they can stay together, they've got each other, and Noreen is a real little mum herself.'

Only a week later I had another phone call about Noreen, Linda and Baby Boots. This time it was from their new foster-carer. They had been found a placement together, so I felt that, in a roundabout way, I had done my best to help them.

'I hope you don't mind my ringing you out of the blue, but another foster-mum friend of mine gave me your number.'

'Yes?' I said, feeling guarded. 'What's it about?'

'You'll never believe what's happened,' she began. 'It's the three you had with you a few months ago. Their mother got this top lawyer again . . . and she's got the children back.'

'Oh no! Those poor kids.'

'Yes. It's all wrong, isn't it? They should never be going back to her. She'll only neglect them again, like she's always done.'

Not long after, I heard through the fostering grapevine that they'd gone back into care yet again; this time quite a long way away, and I never heard what happened to them after that.

'Lost in the care system,' I said to Mike. 'It seems so wrong.'

13

Fetch the Police!

The bigger Gilroy grew the more difficult he became. He was so boisterous, putting it mildly, that he was always in hot water. He could often be quite hostile too if he felt like it, pushing the other children over as hard as he could, taking or deliberately breaking their things, making cruel comments that upset everyone, including adults, and generally looking for trouble.

Once, when a pregnant social worker came for a visit, he took one look at her bump and said, 'I hope your baby dies.' The poor woman went white, then burst into tears, as if it were a curse. I had to send Gilroy up to his bedroom and comfort her, but of course he kicked up and trashed his room completely.

Another time, when we were at the supermarket, he shouted at a disabled man: 'Cripples shouldn't be allowed in shops.' The man was understandably very upset, and so were other customers, so the manager insisted I take Gilroy out of the store and never bring him again.

There were many other instances of this kind, and it became increasingly difficult to take him anywhere, or to have anyone round to our house.

It wasn't just Gilroy who was difficult to deal with. His mother could be even worse – obstreperous was putting it mildly. A few weeks after the episode with the bunk beds, she turned up unannounced, wanting to see him. She knew she had to get permission from Social Services, because Gilroy was on a full care order and his mother was only allowed to have supervised visits. But she ignored this.

She was drunk when she arrived, banging on our front door non-stop, until I came and opened it on the chain.

'I want to see my f****** boy!' she yelled.

'I'm sorry, Kathleen,' I said in my firmest voice. 'You know I can't let you in to see Gilroy without first getting written permission from Social Services. What you need to do is to go down and get them to do you a letter and bring it back here. Then you can come in.'

She swore another string of non-repeatable words at me, so I shut the door, kept the chain on and double-locked it. I checked the back door too, and all the downstairs windows.

As I turned, I saw Gilroy, sitting on the stairs, close to tears. He was a tough boy, who would never have let the others see any chink of weakness in him. But this day, away from the rest of the children, a tear or two trickled down his ashen face, as he sat, rigid, on the stairs. Then suddenly, he seemed to change.

'Why can't I see my mum?' he challenged me.

'Because she can't come in without permission from the social workers,' I explained.

'I f****** hate you!' he shouted and stomped up the stairs to his room, where I heard him crashing things about. Not for the first time.

I'd have to deal with that later, because at that moment, there was a loud commotion outside in the street. I peeked out of one of our front windows and saw her having a go at our old friend the milkman, who had just turned up at that moment in his float. She ranted and raved at him, so loudly that Gilroy stopped his destruction, came out of his room and stood at the top of the stairs, listening.

At that moment, his mother took a milk bottle out of one of the milkman's crates and threw it as hard as she could at our house. Then she threw a few more, and worked her way through all the crates. I think she must have been aiming at the windows, but fortunately she was too drunk to aim straight, so they all broke against the brickwork, streaming milk down the walls, while the jagged pieces of glass fell to the ground beneath.

'Let me in, you f****** c***,' she screamed.

I phoned Gilroy's social worker and told him. 'She's gone too far,' I said. 'She's violent, and probably dangerous. We need the police up here.'

'Oh, don't do that,' he said. 'I'll come up straight away and sort her out.'

'I don't think you'll be able to. I'm afraid somebody is going to be hurt. I could smell the alcohol when I opened the door, and had to close it again quickly to protect the children. She was swearing and shouting threats at me. She even tried to attack the poor milkman. You wouldn't be able to get near her, or the front of the house.'

'You've got a back door, haven't you?'

'Yes.'

'Well, go out and try to stop her.'

'How could I do that?'

'Talk to her.'

'No,' I refused. 'I'm not going out to her. It would be dangerous. She's absolutely lost the plot.'

By now, with all the milk bottles broken, she started banging on the windows with her fists. Gilroy had come downstairs again and was petrified with fear. Embarrassed too, I'm sure. He was horrified at the fuss his mother was causing. As she battered the hall window, Gilroy edged slowly backwards, leaning against the wall, shrinking away from his mother's onslaught. That's a sure sign that a child is traumatised.

The children were all at home, because it was half term, so I took Gilroy by the hand and led him out to the kitchen, at the back of the house, where I had told all the others to stay. I checked again that I'd properly locked and bolted the back door. Then I phoned Mike at work.

'You've got to come home,' I said. I'm sure he could hear the panic in my voice. 'And you'll have to be careful because Kathleen Dobbs is fighting drunk and in a terrible strop, trying to break our front windows.'

'Have you rung the police?'

'No. Gilroy's social worker said not to.'

'Well, ring them now, straight away, and I'll be home as soon as I can.'

Just as I picked up the phone to dial 999, I heard the sirens approaching. I went to have a look, as two police cars screeched to a halt at the front of our house. Straight away, they put up a cordon across the road on both sides, to keep curious onlookers out of danger. I went back to make sure the children were OK.

'It's all right,' I told them. 'The police are here now. So they will keep us safe.'

'I bet there are at least six police cars,' said Ronnie in great excitement. 'We'll probably be on the News!'

Gilroy was usually our biggest doom merchant, but not today. He edged himself closer to me, with his head down and his eyes to the ground. For once, he was silent. I felt so bad for him. He was in complete shock. How could any parent do this to their child?

Mike and the social worker both turned up at the same time and, when they explained who they were, the police let them through the cordon and signalled that it was safe for me to open the front door and let them into the house. As I did so, I saw to the right a policewoman and two policemen taking Kathleen in handcuffs towards their car.

'They've arrested Mrs Dobbs and are taking her down to the police station,' explained Mike.

'I've just come in to see how Gilroy is,' added his social worker.

'Frightened to death,' I said.

'No, I'm not!' Gilroy insisted, gathering some bravado. 'I'm not frightened.'

'No, we'll all be fine now,' I reassured him, and all the kids. 'I'm sure it will all turn out all right for your mum,' I told Gilroy. 'Now that she's calmed down, she'll be fine. I expect they'll just ask her some questions, then take her home.'

The social worker gave me a doubtful look, but knew better than to contradict me in front of the boy. 'Well,' he said. 'Now that I can see that Gilroy is OK, I'll go on down to the police station and see if I can have a word with Kathleen.'

It was my turn to be doubtful. But I said nothing. Gilroy had been through enough. He was putting on a brave front, but I knew his brain must be in a turmoil of distress. For once, I felt very protective of him. He was only a child, just six years old. But, when it was all over, it didn't take him long to regain his usual strength . . . and malice.

A few days later, I was tidying up the children's rooms when I noticed that Gilroy's pillow looked very lumpy, so I smoothed my hand over it, but it wouldn't flatten. I lifted the pillow and found a hoard of knives underneath – table knives, kitchen knives that he must have stolen from downstairs, and a small selection of pen-knives, presumably also stolen from shops or at school. This discovery sent a chill down my spine. And when I looked in his drawers, he had boxes of matches and bits of burnt paper hidden among his clothes.

I was shocked. I took them all away, but what if I hadn't found all this? What was he going to do? Then I realised . . . it must be a reaction to the incident with his mother and the police. Gilroy had been a desperately unhappy little boy in the days since that happened, even more so than usual. He was obviously disturbed. When he wasn't being sullen and withdrawn, or hyper and uncontrollable, he was on a mission, trying to find ever more devious ways to upset or even hurt other children.

The worst thing he did at that time involved our youngest foster-child, Laurel. She was only about eighteen months old, and I remember she was standing at the top of the landing, calling me. Just as I reached the bottom of the stairs, I saw Gilroy run up behind Laurel and give her a sharp push that sent her tumbling off the top step and all the way down the stairs, bumping on her bottom, fortunately padded by her nappy, and knocking one arm and one leg hard against the banisters as she hurtled towards me. I don't know how I did it, but I managed to catch her. It was just instinctive I suppose. I caught her full weight in my arms – fortunately she was quite light, but it still sent me reeling, so I was glad I managed to hold on to her. I knew she could have been hurt very badly.

She wailed at the top of her voice, and the more she wailed, the wider the smile stretched on Gilroy's face, as he stood looking over the banisters at us. She was obviously hurt, so I phoned her social worker and then I had to take her down to the hospital to be X-rayed.

I had to take all the kids, including Gilroy, down with me to A&E. When they saw the motley crowd of us coming in, they took Laurel through straight away. Fortunately, although she was badly bruised, and they had to put her wrist in plaster for a hairline fracture, nothing major was broken and she had no internal injuries.

When I got them all back home again, I called Gilroy's social worker and explained what had happened.

'I think you'd better come round and have a serious talk with Gilroy. It's not just what happened to Laurel today. There's definitely a problem here. He's been hiding boxes of matches and sharp knives in his room. And he's being spiteful and nasty to the other children. When I'm not looking, I'm sure he does things to them. I hear their cries and see their bruises when he hurts them. I think you need to talk to him.'

Several weeks later, I had a letter asking me to be a witness at Gilroy's mother's trial. Apparently, the police had charged her with drunken affray and threatening behaviour, or something like that.

'Why didn't you let Mrs Dobbs in?' asked the barrister.

'Because when she arrived she was drunk,' I explained.

The judge intervened. 'How do you know? Are you an expert on alcohol consumption?'

'No. But I could tell she was drunk.'

'You can't say that, Mrs Merry.'

'But I can . . .'

And when we got outside, Gilroy's social worker said, 'You can't say that. You've got to say that you could smell alcohol and that she couldn't walk straight and she was slurring her words. But you're not a medical expert, so you can't say she was drunk.'

'For goodness sake!' I said to Mike that evening, after the kids had gone to bed. 'What does it matter what words I used? She was definitely drunk.'

'So what was the verdict?' he asked.

'Oh, I don't know. I couldn't stay to the end. But I'm sure they must have found her guilty.'

'Well, as long as she learns her lesson,' said Mike.

'Some hope!' I sighed. 'I wonder what she'll get up to next.'

14

Piggy-Bank Raid

Daisy and Paul's social worker made one of his rare visits to see the children.

'It's good to see you, John,' I greeted him. 'You haven't been for ages. Have you come to check whether I've murdered them yet?'

'No,' he laughed. 'We have so many cases where foster placements are going wrong these days, but I know Daisy and Paul couldn't be in a better family.'

'So does that mean you can have a day off when you should be visiting them?' I teased him.

'Chance would be a fine thing,' he said. 'But I have to check up and write a report now and then, that they're still being fed and watered and that they're growing well!'

'You make them sound like plants – if only it were that simple!'

Over the six years Daisy and Paul had been with us, they'd only seen their father about three times, and his last visit must have been two years ago. So it was quite a surprise when he turned up out of the blue one Sunday afternoon, as shifty as ever, with a young lad of about fifteen, who had a look of Paul about him.

'This is my nephew, Carl,' he said. 'The kids' cousin. Can we come in and see them?'

'Well, you should have called me to make sure, and then I could have got them into some decent clothes for you.'

'Never mind about that,' he said, waving his hand. 'We won't stay long.'

I felt distinctly uncomfortable about letting them in, especially as I knew nothing about this boy Carl, but I felt I had to for the children's sake, so they could see their errant father. I showed them into the playroom to wait, while I went to call Daisy and Paul in. Luckily Mike was home, being a Sunday, so I had a quick word with him, out of the kitchen window, to put him in the picture.

'I don't think I should leave Rocky and this young cousin alone with Daisy and Paul,' I explained. 'It doesn't feel right, somehow. What do you think?'

'No, they don't even know him, do they?'

'I don't think so. They certainly won't remember him.' I paused. 'And there's something about him that makes me feel . . .'

'Threatened?'

'Not quite, but definitely uncomfortable.' I paused. 'And I don't trust Rocky either.'

After all these years of fostering, I had developed a sixth sense about people. And I had a funny feeling about this boy, Carl. A chip off his uncle's dodgy old block, maybe.

So I tagged along when the kids took their dad and cousin up to see their bedrooms, and showed them all their things. Paul showed him a Lego model he had made, but when he gave it to his father to look at, Rocky managed to break it. Daisy tried to show him her schoolwork, some of her drawings, her knitting . . . but he barely looked at it, preferring instead to sit on her bed and adjust his watch. I left the room for just a couple of minutes, to collect a laundry basket, so I didn't hear everything they said, but I don't think I missed much. Then they all came down again and out into the garden. I took out drinks and snacks, then went back to the kitchen to get on with the chores. I knew Mike was keeping an eye on everyone, so I put the radio on while I did some ironing.

At one point, Carl sauntered in and through the kitchen. 'Just going to the toilet,' he said with a sly smile.

'It's on the right of the stairs,' I told him.

A few minutes later he came back through and out to the garden again.

Just as I turned the radio off to go out and see them all in the garden, Rocky and his nephew came into the kitchen with Daisy and Paul trailing behind, more or less ignored.

'We've got to go now,' said Rocky. 'I'm working at six and I've got to take Carl back first. Thanks for the drinks.'

'That's OK. But you've only been here half an hour. It's a shame you couldn't stay longer. I'm sure Daisy and Paul would have liked to spend more time with you.'

'Next time,' said Rocky.

'Any idea when that will be?' I asked.

'When I'm up here again, I expect,' he said in his usual, offhand way.

So we stood at the front and waved them off in Rocky's wreck of what had probably once been a flashy car. I suppose it would be a collector's car by now, but it badly needed doing up. It sounded pretty rough as it chugged away, with its rear bumper dropping loose at one end.

Later that evening, when they'd had their baths and were getting ready for bed, Daisy and Paul came running down the stairs, holding their red post-box piggy-bank. They shared it between them and Daisy, always the methodical one, kept a note of the amounts when either of them put money into it, so that they knew what they both had in it. It was usually small amounts, like bits of pocket-money. Or when my father used to come and visit, he always gave every child sixpence or a shilling to put in their money-boxes. For some reason, one of them must have picked up the piggy-bank at bedtime.

'It's empty,' wailed Paul.

'All our money has gone,' added Daisy, clearly upset.

'Somebody's stolen it,' cried Paul.

'Come and sit down and let's think how it could have happened,' I suggested.

So we sat together at the kitchen table, and I called Mike to come and join us.

'Are you sure you had money in it?'

'Yes, replied Daisy. 'There was two pounds, three shillings and sixpence in it.'

That was a lot of money in those days – more than the cost of a pair of adult shoes – so I could understand their consternation.

'You must have been saving that for a while,' Mike said with a look of admiration.

'When did you last check it?' I asked.

'This morning.' Daisy got out her notebook. 'Look. I check it every morning when I first get up. I counted it and it was all still there, so I ticked the page, see?' She showed us her neat writing, with the amounts and each day's date with a tick against it, the last one being that morning's.

'Well done, Daisy. That's very efficient.'

'Then I put it away again in a secret place,' she explained.

'But we got it out to show Dad,' added Paul.

'So it was on my desk. Anybody could have seen it.'

We tried to work out what could have happened.

'It must have been AJ.' Paul was convinced.

I had to agree that it could have been AJ, who used to steal things every day when he first joined us; but he seemed to have gradually changed his ways over the five years since then. Still, he had been the first person to come into my mind.

'I agree. It could be AJ,' Daisy agreed. 'None of the others would have stolen our money, would they?' she said with a sad expression.

'What about Gilroy?' suggested Paul. 'He wouldn't care.

But if it was him, he would probably have broken the piggy-bank too.'

'That's true,' I agreed.

'Whoever it is, you've got to make him pay it back,' insisted Paul, greatly aggrieved.

'I know you feel very cross and hurt by what's happened, but we have to do this in the right way.'

'Call the police!' Paul demanded. 'We've got to call the police.'

'I'll tell you what,' I suggested. 'Let Mike and me have a think about it, and we'll call John, and ask him what he thinks too. If we can't find out who did it, Mike and I will put that money in your piggy-bank ourselves. We'll make sure you don't lose your savings.'

'Thank you,' said Daisy with a smile of relief.

'Yes, thank you,' agreed Paul.

'And don't tell anybody what's happened, until we tell you it's OK,' I added. 'Until we've decided what to do.'

When all the kids had settled down to sleep, I called John, hoping he might be on late duty. He wasn't, but the woman who answered the phone said she would pass on the message to him and ask him to come round first thing in the morning, before the children left for school.

So early Monday morning, John came and we sat down in the kitchen with all the children round the table. He explained to all of them that the money was missing and showed them Daisy and Paul's piggy-bank, which of course most of the children recognised.

'Can any of you tell me anything?'

Nobody spoke. I was watching both AJ and Gilroy closely, without it being too obvious. They both looked as surprised as the rest when John told them and neither of them looked shifty or uncomfortable, so I felt it was unlikely to have been AJ. Gilroy would probably have had the capability to brazen it out, but I didn't think he was quite that crafty. After all, he wouldn't be afraid to own up, if he felt like it, and damn the lot of us with his foul language, which of course he'd learnt from his mother.

Mike took the older ones to school and my friend Val came to play with our three pre-schoolers – Laurel, Alfie and Mandy. This allowed me some uninterrupted time to talk it all through with John in the sitting-room.

'What's your gut feeling?' I asked him.

'Well, I wonder whether it might have been Rocky. He hasn't been for ages, then he comes yesterday, the children take him up to their bedrooms, they tell him about the piggy-bank, he stays a short while, then he's off again.'

'But why would he steal from his own children?'

'Why wouldn't he? He's always short of money.'

'But he said he's working.'

'Yes, that's what he said. But are you sure?'

'Mmm. I hadn't looked at it that way.'

'Well, there's nothing we can do about it now. But if Rocky comes back again, do not let him go anywhere in the house without you. Don't let him out of your sight – even stay close to the toilet door.

'What you said then . . .'

'Yes?'

'It reminded me – Carl, their cousin, came in and went to the loo while everyone was outside . . . or at least he said that's where he was going.' We exchanged glances.

'I'm afraid we may never know,' said John with a shrug.

After John had gone, I searched the children's bedrooms – every inch in AJ's and Gilroy's. But I found nothing more than the odd penny or thruppeny bit.

So I told all the children at teatime that we hadn't solved the crime, but we would replace the money Daisy and Paul had lost, so that they didn't lose out.

Just a few days later, when I had almost forgotten about it, I had a call from Carl's mother. She had found some money in Carl's bedroom and she knew it wasn't his. Could he have acquired it when he came to visit Daisy and Paul? I said yes and explained a bit about it, then thanked her. She promised to send me the amount taken in the form of a postal order.

'When do you think Rocky will come again?' asked Mike that evening when the children were all in bed.

'I'm not holding my breath!'

'It's Daisy and Paul who miss out on having a parent.'

'They didn't seem too bothered about him on Sunday, when he showed so little interest in them. I think they've lost faith in his promises over the years.'

15

Expelled

Daisy had joined the Brownies the previous year and loved it. She had already gained her booklover and artist badges, and now that she knew how to knit, she was working towards a badge for that too. She wasn't a leader, or an instigator, so she probably wouldn't be a sixer, but she loved making things, and they did a lot of that at Brownies.

Paul started going to Cubs, which he also loved, but for very different reasons. He was never a child who wanted to sit still and do something studious, like Daisy. He was an action-man, right from the start, and his main aim in life was to have fun, being as active as possible.

So I wasn't surprised, when I collected him and Ronnie from Cubs one day, to be met at the door by the cub leader.

'I'm glad I've caught you, Mrs Merry. I wanted to have a word with you about Paul.'

'Oh yes?' Looking at his serious face, I could already guess what was coming.

'Paul is a very lively child, which is fine . . . But the

trouble is we can't get him to sit still for a moment! AJ and Ronnie are restless too, but Paul is incorrigible. We simply can't keep him in order.'

'No, I don't know how they manage him at school, but probably by the time he gets here, he's had enough of inactivity, like most boys.'

'Yes, I can understand that, Mrs Merry. But he's almost wild by the time he gets here. We're used to coping with the usual rough and tumble, which both AJ and Ronnie are always in the middle of, but Paul is completely over the top. He's a daredevil when he's here, and tries to get the other boys to join him. We've been trying to calm him down enough to start working on a badge, but maybe he's too new to take that on. The problem is that all the other boys are working well towards their badges and we help them to do that. Paul has been quite disruptive during these sessions, which has upset some of the other children, especially when he has trodden on their hand-made models, or splashed all over their writing, or whatever.' He paused. 'But today we had an unfortunate incident.'

'Oh?'

'One of our older Cubs is doing his astronomer's badge, so we borrowed a telescope and set it up in the car park to see what stars and planets this boy could identify. But out came Paul and started careering around between the cars. My assistant couldn't stop him. It was just high spirits, I know, but he ran straight into the telescope, knocked it to the ground and broke it.'

'Oh no, I am sorry. He can be so reckless sometimes. But

I'm sure it would have been an accident. We'll pay for the damage.'

'Thank you. But I'm afraid Paul is just too boisterous for us, so we must ask you not to bring him to Cubs any more . . . not until he has calmed down a bit. Maybe next year? I'm afraid he is just too hyper for us to manage at the moment.'

So there it was – having once been excluded from pre-school, Paul was now expelled from Cubs at not quite seven years old!

Daisy came home from school with a note one day. 'We're going to do a play,' she said. 'And I'm going to be a Dutch girl.' Her eyes sparkled as she told me. I had never seen her this excited. I read the note, explaining that it was going to be a performance by the whole class for an assembly, and asking parents to make or provide the appropriate clothes.

'I've got to wear a pretty blouse and skirt to be a Dutch girl,' she enthused. 'And we all have to wear plaits. Can you make them for me, please?'

'Yes, of course.' I laughed. 'So you will be able to wear long hair at last!'

'And can I have them blond, so it looks like my hair?'

'OK, I think I've got a ball of yellow wool, so you can help me make them. And I'll sew you a Dutch-style blouse and skirt outfit as well.'

So that's what we did over the next few days. She tried everything on when it was finished and it all looked perfect.

'I love the plaits,' she said, looking at herself in the mirror. The way she had them, attached to an Alice-band, with just her blond fringe showing, framed her face, so that she couldn't see her awful haircut. 'Thank you,' she said with a lovely smile and a hug. She was more demonstrative that day than I'd ever known her.

'Right, take off your outfit and I'll put it away for Friday.'

'OK. But can I keep the plaits on?'

So that's what she did. The performance came and went, and the Dutch girl outfit was put away in her drawer to wear again if she wanted to. But the plaits were always with her. She wore them at home and she wore them to and from school. She wore them for weeks, turning into months.

Several months later, I went up to the school for parents' evening. When I reached Daisy's teacher, we talked about her work and how well she was doing in everything.

'Well, that's all good news,' I said with a smile. 'I wish I got that with all my kids!'

'But there is one thing I wanted to discuss with you, Mrs Merry.'

'Oh yes? What's that?'

'Daisy's plaits – she keeps them in her desk every day and insists on wearing them at break-times. She'd wear them in the classroom too if we let her.'

'Really?' I was surprised that Daisy had become so attached to them at school as well as at home.

'So, could you please ask her not to bring the plaits to school anymore? This has gone on for too long now, and some of my colleagues are rather concerned about it becoming a bit of an obsession.'

The next evening, I had a chat with Daisy. 'I'm so pleased with how well you are doing at school, Daise,' I began. 'Your teacher showed me some of your books, and the marks you've been getting. I'm very proud of you for working so hard and doing so well.'

'Thank you,' she smiled, her self-esteem quietly boosted.

'But there is one thing,' I continued. 'It's those plaits I made you. Now, we don't mind if you want to wear them at home, but the teacher doesn't want you to have them at school any more. So just keep them at home and you can wear them here when you want to.'

'It's only because I'm not allowed to have long hair,' she explained.

'Yes, I know, Daise. But not away from home, OK?'

She gave a big sigh. 'OK.'

The next time John, her social worker came to the house, a few days later, Daisy had her plaits on.

'Daisy's still acting the Dutch girl, is she?' he asked with a smile.

'Yes, but only at home now.' And I told him what her teacher had told me at parents' evening.

He nodded his agreement. 'It's time these plaits were taken away and burnt!'

'I can't do that, John. I can't . . .'

So she carried on wearing them all day, every day at home, until they started to become so tattered that they began to fall apart.

'Can we mend them?' she asked me one day, with a forlorn expression.

'No, I think they're beyond repair, Daise.'

'But I want to keep them,' she pleaded, close to tears.

'Well, why not put them in your memory box?' I suggested.

'Oh yes!' her face brightened. 'That way I can still try them on sometimes, to cheer me up.'

I used to give every child a memory box, no matter how short a time they were with us. We used to put photos in them, along with bus and train tickets, certificates from school, entry tickets to places we'd visited, plus posters, programmes, hair ribbons, masks, letters, badges, small gifts, a favourite comic or book, things they'd won at the fair (other than fish!) – all sorts.

Sometimes on Sundays, when the weather was bad, I used to ask the children to bring down their memory boxes and we all sat round the kitchen table, sharing their memories and taking out some of their treasured items to show, as well as adding new ones. Out would come the funny stories and we all enjoyed laughing together. Everyone loved these sessions, apart from Gilroy, who was becoming gradually more morose and seemed to be listening to his own thoughts more than to anyone else.

Whenever a child left, they took their memory box with them to help them remember the fun times they'd had with us. And for some children, like Daisy and Paul, their memory boxes held all the memories they could remember, having come to us at such young ages and stayed for so much of their childhood. We hoped they would be able to keep them long after they left us, and continue adding to them.

16

Revenge

Ever since Gilroy had joined us, his mother had been the bane of my life. But we'd had a welcome lull since the court case, when she had been convicted and ordered never again to come within 100 yards of our house. She had kept to it, so far, though her frequent abusive phone calls had been almost as bad.

One day, however, there was a persistent knocking on the front door. I peeked out of a window and saw her standing there. So I went to the door and fastened the chain before opening it a crack. It was awkward trying to talk through that crack, with her on the doorstep. But I knew I couldn't let her in without permission from Social Services, and anyway, I wanted to make as sure as I could that she was in a fit state.

'I've come to take Gilroy to the fair.'

'Now, come on, Kathleen. You know there's a court order—'

'F*** the bleeding court order! It's time up now.'

'Really? I thought it was continuous.'

'You don't know nothing. You're as f****** bad as they are.'

'Well, I can't let you in without a permission letter from Social Services . . .'

'Blow that for a f****** lark! I'm not bloody well going down there.'

'Well, I was about to suggest that I bring you the phone and you can call them from here if you like.'

'What bleeding good would that do? And what business is it of theirs anyway? A load of stuck-up cows! They don't know f****** nothing about kids.'

I focussed on her first question. 'Well, I know you're supposed to have a letter, but if they can give me permission on the phone, I'm willing to let you in.'

'Huh!' She obviously didn't think much of that.

'But I can't let you take Gilroy out without written permission.'

She finally paused to think that through. 'But I could come in and see him?' She realised that, if she played ball, she could get some of what she came for.

'Yes, we can get some toys out and you could sit and play with him.'

She looked doubtful. 'But I'm not a bloody child!'

'I didn't mean that. I just meant you could help him play.'

'He don't need no help from me,' she snorted. 'But still . . .'

'I'll just close the door while I get the phone,' I said. I had once before stretched the phone cord to the door, when Rocky turned up drunk, so I knew it would reach. 'Here's the phone and here's the number,' I said, taking the chain off and handing it all to her.

She called Social Services and asked if she could visit and they said yes, as long as I agreed. They then spoke to me and said I could let her in if I felt it was safe, and that was it. I just hoped I was doing the right thing.

I don't know what it is with some parents when they come to see their children. They're often nervous, as if they're going to be watched and judged, though I was always pleased to see them together. I think a lot of them have had a drink before they come, thinking it would steady their nerves, not realising it would make them worse. And of course, I'd had first-hand experience of Kathleen and her drink problem. I could smell it now, but her eyes looked to be in focus and she was standing unaided, so I decided to let her in. I thought it might help Gilroy, whose mental health was causing me some concerns at that time. Perhaps seeing his mum would relax him, I thought, but I should have known better.

We had a big, family kitchen, so I could go and busy myself at one end of it while they sat at the other. I made her a coffee and handed it to her.

As I rolled out pastry and made some tarts for tea, I watched Gilroy sullenly settle himself on the cushions by the toy box, next to his mother's chair. Not a word, or even a look passed between them – in fact they barely interacted at all, except when Kathleen gave her son a packet of sweets and he snatched them from her, guzzling them all in one sitting.

I saw Kathleen getting a packet of cigarettes out of her bag.

'Sorry Kathleen, but we have a no-smoking rule in the house, to protect the children's health,' I said

'F****** health,' she moaned, then took a small mirror out of her bag and began to refresh her make-up. Meanwhile, Gilroy built a tall tower on the floor with some wooden bricks, then stood up, drew back his leg and gave them an almighty kick, so that they went everywhere. The noise and sudden disarray made him smile. But one brick hit his mother and she immediately slapped his head. She swore at him and he made a face. They were the first words between them in fifteen minutes.

Once I'd put the tarts in the oven, I went over to join them. 'Why don't you tell your mum about the model ship your class are making at school, Gilroy?'

'We're making a pirate ship,' he said, grudgingly. 'When it's finished . . .' he paused, looking at his mother, who was looking at her watch. 'We're going to smash it to pieces,' he shouted, acting out an explosion, with all the sound effects.

I felt for Gilroy. Why did his mother bother to come, if she wasn't even going to take any interest in him? But it was probably Gilroy's best visit from his mum. They had nearly half an hour together in the same room. Nobody got into a temper, there wasn't much swearing and no one was hurt. Sadly, there was hardly any affection at all – only the sweets. As I showed Kathleen out of the door, I breathed a sigh of relief.

Gilroy's mum did try once more to visit, but she shouted and swore at me and called me names as loudly as she could.

I could smell the alcohol much more strongly this time, just through the crack of the door with the chain on.

'Let me in, you f****** c***.'

'I can't. I am not allowed to let you in when you're like this. You've got to get a permission letter from Social Services if you want to come again.'

'F*** you!' she yelled and tried to kick the door down.

As I closed it I turned round to see Gilroy sitting on the stairs, his face bright red with anger as he punched the step repeatedly with his fist.

'I'm sorry, Gilroy,' I said. 'But I couldn't let your mum in when she was in a temper like that. It would have frightened the other children.' I felt so sorry for him and went to give him a hug, but he backed away up the stairs. I'm not sure if it was my imagination, but there was something very unsettling in the way he stared at me before he turned and ran off down the landing, then slammed the door. Seconds later, he kicked off and trashed his room as he'd done before, the crashing sounds reverberating around the house.

Paul was always the happy-go-lucky one of the family, with a strong sense of fairness. He would always stick up for his friends, or any of the other kids, if he felt they had been treated unfairly. So that evening, when Mike was reading the bedtime story to the little ones and the others were all in their rooms, I went along to get Paul, who was now sharing again with AJ and Ronnie, leaving Gilroy on his own at the end of the corridor, away from everyone else, just in case.

'Do you think you can help me, Pauly?' I asked him, as I took him into the spare room to talk. 'I expect you heard Gilroy trashing his room earlier?'

'Yes, everybody could hear it.'

'And I know you helped Mike and Gilroy clear up the worst of the mess and mend his bed so he could sleep on it. Mike says you did a grand job there.'

'Thank you,' said Paul with a smile. 'I like mending things.'

'Yes, maybe you can do more of that when you grow up. But right now, I want your help in another way.'

'What way?'

'Gilroy was very upset this afternoon, when his mother was in such a rage that it wasn't safe for me to let her in. It wasn't Gilroy's fault that his mother was like that, so I think he needs a friend at the moment, to help take his mind off it.'

'Do you want me to share a room with him again?' He looked a bit worried.

'No, nothing like that. But you're the same age as him and you used to get on well, so if you could try to include him in your games and help him to have some fun again, like he used to, that could really help him. What do you think?'

'Yes, I guess so. As long as he's not too mean. Shall I tell Ronnie and AJ too?'

'Yes. Let's go up and tell them together.'

The next few days were tricky ones for Gilroy. When he was out playing with the boys and they were having raucous fun together, he was fine. But in between I often saw him sitting with that look in his eyes, chewing his lip and making fists with his hands as his resentment and anger resurfaced.

I checked his room every day, for anything that might be damaging, and I kept a closer eye on him than before, to make sure he didn't take his anger out on the little ones. But, luckily for the other kids, he chose to attack the toys instead, breaking a couple of the trikes and a sit-on digger, much to the small children's indignation; but we bought them a few replacements at a second-hand shop, so they didn't lose out for long.

'Kathleen's an alcoholic, you know,' said Gilroy's social worker when he visited a few days later. He probably shouldn't have told me that, but I expect he assumed it was all right, since I'd been at her trial. Apparently, after I'd left the courtroom, a policeman had reported that Kathleen had been in trouble with the police before for being drunk, and a doctor testified that she had been sent for treatment for her alcoholism, but stopped attending.

Now, looking back, I realise that she had mental health problems as well. She was a very, very difficult woman.

The phone rang one day soon after that and a sharp male voice spoke in a hurried tone. 'I've abducted your foster-daughter Daisy from her school. You'll never see her again.'

'What?' I shrieked and the phone went dead. I froze in shock. Then I heard myself screaming. I panicked . . . unable to catch my breath. But I knew I had to keep my head, somehow. There was no one at home but me and the three little ones. What should I do? I was in a terrible turmoil, but I had to act quickly.

I had to get down to the school, straight away. But I couldn't leave the children.

No, I had to phone. But who should I phone first? I dialled 999.

'What service . . . ?'

'Police, quickly.' My heart was pounding. The wait seemed endless as I watched the slow second hand on our hall clock.

'Hello—'

'You have to help me,' I interrupted. 'My daughter, my foster-daughter – she's been kidnapped. I've got to go down there.'

'Where?'

'Park Primary School.'

'Right, we'll meet you there, and we'll organise a search.'

'Please hurry.'

I grabbed three-year-old Mandy and four-year-olds Alfie and Laurel as fast as I could and ran round to Edie and Frank next door. I rang the bell. *Please let them be in. Please . . .*

The door opened.

'Edie, can you have the kids? I've got to go down to the

school. It's urgent. Daisy's been abducted. Here's the key if you want to take them back to our house.'

The police had already arrived when I got to the school. I ran in. 'Oh my God,' I screamed at the secretary. 'Why did you let this man take my Daisy?'

'Er, no, Mrs Merry. She's in her classroom.'

'You mean you still haven't noticed?' I was beginning to feel hysterical. 'She's been kidnapped!'

'No, it's OK, Mrs Merry. She's fine. Daisy hasn't been kidnapped. She's here and she's safe. It must have been a hoax.'

'I don't believe you. Are you SURE?'

'Yes, certain.

'I've got to see her,' I shrieked. 'I've got to see her.'

'It's all right. Calm down, Mrs Merry. The police alerted us and we checked straight away. She was here all the time. Let me take you to see for yourself.'

So we went down the long corridor, with me racing ahead. When we reached the classroom, the door was open and I walked in. Straight away I could see Daisy, in a world of her own, reading in the book corner. It was a HUGE relief. She didn't even notice me, so I left quietly and walked back with the secretary.

The police were talking with the headteacher when we reached the entrance hall again. A policeman and a policewoman.

'It's all right,' I told them. 'She's here. Phew. Panic over.'

'But somebody has played a very cruel trick on you, Mrs Merry. We need to see if we can stop him doing it to anybody else. We need you to tell us all the details about that phone call. You might be able to give us vital clues to help us try to track him down.'

'Yes, of course,' I agreed. I would have done anything to make sure nobody else had to go through the trauma I had just suffered. 'But I don't understand who could have done it,' I said, still in a flustered state. 'And why? I mean . . . do you think he got some kind of a kick from trying to destroy me like that?'

'I can't say, Mrs Merry.'

Just then, the secretary brought me in a cup of tea.

'I don't know whether you take sugar, Mrs Merry, but I think you need it for the shock.' I thanked her.

'Do you think you have any enemies?' continued the policeman.

'No, not at all,' I said. 'Except maybe the neighbours we had at Sonnington, who didn't like our kids, but that was a long time ago!' I smiled. 'And they wouldn't have done this.'

'Well, the man who rang you obviously knew you had a daughter called Daisy and the name of her school.'

'But I don't think he said the name of the school,' I replied, trying to think back to his actual words. 'Wait a minute . . . yes, it must be someone who knows us, because he knew that Daisy is my foster-daughter. That's what he said: "your foster-daughter".'

'Right,' said the policewoman. 'Let's write all this down in a statement, Mrs Merry. And we'll ask you to sign it. Will that be all right?'

* * *

'What a shock!' said Mike, when I told him the whole story later that day. How are you feeling now?'

'Still a bit wobbly inside, I suppose, but I can't tell you how relieved I was to see Daisy sitting there safely in the classroom, completely unaware of all the fuss.'

'Any ideas about who this man could be? Did you recognise his voice? Or do you think he was disguising it?'

'I don't know. I'm trying to remember. It was so quick. He just said those terrible words, quite rushed, then hung up. I went into panic mode, so no, I don't think it was a voice I knew.'

'Was it a local accent?'

'Yes, I think so. I didn't notice, so it probably was. But the police seemed to think it could be someone who knows us. Someone with a grudge. Someone who was deliberately getting back at me for something.'

We sat in silence for a few moments, racking our brains. Then it came to me.

'You don't think Kathleen Dobbs could have anything to do with it, do you?'

'Gilroy's mum?' asked Mike. 'But it was a man's voice, wasn't it?'

'Oh yes. So it couldn't have been her.'

'You could mention her to the police though, just in case.'

So the next day, I rang the police station.

'You've beaten us to it, Mrs Merry,' they told me. 'We were just about to call you. We've had a breakthrough, and we're ninety per cent sure we've found the culprit. Can we come round and explain?'

'So you see,' said the male police officer I'd met at the school the previous day, 'we just had a hunch about this case. One of my colleagues attended when you had all that trouble with a woman who was drunk and hurling milk-bottles at your house. Do you remember?'

'I'll never forget!'

'Well, she has a cousin, who's known to us. He's a bouncer at a local club. We took him in for questioning this morning, and she's also been interviewed at the station by two of my colleagues. I've just heard that she admitted putting him up to it. He was the one who phoned you and they've both been arrested. They planned it together, to frighten you.'

'Well, they succeeded,' I said with feeling. 'I've never been so frightened in my life.'

'So, have the police charged Kathleen and her cousin?' Mike asked me when I phoned him at work to tell him the mystery was solved.

'Not yet. They wanted me to take her to court and I said no.'

'Why on earth did you refuse?'

'Because Gilroy has a hard enough time as it is, without us making it even worse. If she was put in prison, he wouldn't see her at all. It might be hard for us to swallow, but she's all he's got, apart from us.'

We finally heard that the police had taken action themselves and secured a lifetime ban on Kathleen Dobbs coming down our road at all, on pain of imprisonment. I had to agree that I was pleased about that. It made us all feel safer.

If she wanted to see Gilroy, she had to book a time with the local authority. Then his social worker would come and fetch him and supervise their visit at the family centre.

Unfortunately, that made things even worse for Gilroy. She would arrange a date and time and I'd get Gilroy ready to be picked up. He and his social worker would be waiting at the family centre and she didn't turn up. This happened nearly every time. The poor lad hardened and grew more defiant and angry with the world every day. He was a troubled boy and we had to help him as best we could.

All the children we had at this time had been with us for at least two years, so it was the most settled we had ever been. Others had come and gone, and we currently had one place, but we thought maybe it was a good time to think about taking all the children away on a holiday in the summer. It would be the first time, so it would need a lot of planning.

'What about Bournemouth?' asked Mike.

'Good idea. We'll need at least two caravans,' I pointed out. 'It will be quite a squash . . .'

'Hey kids,' said Mike at teatime the next day. 'Would you like us all to go on holiday together this year?'

'YES!' they all shouted in unison, highly excited, jumping and laughing and dancing and cheering . . . all except for Daisy, who stood back and watched all the fun – with a big, beaming smile on her face. So it was unanimous.

Now all we had to do was organise the finer details . . . and pray hard not to lose or maim anybody for the whole holiday. Quite a daunting prospect!

17

Jekyll and Hyde

'I've heard such good things about you,' said the educated voice on the phone. I know you're a foster-parent, but would you consider child-minding?'

'Well, I started off with child-minding.'

'Please say you'll do it. I'm at my wits' end with my eighteen-month-old. He's adorable when he's asleep, but a nightmare all the rest of the time. And I have to work.'

'What do you do?'

'I'm a university researcher, so even when I can work at home, I do have to concentrate. I need a wonderful fairy godmother to take Max on and tame him. I know that's a huge ask, but I wonder if perhaps you could have him for a few days to start with, and see how it goes?'

'Well, maybe, but I think I'd better discuss it with my husband.' I didn't tell her that Mike always said yes – he must be the most tolerant man ever.

'And could you maybe . . . I know it's a bit of a cheek, really . . . but as you are a foster parent, do you think it might be possible . . . if you've got enough space . . . to have Max to stay over occasionally, to give me a break?'

She paused. 'Of course, that bit is not essential. If you can only do the day-care, that would be great for me anyway, but if you could do the odd night as well, you would be my lifesaver.'

'OK, I'll talk it over with Mike. Can I let you know tomorrow?'

'Yes, perfect. The sooner the better. My name is Vanda, by the way, and this is my phone number . . . Thank you so much for not saying no. I can't tell you what a relief it is that you're even considering him.'

She sounded such a lovely person, this woman who had phoned out of the blue. But experience had taught me to be wary. I have to say, I don't always learn from my mistakes, although I do try to; so I had an idea.

'I know you said you have a lot of work on, but if you can spare half an hour this afternoon, why not bring Max round for a cup of tea? That way I can meet you both and it will be easier to tell my husband about you.'

'Well, that was an interesting visit,' I told Mike later on. 'I could hear this child screaming and kicking off inside their car as soon as they turned into our drive.'

'You mean something more than interesting, don't you?' Mike knows me so well. 'I bet you were doing your amateur psychology thing on them!'

I laughed. 'Yes, you're right. But it was fascinating to see just how naughty that child is when his mother is in the room. He was throwing things everywhere, having tantrums, trying to hold her mouth closed to stop her speaking and bawling loud enough to disturb Edie and Frank next door. But the moment his mother left the room to go to the loo, he immediately became a sweet-natured, smiling cherub who played beautifully with me. As soon as she came back into the playroom, he switched back to being a little devil.'

'Are you sure you want to take on this Jekyll-and-Hyde child?' He looked doubtful. 'After all, you've already got your hands full with Gilroy, AJ, Paul and all the rest. Why make life harder for yourself?'

'Well . . . I liked Vanda, and I liked her son, when she wasn't with him. I want to watch him, to see how his brain works. And anyway, I love a challenge.'

'You can say that again!'

'So you don't mind?'

'Of course not. When did I ever mind?'

The first day I had Max, he was awful when he arrived, but as soon as the front door closed behind his mother, it was like pressing the 'off' switch. This lovely boy with blond curls was the most amenable child ever.

'Come on, Max,' I took him into the playing end of the kitchen. We got out some chunky wooden shapes and made a funny building, then we got some cars out to whiz and clatter around on the tiles.

'Would you like something to eat?' I asked.

He nodded.

'Some cereal?'

'Es pees.'

He hardly stopped smiling and he was obviously enjoying the toys, playing happily with our other pre-school children, four-year-olds Laurel, Alfie and Mandy. In fact, he charmed them completely.

'Right, you four,' I said. 'It's time to clear away the toys, so we can go out for a walk.'

I was impressed to see Max toddling about, dextrously picking up cars from all around the kitchen and putting them in the toy box.

I waited all day for this obnoxious tearaway to emerge, but there was no sign of the bad Max. He was obviously saving that for later. His mother was due to come for him at six. So after he'd had his tea with us, he went and sat on the window seat in our hall. Daisy and Sheena sat on either side, doing rhymes and actions with him to keep him amused. He giggled away until he heard the sound of his mother's car.

I saw the switch-on moment when he turned into his tempestuous alter-ego. Before I could even get to the door, he was banging and kicking it. And when I opened it, he started hitting and kicking his mother, shouting and roaring in his fury. The girls and I were gobsmacked.

'Oh dear,' she said. 'I'm so sorry. Has he been like this all day?'

'No. Honestly. He's been as good as gold. Absolutely brilliant. No trouble at all. I can't believe the sudden change in him.'

'So can I bring him again tomorrow?' She looked doubtful.

'Yes, of course.'

When he arrived the next morning, it was bedlam when he came in with his mother, and as soon as she was out of the door, it was as if someone had sprinkled angel-dust on him. Again, he was smiley and gleeful all day. Whatever was it that changed him in a flash like that?

Over the next few weeks, we even had him one day each weekend. We took him swimming, to the park, to the zoo, to all the places the kids wanted to go, and he was never any trouble. Everybody loved him, except Gilroy who was always waiting for the chance . . . so we made sure to keep them apart. Even strangers would come up to us and say what a lovely boy he was, with his blond curls and dimples, and how well behaved he was.

At first, I assumed his mum was a single mother, but she had a good-looking young man with her one day. 'This is Max's dad,' she said. 'My husband Mark. He's a musician.' He smiled as we shook hands.

The following Friday evening, when Vanda came to pick up Max, she said, 'We've decided to go on a week's break to Scotland. It's a spur-of-the moment trip. Mark's not keen, because Max is such hard work, but maybe he'll be better when we're away from home.' She paused, looking uncertain. 'The only trouble is, Max doesn't want to go. I think you give him such a good time here that he doesn't want to miss out.'

'Well . . . I've got one space, so he could stay here if you like, to let you have some time to yourselves.'

She wavered for a moment. Then made her mind up.

'Thank you very much. It does sound tempting, but no. I think we need some time together as a family, the three of us, to bond together.'

I wondered how Max's behaviour might affect the family dynamics. I had a suspicion that he had rocked his parents' relationship. His mother worked during the day, and his father worked mostly in the evenings, so maybe they weren't able to spend much time together.

'Well,' I said, 'I hope you all have a really good, relaxing week. I'm sure Max will appreciate having you both to himself.'

They went on the Saturday. But on the Tuesday, I had a phone call.

'Trisha, is it possible for Max to come back to you tomorrow?' Vanda sounded more stressed than I'd heard her before.

'Yes' I said. 'But what's happened? I thought you were going for a week?'

'We hired a caravan, and he's totally wrecked it. The whole caravan – totally destroyed.'

'Max?' I gasped, in disbelief, trying to picture this toddler wreaking so much havoc.

'Yes.' I heard her sharp intake of breath.

'How awful!' I sympathised.

'Yes, it was. And we've been in trouble because of it. We had to leave the site yesterday.' She burst into tears. 'Mark is absolutely furious,' she sobbed. 'Incandescent with rage.'

'Oh no.'

'It's been awful, Trisha. Terrible.'

I didn't know whether she was talking about Max's behaviour, the caravan site manager, or her relationship with her husband. Maybe all three.

'Bring Max tomorrow,' I said, with a soothing voice. 'It sounds like you've got a lot to sort out. He'll be fine here.'

'Thank you so much, Trisha. You're a rock. I don't know what I'd do without you at the moment.' I could tell she was still crying as she put the phone down.

Next morning, in walked Max, with a big smile on his face. He was an absolute poppet, all day long. When it was lunchtime, they all had different coloured bowls or plates. So Max would go and get his own bowl and carry it proudly to the table. I couldn't believe this was the same boy who did so much damage on holiday with his parents.

For some time I had been worried that our 'bush-baby' Laurel, now nearly five, still hadn't been put forward for adoption; but now at last it was all being sorted out.

She was a lovely child with a pretty face and a sunny personality, so we weren't surprised when a young couple came to meet her, along with her social worker, to start to get to know her and to see if they'd be a good fit.

I could see it working straight away. They were perfect for Laurel and she for them, as they sat on the playroom floor and played with the toys together. Later, they played outdoor games in the garden, all three of them enjoying their growing relationship.

'How long will these visits go on?' I asked Laurel's social worker.

'Oh, several weeks of them seeing her here, then a few more when they can take her out during the day if they want to. Then maybe they'll do a couple of trial home visits, to see how that works out. Even if all goes really well, it would probably be the autumn before all the stages are completed and the adoption can go ahead.'

'Oh, that's good,' I said. 'We are hoping to take all the children on holiday together in the summer. We wouldn't want to leave Laurel out.'

'That's a great idea for the children,' she said, then gave me a look. 'But you must be mad! It won't be much of a holiday for you and Mike with all these kids and their different needs!'

'I know, but we'll love it just as much as they do, playing all day by the sea!'

'What about Gilroy?' she asked. 'How will you manage him? Will the children be safe with him there? Remember what he did to Laurel last year, when he pushed her down the stairs?'

'Yes, I know he can be difficult, very up and down, but he's not been too bad lately, and we'll keep a close eye on him. He's part of our family and he deserves a holiday as much as the others.'

I told Mike about this later.

'Perhaps we should put reins on Gilroy.' he suggested with a laugh. 'Like they used to do with toddlers.'

* * *

The summer was approaching and Mike booked two large caravans, adjacent to one another, on our chosen caravan site in Bournemouth for a week. Next, he mapped out the route to get there, with lots of stopping places with facilities on the way. We didn't have Satnavs in the 1970s – we had to rely on good old road maps.

As the date grew nearer, I started making lists, of all the things we needed to take, food to buy and all the other jobs we had to do, like getting permissions from Social Services and all the parents who were contactable. I can't actually remember whether Rocky answered with his permission for Daisy and Paul. But we would have taken the risk and included them anyway.

We still had just the nine foster-children, aged between four and ten: Ronnie, AJ, Sheena, Daisy, Paul, Gilroy, Laurel, Alfie and Mandy. They were all very excited and the older ones were crossing off the days on their calendars. Even Daisy was quite animated and clearly enjoyed all the build-up.

'You can all choose out of your own things what you want to take on holiday and put them on your beds,' I told them, 'so I can see if anything needs washing or ironing.'

An hour or two later, when they were all outside again, I did a tour of inspection. This was when I discovered that Laurel had put out all her summer dresses, but no knickers. Paul had put out plenty of toys and games on his bed, but no clothes at all and Daisy had put out eight books to read and only one top and shorts. And there were other variations in between.

'You've all got to take some outfits of play-about clothes, and one good set of clothes, in case we want to go somewhere special,' I told them at teatime. 'And Laurel, you need to take some knickers, too.' Everyone giggled.

'Paul, you didn't put out any anything at all to wear. Don't worry about toys and games. We'll pack those separately. Just make sure you take some clothes. We don't want you running around naked!' More giggling. 'And Daisy, you won't be able to carry your case with all those books in it, so take out half of the books and put some more clothes in instead.'

Next it was time to raid the toybox. 'Right,' I said. 'You can each choose one toy or game. And we'll take some extra things that everyone can play with.'

Toddler Max was still coming three or four days a week. He must have felt a bit left out of all the increasing excitement, although I tried to distract him onto other things. I asked the others to try not to talk about the holiday in front of him, but I don't suppose they took much notice and I felt bad that we couldn't include him.

'Max was looking a bit down in the dumps today,' said Mike, just a few days before the holiday. 'It's not like him – he's usually such a happy-go-lucky little lad.'

'Not according to his mother,' I said. 'And I've seen it for myself. He really lays into that poor woman. And I think he's driven a big, fat wedge between his parents since he trashed that caravan.'

'Good job he's not coming with us, then!' Mike laughed. 'But we'll miss his cheery smile.'

'Maybe we can take him with us? I thought out loud.

The next morning I asked Vanda, 'You know that we're going on holiday for a week on Saturday?'

'I'm dreading it already!' She gave a heavy sigh. 'I don't know what I'm going to do with Max. But I hope you all have a great time.'

'If we have enough space,' I suggested, tentatively, 'would you like us to take him with us?'

'Oh . . . no, I don't think it would be possible.'

That surprised me. 'Really?'

'We're still having to pay for all the damage he did when he trashed the caravan we hired on our holiday . . . We can't afford any more expense at the moment.'

'Oh,' I assured her, 'it wouldn't cost you anything. We're going anyway, all in the van, so one more wouldn't make any difference. And the caravans are booked as well, so it's only a case of squeezing him in. We'll work that out somehow.'

So when we set off on the following Saturday, Max came too.

18

Taking Ten to Bournemouth

It was a long journey south from the Midlands to Bournemouth, with all the children in the back, together with all their luggage, potties just in case and some large play equipment for the beach. We had to make toilet stops every forty-five minutes on the way, and a couple of other stops because I get car-sick. I had the map, but luckily Mike had learnt our route, which is just as well because I'm dyslexic.

I won't say it was easy taking a barrel of monkeys in the back of a van, crowded round with stuff. 'Don't anybody ask me "are we nearly there yet?",' I said. 'Because we won't be.'

'Not ever?' asked little Mandy, who was rehearsing to set up the British Logical Thinking Association – as soon as she could spell it.

'OK, Mand. You win. We will get there . . . but not for a very long time.'

'How many hours?' she persisted.

'Is it a leap year?' I replied, but fortunately that was lost on her, at that age.

* * *

For our lunch stop, Mike had chosen a place where there was a picnic area with lovely views and a large grassed area for the kids to play an impromptu football match, in between sandwiches, snacks and drinks.

When we reached the spot, there were lots of family groups of three or four dotted about, and not much space for us. I exchanged looks with Mike.

He weaved his way around them. 'We'll just park here,' he said, stopping right in the middle.

I gave one nearby family a smile and we exchanged hellos as I went round to the back of the van and opened the doors. It was like a scattergun explosion. Out poured the ten children, all the picnic things, all the balls and bats and skipping ropes and all the toys . . . and all their pent-up noise and energy.

'Well,' I said to Mike as people edged further and further away. 'We cleared this space quicker than a bomb-disposal unit!'

We had set off at eight in the morning, and it was late afternoon by the time we arrived at the site in Bournemouth.

We reported at the reception hut, and were told where to go. But there must have been a mix-up, because these two caravans were much smaller than we'd been led to believe they would be. How on earth were we going to fit everyone in?

'Do you think we can manage?' asked Mike, scratching his head.

'Well, somebody will have to sleep in the broom

cupboard,' I said, opening the door of the narrow space where the cleaning things were kept.

Ronnie laughed, and they all joined in.

'No, I'm serious. Look,' I pointed at the beds. 'We haven't got enough beds for everybody to sleep in, so you can all take turns, one night each in the broom cupboard.'

The children all looked at me, then at the cupboard, so I kept my face straight. 'Right, let's see who can go first . . . Paul, you come and try it out. You'll have to stand up, like the brooms.'

So, slim, wiry Paul squashed himself in sideways as far as he could.

'Yes, that's it, so you can do tonight. Daisy, you can go next. Then Sheena, Ronnie, AJ and Gilroy, you can do a night each.' They really believed me!

There was a double and a single bed in one caravan, and just a double in the other, so we topped and tailed the kids, four in each double and two in the single. And we put the settee bits together for Mike and me to sleep on.

None of the 1960s caravans on this site had bathrooms or toilets, so we all had to troop across to the wash-house, where the water was usually cold. But the kids had great fun splashing about in the showers.

The first morning of our holiday, we all trooped down to the beach with our stuff. All the kids, even the little ones, had to carry something. I can remember how excited they all were. Most of them had never seen the sea before, or felt the sand under their feet. Everybody was laughing and even normally quiet Daisy was joining in with the banter.

We found a good place to settle ourselves. Then we told them all to lie down, and Mike and I tried to bury them in the sand – well, not quite! When I think how dangerous it could have been . . . It wouldn't be allowed nowadays. But we just gave them a light covering, up to their necks, and they only stayed still for a few minutes, before wriggling free to have a runabout on the beach and down to the sea's edge.

We had all the beach toys with us, so they spent the day playing beach games, making sandcastles, having a paddle or a swim and eating ice creams. It was all so new that we didn't have any trouble. Max was good as gold. AJ didn't steal anything from anyone (as far as we knew). Even Gilroy, away from home, was a happy child, for the first time in months; carefree, full of smiles and just enjoying himself with the boys.

At one point Paul became a bit too energetic, as usual. He started throwing handfuls of sand, and the others complained. I was about to tell him off, when suddenly there was a scream from Laurel as she put her hands to her eyes.

I dashed across, as quickly as the soft sand would let me. 'What's the matter? Did you get sand in your eyes?' I asked, as I sat down to give her a soothing cuddle.

She leant into me, but carried on screaming, so I left Mike to look after the others and rushed Laurel straight up to the first-aid tent at the top of the beach. The two first-aiders tilted her head and trickled water into her eyes to wash away the sand. Gradually, her screams subsided, reducing to whimpers as the treatment took effect. I carried her back down the beach, where she gave a hard stare to Paul who was lurking by our windbreak, looking suitably crestfallen.

'You hurt my eyes!' Laurel accused him.

'I know,' he said in a genuinely sympathetic voice. 'I'm sorry.'

The rest of the morning passed without any major incidents. Most of the children were in and out of the water all day and even Alfie's elephant got her toes dipped in the sea. But I remember how we had to take turns to carry Mandy down to have a paddle, because she hated to feel the dry sand between her toes. And we had to spread out our largest towel for her to sit on.

Later in the afternoon, we got out the nets and took them crabbing. They loved that and everyone wanted to be the first to catch a crab. I think Gilroy and Paul both caught one.

'Now you have to put them back,' I said.

'Why?'

'Because it's a living creature and you've got to be kind to it.'

'Why?' asked Gilroy.

'Some people must take them, 'cos you can eat crabs,' added Ronnie.

'Only fishermen,' I said. 'It's against the law to keep them.' Of course it probably wasn't, but it's amazing what you can get away with when the kids don't know any better. 'You can take your bucket and you can take some shells, but that's all.'

When we finally went back to the caravan site, the older children ran off to the playground for half an hour, and Mike took the little ones for a go on the toddlers' swings, while I rustled up something to eat. Any cooking had to be very basic on the little stoves we had in caravans in those days – no home cooking, or anything like that. Just tins and packets and lots of fruit, bread and cereals. I'm sure we had more canned soups than were good for us that week.

The second morning it was raining, so I got out all the bits and pieces I'd brought for them to do. We had a games compendium for the older ones to play with Mike, which kept them occupied for an hour or so, while I helped the little ones to do some colouring, and cutting patterns with the alligator scissors.

'Let's play hide 'n' seek,' suggested Paul when he tired of the sitting-down games. So Ronnie volunteered to go and close his eyes. We had top storage lockers in the caravans, so Paul picked up Max and stuffed him into one of those. Max loved it. 'Now, don't fall out,' said Paul. And he didn't.

I know it seems unlikely, but you'd be surprised how many places you can find to hide in a caravan! Everything was fun to them, even in the rain, and they all played well together . . . most of the time.

Luckily, the weather cleared up by lunchtime, so we packed everything up again and went back down to the beach, which was always their favourite place.

We didn't have much money, but we used to allow them all a few pennies every day of the holiday, and they could each decide what they did with their money. Some of them spent it straight away on ice creams, while others saved it for when we went to the fair, which we planned to do on the last day.

On other days, we went off in the van to a different beach at Poole, or to the cinema and various other places.

The scary thing about taking so many foster children on holiday like that was the responsibility. Somehow it's worse when it's other people's children. We always worried and I had to try and watch them all, wherever we were, checking that they were all still there, and being over-protective. What if one of the kids had an accident, or we lost one of them? We were so far away from our local authority. And we had no way of contacting anybody ourselves. We didn't have mobile phones then. If anything had gone wrong, we would have been hauled over the coals, so we had to watch them all the time.

The caravan site was near the end of the cliffs at Bournemouth. It was a beautiful spot, with views out to sea. When we came back from an outing one afternoon, Mike and I were unpacking the picnic stuff from the van when Daisy asked, 'Where's Mandy?'

'Isn't she with you?'

'No, she was with us, but now I can't see her.'

'Oh my God!' I panicked.

'Daisy, you and Sheena go and look for her in the toilet block. Ronnie and Paul, can you check inside and underneath our caravans please, in case she's hiding.' Everybody had somewhere to look, and I took seven-year-old Gilroy off with me to search around the far end of the site, while Mike took the little ones, meandering round the area near the caravans, to look for her and to ask if anyone had seen her.

I was getting frantic. Mandy was only four. There was no gate security or anything like that, so anyone could be roaming around, perhaps preying on little children. The longer she was out of our sight, the more desperate I felt. And Gilroy didn't help.

'She's gone for good,' he announced triumphantly. 'She's probably fallen off the cliff and into the sea. She's drowned. She's dead and washed out to sea!' He was enjoying this. 'I bet you she's dead. Let's go and see.' He tried to pull me towards the cliff edge, but I was too terrified to look.

I took Gilroy back towards our caravan and we started going down the rows. But I couldn't stop thinking about what he'd said, and my own fears. Surely she couldn't have fallen off the cliff? What if someone had taken her, kidnapped her? *Oh no . . .* I was panicking again – running around like a headless chicken.

Meanwhile, Mike had gone to the reception office and had a call put out on the Tannoy, to anyone who had seen a lost four-year-old called Mandy.

Just as the announcement stopped, I heard Mandy's voice. Was I imagining it? I was sure it was her. But where was it coming from? I looked all around, but I couldn't see her. Was my mind playing tricks? No, there it was again, coming from the open doorway of a stranger's caravan. I rushed to go up the step, ready to save her . . . only to find her sitting down with a drink in one hand and a chocolate biscuit in the other, making herself at home, having a chat with a kindly looking elderly couple.

'Mandy, we thought we'd lost you,' I said with surge of relief.

'We thought you were dead!' added Gilroy, looking disappointed. 'We thought you had fallen off the cliff and drowned in the sea.'

Paul and Ronnie arrived behind us at that moment.

'Oh good,' said Paul. 'She's not dead.'

'Your little girl just came in through the door, explained the woman. 'She was so sweet. She just said she was thirsty. So I gave her some lemonade.'

'Thank you,' I said. 'That was very kind of you, but . . .'

'We were having a lovely chat, weren't we, Mandy?' said the man, smiling.

Mandy gave me a look as if to say, what's all the fuss about?

I was just so relieved and delighted to have found her that I didn't have the heart to tell her off for going into a different caravan or for talking to strangers. Not at that moment, anyway. That would have to come later. I just picked her up and gave her a big hug. Phew! She had been safe all the time, and we didn't have to answer to Social Services after all.

On the last day of the holiday, as promised, we took all the kids to the fair. All week I'd been telling them that if they didn't spend all their pennies on ice creams or sweets, and saved up this much money, they could maybe have five goes at the fair.

They chose their goes carefully. Some went on the merry-go-round while others did games like hook-a-duck, or the older ones went on the dodgem cars, but we wouldn't let them do the shooting, which particularly upset the boys.

'Spoilsport,' accused Gilroy.

'Why can't we do the shooting? It's not a proper rifle anyway,' moaned Ronnie.

'I wanted to knock down some ducks,' added Paul.

'Come on, kids,' said Mike, coming to my rescue. 'I'm going to have a go at the huge hammer to see if I can make the thing go up to ring the bell.'

So we all went over to watch him roll his sleeves up and flex his biceps, building up the tension.

'Come on, Dad,' shouted Ronnie.

'Hit the bell,' chorused Gilroy and Paul, at the tops of their voices.

'Careful you don't hit your foot,' I warned, much to the children's amusement.

'Ohhh,' said Daisy, disappointed that Mike hadn't managed to make the bell ring.

'Have another go,' yelled five-year-old Laurel, jumping up and down with excitement.

I don't think Mike ever did make the bell ring, but everybody enjoyed watching him try. I've never liked fairgrounds, so I didn't go on anything. But Mike was very good, going on all the rides with the kids, to keep them company. I think he enjoyed himself as much as they did, being a big kid at heart.

I just held things and tried to watch them all, though it was a nightmare trying to keep track of them all among the crowds. They kept darting off to look at different stalls. 'Oh my God!' I kept saying to myself. I was so relieved when we finally got out of there, with everyone safe and sound.

But then, disaster! Well, it was to four-year-old Alfie. 'I've lost my Ellie!' he wailed.

'Where did you last have it?' asked Mike.

'I can't remember,' he whimpered, the tears falling down his cheeks.

'He had his elephant on the cup-and-saucer ride with me,' said Ronnie.

So we all went back to that ride and asked the man who was operating it. As soon as it stopped he put the brake on and switched it off.

'Go and have a look,' he said. So we did.

'Here it is!' yelled Paul, triumphantly holding up Alfie's rather bedraggled cuddly elephant. He brought it over and put it into the younger boy's hands.

'Thank you, Paul,' said Alfie, smiling through his tears. He held Ellie tight and off we went again.

Next morning, we packed everything up and started out on the long journey back home, with the kids playing and singing in the back of the van.

We laughed about that holiday for years: 'Do you remember when you had to sleep in that broom cupboard?'

When we arrived back home again, at five o'clock on the Saturday afternoon, Max's mother Vanda was in her car outside, waiting for us.

'What's he been like?' she asked in a tentative voice, as the children tumbled out of the back of our van. She leant towards Max for a hug, but he took one look at her, turned and scrambled over the seats into the front, then climbed out on the far side.

She turned back to face me, close to tears.

'Honestly, he has been very good company and has played well with everyone. He's eaten everything I gave him and he hasn't been a problem at all.'

'What about the caravans?' she asked.

'He didn't do any damage this time,' I said.

'Really?' She looked crestfallen.

'I expect he was just too busy playing with the others.'

'I can't believe it,' she sighed. 'I cannot believe it.'

'He obviously likes having other children around him, and he was the youngest, so they all spoiled him.'

I felt really sorry for her. It must have been heart-rending to learn that he was well behaved throughout for us, when he was always so horrendous when he was with her. And his rejection of her greeting, after a whole week apart from her, must have been devastating, but she tried not to show it.

'It looks like he doesn't want to come home!' she tried to smile. 'How am I going to get him out of the house now?'

I knew that was a throwaway remark, to reduce the tension, but I'm sure she really did want to take him home with her that evening.

'We'll go and extricate him for you,' I reassured her. 'He's had a lovely week. I expect he'll tell you about it himself.'

'I very much doubt it,' she sighed. 'I've never had a normal conversation with him. He's like a wild animal in our house. I can't believe that he was so good for you, but I'm very glad.' She looked thoughtful. 'You're right. Maybe that's what he needs – other children.'

'Let's go and find him,' I suggested. 'Unless you don't mind him staying the night here first – we'd be happy to have him if you want. I'm sure they'll all sleep well tonight. You could fetch him tomorrow morning, when we've sorted out all his things to take home.'

Her face lit up. 'Oh, really? Are you sure you don't mind?'

'Yes, that would be fine.'

So Max stayed the night and left with his mother in the morning, a little more subdued than usual, until he got in her car. As she drove off, I had sensible eight-year-old

Daisy standing with me and we could hear him shouting and bawling half-way down the road.

'That boy needs to realise how lucky he is to have a mother,' she said.

19

Psycho

A couple of weeks after we came back from our holiday, we received a letter informing us that Laurel's adoption had now gone through and that her adoptive parents would like to come the next day to take her home with them for good.

As always, my first response was a contradiction of feelings – sad that, after five years, we would be losing our lovely Laurel, who had had no family at all, except for us. We would probably never see her again. But delighted for Laurel as this was a real family for her at last, and her adoptive parents were lovely people – she had really scooped the jackpot with them.

First I told Laurel, who already knew it would probably happen soon. I could see she had mixed feelings too, but I encouraged her to look forward to having a proper mum and dad of her own. Her eyes brimmed with tears, but we both wiped them away.

'Just think,' I teased her. 'You won't have to fight for space in the bath, or for the biggest slice of cake . . . you won't even have to sleep in a broom-cupboard!'

She grinned. 'But I'll miss you,' she said. 'And all the fun.' I will always remember her dimples, as clearly defined as when she first came to us, at two or three days old.

We had a breakfast 'goodbye' party and all lined up outside the house to wave her off with her new parents. It was a bitter-sweet morning for children like Gilroy, AJ, Paul and Daisy, who had known little if any love from their parents and rarely saw them.

Not long after the holiday, Max's parents decided to move house, to a new area, so Max stopped coming. Vanda stayed in touch for a while, and they had another child, a baby girl this time. Apparently, he began to settle down better after they moved.

'I expect he's growing out of his terrible tantrums now,' I said.

'Yes, thank goodness. But you were our saviour during that horrendous time. A true fairy godmother.'

'You obviously don't know me well enough!' I laughed.

'Well, whatever he grows up to be,' she said, 'it will be at least partly because he had all that wonderful time with you and Mike. I'm sure he learnt a lot from you.'

Many years later, I met someone who knew Max's family. She told me that he had grown up very well. He was very intelligent and had an executive job in a major company. I smiled as I thought back to that charming two-year-old who'd been such a devil with his mum.

* * *

The weeks passed by. Christmas and New Year came and went, with great frivolity. But as the new year began, Gilroy was giving us more and more grief. His whole personality seemed to be disintegrating as he became suspicious of everyone's motives.

'You're all ganging up on me,' he would say. 'I don't care if you all hate me. I hate you even more.' He paused. 'You wait and see . . . I'll get my own back on the lot of you.' He was angry as a silverback gorilla, and took it out on everyone. He didn't seem to care.

Not a day went by when he didn't hurt one or other of the children. They were all fair game to him, even the older ones. He was the bane of poor Daisy's life. Being the quiet, conscientious one, who liked to be left alone to do her homework, to read or draw, or to write her stories, Gilroy plagued her at every opportunity. He scribbled on her school-books, tore up her artwork, took pages out of the book she was reading, even if it was a library book, and trashed the neat bedroom she shared with Sheena.

But Daisy wasn't the only one who suffered from his wrath. We all did. He attacked every one of the children, even Alfie, who used to shout out in a terrified voice whenever Gilroy approached him, which of course stoked him up even further. We had to make sure that one of us was always there to protect Alfie, Mandy and all the others from Gilroy's vicious pinches or sudden shocks. He even tormented Mike and me whenever he could. One day he took my basket of newly washed and ironed clothes down the garden and threw them into a muddy puddle. Another day, while I was out of the room for a minute or two, he strung a length of wire quite low across the kitchen doorway. I'm sure I would have tripped over that wire and fallen heavily on the tiled floor, if I hadn't seen the dog jumping it in front of me. Later that same day, Gilroy used a piece of jagged metal he'd found to make a long scratch all the way down one side of our van.

It was getting so bad that I had to call in his social worker, Des, for a serious chat. I told him some of the latest things Gilroy had done – the hole he'd made in the arm of the sitting room sofa, the smashed television set and his setting Ronnie's shoes on fire.

'I have to check his room and all his pockets for matches every day,' I explained. 'And it's not just us. He even plastered Mike's boss's car windscreen with mud when he called round the other day, then did a moony at him as well. Mike had a lot of apologising to do for that.

'Luckily the man has kids, and a sense of humour!' I paused. 'But the worst thing is the way he deliberately hurts the other children, or gets them into trouble. Poor Ronnie doesn't realise he's being had. Gilroy apparently bet Ronnie a couple of days ago that he wouldn't be strong enough to kick his bedroom door off its hinges. He goaded him into it, so Ronnie, who's a big, well-built boy, gathered all his strength and did it. He kicked the door so hard that the bottom hinge burst and the door was hanging off at an angle. Ronnie was so ashamed when he came and owned up.'

'What about Gilroy?'

'When I confronted Gilroy, he just smirked and said he didn't do anything.'

'Yes, we have a big problem here,' agreed Des. 'What sets him off, do you think?'

'Nothing that I can see. That's just it. His attacks are totally unprovoked . . . and sometimes dangerous.' I paused. 'Do you remember the time I had to take Laurel to the hospital after he'd pushed her down the stairs?'

'Yes, and that was a couple of years ago, wasn't it?'

'Well, he tried to burn down the shed the other day, but it was too wet to burn more than a corner of it. Mike's patched that up now. If one of us doesn't sit on the landing, he creeps into the little ones' room and tells them lurid horror stories and they come down to us, screaming or crying their eyes out, needing cuddles and reassurance.' Des was taking notes as I spoke, so I paused to let him get it all down. 'Up till now, he's not been too bad at school, but one day last week, he threatened his teacher with a knife. I don't know where he could have got that from, because I always check through his bag before he leaves for school. Another day, he bunked out of school and ran all the way down to the police station. He told them that I was keeping him prisoner in his bedroom, but he'd managed to escape. That led to the police visiting his school as well as us, but they quickly discounted his story, thank goodness.'

'Why didn't you tell me all this before?' asked Des, looking shocked.

'Because I thought we could get it under control, but I was wrong. Now I realise we can't go on like this,' I said. 'He's getting bigger, stronger and more threatening every day. I worry that he'll set the house on fire next, and I have to keep counting the knives. Mike's locked all his tools away, but we can never be sure. The other children are all scared stiff of him, and it's just not fair to expect them to go on taking this kind of punishment.'

'What have you tried so far?'

'Oh, Des! All the usual strategies. The things that work with everyone else, but they don't work with Gilroy. In fact, they seem to make him even worse. Or perhaps it's because he's getting worse anyway. He's lost interest in all the things he used to enjoy, like football. He was mad on football, but now he just doesn't care.'

Des came to a decision. 'I think we need to have him assessed straight away. I'll make an urgent request. Do you think you can cope for another day or two?'

It all happened very quickly. The next day was a Saturday. A psychologist and a paediatric mental health worker came to assess him separately at our house, so that they could observe how he was with the other children. They interviewed us and sat with him as well, trying to talk with him. Somehow they persuaded him to do various game-type tests, so he didn't realise he was being assessed, but I'm sure he knew what was going on. He started to act up. Everything was f****** this or f****** that. He told the psychologist she was fat and needed to lose weight. He accused the mental health worker of being 'a f****** paedophile'.

That evening, Des phoned us. 'The experts agree on their diagnosis,' he said.

'What's that?'

'They say Gilroy is schizophrenic.'

'Really?' I was shocked. 'But I thought it was only older teenagers . . .'

'Usually, yes. But Gilroy is an unusual case.'

'I knew something was badly wrong, but I never thought of schizophrenia.'

'And that's not all,' added Des. 'But I'll tell you more about that on Monday.' He paused. 'Do you think you can manage him until then?'

'We'll do our best. But what's happening on Monday?'

'We're having a meeting about Gilroy's future placement. His needs are too great for a foster home, even your home, Trisha. You and Mike have been marvellous with him, especially taking him on holiday with you all.'

'He wasn't much trouble at all on holiday. He really enjoyed it.'

'Well I'm glad he did. But I might as well tell you now – I'm afraid the experts fear that he is becoming psychotic and he needs to be in a secure unit where he can have treatment. It will be best for him and it will be best for your other children too.'

'Yes,' I sighed. 'I suppose so.'

'Don't tell Gilroy himself yet, but we will try to find him an immediate placement and take him away on Monday afternoon if we can. Not a word to anyone except Mike, until I confirm it after the meeting.'

'I didn't know children could become schizophrenic so young,' I said to Mike, after the children were all in bed.

'Well, he's eight now.'

'Yes, just a child. A boy who should be carefree and curious, mischievous and kind to animals – that's what most eight-year-olds are. Look at Paul. He's no angel, just a typical, boisterous, lovable boy. Poor Gilroy. I don't think anybody could call him lovable right now. But he is, underneath.'

'And we love him,' agreed Mike. 'So did Des say what they are going to do? Will he have to take medication or something?'

I told him what Des had told me: that in the experts' opinion, Gilroy wasn't well enough or safe enough to be in a foster home, and that they were having a meeting on Monday about where they should place him. By Monday evening, he might no longer be part of our foster-family.

I thought about Gilroy a lot over the next forty-eight hours. Had we failed him in some way? Could we have done anything to prevent this happening? I kept looking at the clock on Monday, while the children were at school. I felt mean that I'd driven Gilroy there with the rest of them, without his having any idea that his future was in the balance. I watched him kicking at their ankles as they went into the school yard, while they tried in vain to protect themselves. I knew it had to be, but I did feel profoundly sad about him and about his future.

I wondered whether his mother knew yet. Surely she must have been told as well, or were they going to wait until after the meeting? After all the chaos and upset she'd caused, she was forbidden to come to our house or to contact us in any way, and vice versa. She could only see Gilroy under supervision at the family centre, and I couldn't remember the last time that had happened. At least a year ago, I thought.

Des had said he would ring me after the meeting, and I knew that wouldn't be till at least lunchtime. The afternoon dragged on, the children came home on the school bus and the usual happy chaos took over, albeit with evident tension among the children, who were always wary of Gilroy.

It wasn't until half past five, when I assumed it was too late to hear anything, that the phone rang. I rushed out to the hall to pick it up.

As soon as I recognised Des's voice, I was apprehensive. 'Has anything been decided?' I asked him.

'Yes. That's why it took all day. It was a unanimous decision this morning, but it took all day to find the right placement within reach for his mother to visit.'

'Well, she hasn't seen him for months!' I pointed out.

'I know, but we all agreed that we must encourage her to visit him there, as part of his therapy. It's a good place – a well-respected home, about thirty miles away,' said Des. 'It's too late this evening, so I'll come and pick him up first thing tomorrow morning. Meanwhile, I think we should break it to him together, so that he doesn't just blame you and Mike. Would it be all right if I come over in about half an hour?'

Des duly came and I brought Gilroy into the sitting room, while the others played in the playroom. Edie and Frank had kindly come over to sit with them, which was a treat for all the children, who adored our lovely neighbours.

So Des, Mike and I sat with Gilroy and calmly explained to him together what was going to happen and that it was because we all wanted to help him.

'I don't want any help!' He yelled at us. 'You're all f****** b*******!'

It wasn't an easy evening, with him swearing and kicking off all over the house. We had to separate him from the others and put a mattress in the babies' room, which was empty now. I sat like a sentry outside the door until he finally fell asleep. I don't know what I would have done if he'd attacked me with the matches or a blade, but I managed to handle his efforts to get past me, and I had the bruises to prove it.

Later I found out that when Gilroy went into the home, they put him on some very heavy medication. He was just eight, and they dosed him up with this very strong drug that apparently turned him into a zombie. He moved around very slowly, slurred his speech and lost all his energy. I suppose they thought that would help, but it sounded very drastic to me. I was so sad to think of him, or any child, in that state.

It was only after Gilroy left that I realised how frightened all the children had been of him, and now, at last, they were able to relax. It was a huge release of tension and anxiety for us too – we could all feel safe again. Yet I had a lingering sense of guilt that we hadn't been able to sort him out. He'd been with us for a long time, and I did miss the funny boy he was when he first joined our family.

20

Sex on the Rockery

'Can you take a teenager?' asked the social worker on the phone. 'She's fifteen and needs a temporary placement till she turns sixteen.'

'Yes, OK,' I sighed, wondering what I was taking on. I should have stopped and thought about it at least. We'd never had a teenager before. The eldest of our current children were ten-year-old AJ, nine-year-olds Ronnie and Sheena, plus Daisy who was a mature eight. I had no experience of teenagers at all.

I prepared what had been our box room, full of junk, to be a single room for this teenager. I didn't even know her name yet. I had twenty-four hours' notice, so Mike and the four older ones helped me to empty the room, then find and move some bits of furniture. Mike took the rubbish down to the tip, then bought a bed base and headboard at the second-hand shop, a new mattress and some tins of paint, and brought them all back in the van. We spent the evening painting the room and just had time to air it the next morning.

The social worker brought round this sullen-faced girl with a Cilla Black hairdo and cheap but trendy clothes that didn't leave a lot to the imagination. She twirled a lock of her hair and barely gave us a glance as they came in.

'This is Tracey,' said the social worker. 'She's on a temporary care order till her sixteenth birthday.'

'Hi Tracey,' I said in my usual cheery voice. She turned her head in a condescending way and ran her gaze down my long and wayward ginger curls, and my Laura Ashley skirt.

'The hippy look is out now,' she muttered, with evident disapproval.

'Not with me!' I laughed. 'Come on through to the kitchen. I'll put the kettle on.'

Mike had taken all the kids to the cinema, so it was unusually quiet.

'Are you still at school, Tracey?'

'Not likely,' she said with a scornful glance. 'I left as soon as I was fifteen. I'm an apprentice hairdresser now.'

Just then, Mike and the children came back and into the kitchen.

'Who's she?' asked Alfie, pointing at Tracey.

'It's rude to point, little feller,' Ronnie told him off.

'This is Tracey,' I said. 'She's learning to be a hairdresser.'

'Is Tracey coming to live here?' asked Sheena.

'Yes.'

'Is she going to sleep in our room?' I could see that Sheena was eager to have an older girl in the house, to learn about hair, make-up and fashions. She was taking a close interest in Tracey's bangles.

'No, she's having the little room to herself.'

* * *

Tracey settled in well enough, though she only really communicated with Sheena, who seemed to idolise her, and was always following her around. If Tracey sat on the patio, Sheena came to join her. If Tracey flounced off up to her bedroom, Sheena followed her there, though Tracey often didn't let her in. Then I'd have a tearful nine-year-old would-be-teenager following me around for the rest of the day.

'Why does Tracey close her door?' asked Sheena. 'Nobody else does.'

'Because she's nearly grown up and she needs some time to herself,' I explained. 'I expect you might feel the same when you're fifteen.'

Our teenager's social worker was a real harridan; a strict woman who stood no nonsense. But she was also caring and understood that Tracey had issues, whatever they were. We never did find out her background story – what had happened to her through her childhood and why she came into care with us. Nobody told us anything. But Tracey and her social worker generally got on all right, and the woman seemed to have a good influence on her, and gave us wise advice too when we asked for it.

Tracey used to spend ages in the bathroom each morning, getting ready for her day at the hairdresser's. There was always a queue of children wanting to get at their toothbrushes for a quick teeth-clean before going off to school. They would all be shouting, 'Come on, Tracey', and 'Hurry up' and 'What are you doing in there?' But nothing flustered Tracey. She would come out when she was ready and not before.

Rather than have a confrontation with her about it, we relocated some of the children's wash-things, so that they were in the downstairs cloakroom on school mornings.

Some days, she was a pleasant, willing member of the household and even quite helpful with drying the dishes or just playing with the children, if she was in the mood. But she could be very difficult too. Rebellious, surly, self-obsessed . . . a typical teenager as I look at it now, but then it was difficult to know how best to deal with her. I suppose all parents of teenagers say the same.

Of course she had her own life, outside the house and her job. She had a group of friends who used to go out together on Friday nights. Sometimes they would go dancing, or to a party or the cinema.

One Friday night there was a fair in town, so they all went off to the fairground, done up to the nines, thick with make-up and short on dress-fabric. But it wasn't quite indecent, so we let it pass. After all, she was only three or four months away from her sixteenth birthday, when she would be out on her own, outside of the care system, with no one to tell her what to do or not to do. I couldn't imagine how she would cope with all the bills and anxieties of everyday life on her own, but that was the way it was. Perhaps she would let us help her find a suitable place and set herself up, when the time came.

She popped her head round the kitchen door. 'I'm going now. Byee.'

'Have a good time,' said Mike.

'And be back by ten o'clock,' we said to her as she left.

'OK, ten o'clock.'

Well, ten o'clock came and went, then ten fifteen. We didn't want her walking back on her own from the bus stop that late at night so Mike drove to the stop to meet the last bus.

I heard him turn into the drive so I went to the door, but no Tracey. 'Not on the bus?' I asked him.

'No.' He came into the hall.

I was just about to close the front door behind him, when I heard a strange noise. I turned on the outside light and there, spread-eagled on top of the rockery, with her knickers around her ankles, was Tracey . . . with a man.

I immediately shut the door, and stood with my back to it. I must have turned pale, which is hard for me as I don't have much colour at the best of times.

'What's the matter?' asked Mike. 'Have you seen a ghost?'

'No. It's worse than that. It's Tracey.' And then I saw the funny side of it and dissolved into a fit of the giggles.

'What on earth do you mean?' He still had his serious face on.

'Outside . . . on the rockery . . . Tracey . . .'

Mike didn't wait to hear the rest. He opened the door, took in the scene and bellowed at the top of his voice: 'Tracey! Pull your knickers up and get in here immediately.'

There was some scrabbling about as they knocked a couple of stones off the rockery in their haste. I couldn't imagine why they had chosen that, of all places, when there was a perfectly good patch of grass on the other side, which surely would have been more comfortable. Or perhaps they were into a bit of masochism . . . I didn't dare think about it.

In they both came, the man looking rather sheepish and she with her defiant face on.

I don't know what made Mike say it – we could have been had up for suggesting it, but I heard him say in a scolding voice: 'If you want to do something like that, you've got a perfectly good bedroom upstairs to do it in.'

There was a moment of stunned silence, in which we all digested that, then Tracey went into her affronted voice.

'If you think I'm that sort of a girl! . . . I'd never do it in your house,' she said. 'That wouldn't be right.'

I was about to respond about it not being right anyway, but I stopped myself just in time. It wouldn't have got us anywhere at that moment.

'Come into the sitting room,' Mike said to them both, as if it were an order.

They were on the defensive by then, understandably, and I think the young man, who must have been in his early twenties, was quite surprised that he'd even been allowed into the house at all.

We then had this inane conversation, as if he was our prospective son-in-law or something.

'Where do you work?' Mike asked him.

'The fairgrounds,' he replied. 'Wherever we go. Mostly across the Midlands.'

It became increasingly bizarre as this young man, whose

name we discovered was Lee, began to tell us about his work. Tracey was mostly a spectator, hanging on his every word. We were encountering a new world, as he proudly explained and taught us some of the tricks of his trade.

'Palming,' he said. 'Now that's something we all have to learn to do.'

'What's palming?' I asked, betraying my total ignorance.

'Well, it's . . . Say you are going on a ride that costs sixpence, and you gave me half a crown. You would need two shillings change, wouldn't you? Now let me show you what I do.' He searched each of the pockets of his jeans in turn and seemed not to find what he was looking for.

'Have you got any change, mate?' he asked Mike.

'Yes, will this do?' Mike put a handful of change from his pocket onto the coffee table and Lee took it.

'So I would count out loud, in front of you, the two shillings in small coins in my open hand, like this, so that you can see it.' He deliberately counted out the change. 'Then I would hand it over to you. But what you haven't noticed is that when I turn my hand over to give you your change, that you've already seen, I've put my thumb over a couple of the coins, so only the rest will go into your hand.' He demonstrated this. 'You're not likely to stop and check your change, when you've already watched me count it out before I gave it to you. So that way, I can make a bit of extra money every time.'

'That's so clever,' Tracey said with admiration.

It wasn't what I was thinking, but I had to keep that to

myself. I briefly exchanged glances with Mike, who raised his eyebrows. 'Don't show AJ that one,' I said.

And Lee didn't stop there. He showed us a couple more tricks.

'Clever, ain't it?' he gloated.

It was gone midnight by the time Lee left. Tracey disappeared up to bed, so Mike closed the sitting-room door behind her. We just took one look at each other and burst into laughter. 'What an education that was,' I said. 'Did he give you back your change?'

'Oh, no!' he spluttered. 'And what a little madam that Tracey is.' We both laughed again. 'But I'll tell you what . . . I don't think I'll ever look at that rockery in the same way again!'

21

The Porn Film Kids

Sure enough, as soon as she was sixteen, Tracey was kicked out to fend for herself. Not by us of course. We offered to keep her a little while longer, without being paid, if she wanted to stay. That would have given her time for us to help her find a good, clean bed-sit. But Social Services said they wouldn't allow it as it was their job to resettle her.

However, when the day came, Tracey snubbed us all. The lure of the fairground had won her over. She packed all her stuff, said her carefree goodbyes, went out of the front door and into the heavily tattooed arms of Lee, the fairground man. Without a backward glance, she disappeared down the road in Lee's old banger and we never heard from her again.

The phone went just after breakfast on a Friday morning. I always thought it was going to be somebody new coming to join us. But not today.

'Alfie's mother has remarried and her new husband wants her to have Alfie back,' said the Social Services voice.

'That sounds as if it's the new husband who wants him, rather than his mother.'

'Does it?' asked the voice. 'I'm afraid I couldn't tell you.'

These Social Services staff are taught to be economical with the truth.

'They'll collect him at eleven o'clock tomorrow morning.'

'Right, I'll tell him tonight and make sure he's all packed up and ready in time tomorrow.'

We had met this man when the couple had been to visit Alfie about six weeks before. Alfie hardly knew his mother, so it was a tricky meeting, but the man who was now Alfie's stepfather seemed very kind and interested in him, so I was glad to hear that he'd been approved. I was still concerned about his mother, who seemed such a cold, aloof woman, but perhaps that was just a form of nervousness. I hoped so.

Alfie was shocked when I told him after tea that evening. He clung to his beloved elephant stronger than ever as he went to bed and I tucked him in for the last time. The tears came as I left his room. He had been with us since he was two and now he was six and a half.

When we saw him off the next morning, he clung to me much longer than I should have allowed, but his stepfather seemed touched by that scene. His mother, as usual, lacked any kind of expression in her face, and seemed almost churlish in her manner. But she did hold his hand as they walked across to their car.

'Bye, Alfie,' we all called out, almost in unison.

'Bye, Ellie the elephant,' shouted Paul.

Alfie turned as he got to the car and gave us all a final wave, then a wave from Ellie too.

We were down to just six foster-children now – eleven-year-old AJ, ten-year-olds Ronnie and Sheena, Daisy nine, Paul eight and five-year-old Mandy. But it wasn't six for long.

'According to our records, Mrs. Merry, you have some spare foster-places?' asked the female voice.

'Yes, that's right. I can take up to four more, maximum.'

'Good. Well, we have a family of six . . .'

'Oh no, I'm not allowed to take that many.'

'Yes, I understand that. But a different arrangement has to be made for the three older children.'

I thought that sounded odd, but I focussed on the younger three. 'Yes, I do have space for three. What are their ages?'

'Well,' she hedged. 'It's actually the youngest one for sure – her name is Lulu and she's just three months old.'

'But I said ages ago that I didn't want any babies under six months,' I reminded her.

'I know, Mrs Merry. I saw that against your name, but we're all hoping you'll change your mind on this occasion. This is a bonny baby who hasn't suffered any neglect and is in perfect health. We think you would be the best placement for her, and possibly the next two up.'

'Well . . .' I thought about it for a few seconds. 'All right. I'll say yes then. How old are the other two?'

'Duane is two and Sindy is three.'

'Is that all you can tell me?'

'I'm afraid so, but they will be coming with their social worker. Lulu will definitely stay with you, if you agree, and we will observe the other two interacting with your children, before we make a decision about them.'

That sounded strange. In fact it had never happened to me before. I wondered why she should think it would be necessary now.

As usual, I heard the car and watched as a youngish woman approached our front door, carrying a tiny baby against her shoulder, holding hands with a toddler, with another small child walking alongside.

'Mrs Merry? I'm Susie, the children's social worker.'

I nodded and smiled at the two little ones.

'Hello, come in, all of you,' I said, welcoming them through the door. Then I had a peek at the adorable, sleeping baby. 'What a little angel.'

'Yes, she's the lucky one, we think,' said Susie.

Another odd comment, I thought, but decided it was best not to ask her what she meant straight away. Hopefully I might learn more once the children were settling in and we could talk more easily.

Our children were great and tried their best to help these two new little ones to feel at home. Lulu was oblivious to it all at this point, still sound asleep. I noticed that, when Susie sent them off to play, she was observing them very closely. In fact, she didn't take her eyes off them, until Lulu suddenly woke up, with a wail of hunger.

At just that moment, two-year-old Duane went toddling over to Daisy, who was on a bean-bag at the far side of the room, reading. He clambered onto the beanbag and, before I could alert Daisy, he delved his hand right inside her pants. She shrieked and shot out of the bean-bag. Susie handed the screaming Lulu to me, while she rushed over and picked up Duane, taking him right away from Daisy and sitting him next to her on the sofa.

'You must not do that to other children, Duane,' she said to him in a slightly stern voice. Far from looking guilty, or embarrassed, he seemed surprised, perhaps even confused, that she had stopped him. Susie reached for a couple of cars for him to play with on the sofa, hemmed in by the way she sat.

Meanwhile, three-year-old Sindy was looking through the books. Finally she found one that met with her approval and brought it over to Mike, who was sitting on a big easy chair in the corner, with his newspaper.

'Read the book, for your little friend?' asked Sindy, tapping his leg.

He put down his paper. 'All right then.' He took the book she was holding out to him.

Sindy clambered up on to his lap, so that she could see the pictures, I thought. But as Mike opened the book and started to read, she started to wriggle strongly on his lap.

'What are you doing?' he asked.

'I make your little friend happy,' she said.

He gave me a quick look as he reached for a thick cushion, lifted her off his lap, slid the cushion underneath and plonked her back down. 'There, that's better,' he said.

Susie was busy with the baby and with keeping Duane occupied and hadn't noticed what might have seemed an everyday story-time. I watched Mike start again to read the book to Sindy, but she had lost interest now and climbed down. I took her with me to the kitchen.

'Let's get a bottle out for the baby,' I said to her and she happily held my hand. She seemed such an innocent child, yet I couldn't get that scene with Mike out of my head. I warmed up the milk, then took Sindy back to the playroom to collect baby Lulu. I had sometimes seen small children behave inappropriately before. But what both Duane and Sindy had done seemed different somehow . . . as if deliberate and yet normal for them.

'I think we should take Duane and Sindy to the kitchen with us to feed the baby,' I said to Susie in a low voice that I hoped sounded like it was important.

While I fed the baby and she played on the rug with Sindy and Duane, I whispered to her what I had seen Sindy do on Mike's lap, and what she had said. The exact phrase. I expected her, as a social worker, to show some concern at least, but it was as if she wasn't surprised at all. *What was going on here?* The earlier comments that had puzzled me came back to me now.

'Have these children been sexually abused?' I asked her outright.

'I'm not normally allowed to tell you anything,' she said. 'But in this case my boss said I could explain and apologise if the toddlers acted up.' She paused. 'So, the answer to your question is yes. But it's more complicated than that, I'm afraid, and more terrible too.'

Now I was really on edge, as I waited for her to continue.

'These are the youngest three, but they also have three older siblings, and this has been going on for a long time, without even the neighbours knowing anything about it,' she said. 'But it was the health visitor who found out, when she visited this new baby, Lulu, right in the middle of a shoot.'

'A shoot? Do you mean with guns?' I must have sounded very naive.

'No, a film shoot. As we now know, this couple made their living by making sex films.'

'Of themselves?' I asked.

'Mostly of the children,' she corrected me. 'The parents had trained all their children, even these two.' She looked at Sindy and Duane. 'They had trained them all to do sexual things to each other, and with each other, as well as with them sometimes. And that's not all – they regularly invited known paedophiles to come round and join in.'

I was stunned into silence, hit by waves of shock and disgust. How could any parent do this to their own children?

'They made them for people who paid them a lot of money for each thirty-minute film. They wanted as many as they could produce . . .' I struggled to cope with my anger and horror at what she was telling me. 'And they've been doing it for a long time, ever since the eldest child was born, eleven years ago.'

'What, even with a newborn?'

'Yes,' she said in a quieter voice. 'I know all this must be a terrible shock to you, Trisha. But we all thought you ought to be told, if it seemed necessary. We really hoped you would have all these three younger children for us. I know it's a lot to ask . . . What do you think?'

'I think you're right. It may be too big a commitment, with all our other children to think about,' I said. 'Now that I've seen how sexualised they are, I don't think we can take the risk of having Sindy and Duane. I don't think any foster-carer should. I'm afraid they will need a lot of specialist input before that could happen.'

'Mmm. I thought you might say that. And I do understand. But what about Lulu?'

'Well, I don't suppose she has been programmed yet to all that you've told me about has she?'

'No, we don't think so. The health visitor didn't notice any bruises on her, so we hope we've been able to step in just in time. But apparently they did include their previous babies in some of their films . . .'

'Yes, we'll have Lulu,' I agreed. 'At least we can help her and give her a normal, safe and loving home. But what will Social Services do with all the rest of the family?'

'That's the most difficult thing, I'm afraid. We could try Duane on his own and Sindy on her own in different foster-homes, where there aren't any other children, but even that would probably be too challenging, knowing what they have already been through.'

'What about when they were at school? Didn't their teachers notice their sexualised behaviours?'

'They didn't go to school,' she said. 'That was why we didn't know about them before. Their births weren't registered and they weren't in any of the local authority's records, so nobody knew they existed. Their parents simply never sent them to school, or took them out shopping or anything. They had never played with any other children, so that's why we needed to see what would happen.'

'It's a dreadful situation,' I said. 'I just can't understand how this could have been going on for so long, without neighbours, grandparents or anybody knowing.' I paused. 'What has happened to the parents?'

'They're out of the picture at the moment, and almost certainly will be for several years. They were arrested and charged with a number of crimes against under-age children. They're currently still being interviewed by the police. They hope this couple will lead them to a paedophiles ring as well as to the sellers of their cine-films. We're pretty sure that they won't be allowed bail, given such potentially serious charges.'

'There is one thing that is still puzzling me,' I said. 'Why have you told me all this? Normally, I don't get to know anything about new foster-children, let alone their families.'

Susie smiled for a moment. 'You're right. We have a strict policy not to tell foster-parents anything more than we have to.' She hesitated. 'But we've never come across anything like this before, and we're trying to work out a way to help these children. It would be good to think that the older ones at least could stay together. But how? We can't place all five of them in one foster-home, and who would accept them anyway, with their extreme sexualisation? At the moment, they are all in a police safe house with temporary carers. But we can't leave them there for more than a few days. The police need it back, for use in witness protection.'

'Well, they can't go to foster-homes and I agree it would be best for them to stay together – and away from other children, until they have learnt different behaviours . . . What about having them all in one big house, with live-in foster-carers or social workers, with rotas of visiting carers, teachers, therapists, psychiatrists, psychologists, relief staff and all the other specialists they might need?'

'Well, that's the sort of thing we were thinking about, but it would need a lot of organising and you've suggested some good ideas. Could you come and talk about it with my boss?'

'OK. If you want.'

'You see, that's why I got permission to tell you.' She smiled. 'We need someone with your practical experience. And you're so wise.'

I laughed. 'I don't think Mike would agree with that!'

It was really the job of Social Services to sort out all the arrangements, but they asked me to join their panel to focus on this one family's needs. So that's what I did, after signing a confidentiality agreement. There was a good group of people working together and we planned how best to support and care for these badly abused kids, physically, emotionally and educationally, while also protecting them and keeping them safe. Because I was appalled at what these children had suffered, almost every day of their lives, and all for money, and I felt guilty not to be taking them in myself, I felt that at least this was one way I could help them.

It took a lot of my time and energy being part of this team. We had to set it all up; to find a property, recruit and train specialist staff, order furniture, clothing and supplies, draw up rotas, and everything else. All this must have cost the council a fortune, but they had no alternative. I have often said how let down we have been by some local authorities, but this time I could only praise them for doing their best, as sensitively and proactively as possible.

Meanwhile, Lulu became the spoilt baby of our family and thrived in her new home. She was sometimes fractious, to the extent that I did wonder whether anything had happened to her. But most of the time she was a contented laughing child, who loved all the attention she had from our six older ones . . . and from us.

'Thank goodness they let us keep Lulu,' said Mike.

'Yes. I'm sure it's the best chance for her,' I agreed. 'She's too young to have any memories of what went on, but I can't help wondering how it will affect her in the years to come, especially when she starts asking questions.'

'We'll have to wait till it happens,' Mike said, always the pragmatist.

22

Down the Chute

Daisy and Paul had been with us for eight years now and they were both doing well, in their own ways. For Paul it was being active, being good at sports and having fun. But he was the untidiest child in the house. He was always in scrapes at school and often at home too. But one endearing thing I do remember about him was the way he always owned up – and apologised. He didn't have a devious bone in his body. Whenever I asked the kids who broke something, or who kicked another child, he immediately said, 'It was me . . . sorry.'

Daisy was equally honest and straightforward, but she was the opposite of Paul in almost every other respect. She folded all her clothes neatly; even the dirty laundry, and her shoes, slippers and boots were all lined up with mathematical accuracy in the bottom of her wardrobe.

She always did her homework as soon as she got home from school. She was a child who liked her own company, which all the others understood and they usually steered clear.

I used to teach all the kids to cook, and Daisy was a quick learner, although I wouldn't say she was an enthusiastic baker. Some children would come into the kitchen and say 'Can we make fairy cakes?' Even Paul enjoyed sloshing a bit of cake-mix about, but not Daisy. She only helped me if I asked her, and then she would do it well, but she wasn't the domesticated type. She much preferred to lose herself in a library book. As the expression goes: 'good books are like good friends', and they certainly were to Daisy.

For all the eight years she had been with us, Daisy had been desperate to grow her hair. I tried, several times, to get her social worker to contact the mother if possible and obtain her permission for Daisy to change her hairstyle, now that she was older and painfully aware of how unfashionable it was. She was teased about it a lot at school and I felt I was failing her, not being able to do something about it.

'If you can't contact her mother, couldn't you give her permission to grow her hair?' I asked John.

'You know the rules, Trisha. I can't do that.'

But John didn't visit much – perhaps once every six months, so in between, Daisy and I had this agreement that I would conveniently forget to take her to the hairdresser's for a while. And, as it began to grow, I noticed her looking in the mirror more. If she could have pulled her hair to make it longer still, she would have, no matter how much it might hurt.

I spent most of the weekday mornings sorting things out for Lulu's five abused siblings in the house we had set up for them. We had put a comprehensive domiciliary package in place for them and it seemed to be going well so far, bar the odd hiccups when a teacher was ill, or a carer or therapist got their times muddled.

However, the main problem was that the children's sexual advances towards each other were so ingrained that we had to put in extra therapists and experienced foster-carers to work on containing and hopefully addressing these behaviours, that were obviously normal to the kids. It was apparently all they had known – the focus of every day of their lives. And we couldn't send men in to help at all at that early stage. As far as these children were concerned, all men were only there for sex, after all those paedophiles had 'played' with them, as they put it. Not to mention their own father. It was no surprise that both parents were convicted and given long prison sentences.

Thank goodness Lulu herself was quite placid and easy-going. I timed her main nap for late mornings, so that I could do any phone-calls and cooking for them. A couple of times a week, Social Services sent a support worker round to look after Lulu, so that I could spend the whole morning at her siblings' house, helping the carers and doing some play-therapy with the children. It was often a traumatic experience and every day I saw them I wondered how we could ever turn things round for them, but we had to keep trying. It would obviously be a very long and tricky task. Would it ever be possible to 're-programme' them to such an extent that they could eventually live 'normal' lives? I had to believe we could.

* * *

At home, our children were getting older but not necessarily wiser. We used to give them a bit of pocket-money every week, according to their ages. But one autumn day, Paul wanted to earn some extra money. I don't think he knew what he wanted to do for it, but he was saving up to buy something for his bike. We used to have a chart in the house for earning extra pocket-money. It was 20p in 'new money' for washing up or sweeping the kitchen or for sorting and taking out the rubbish, 25p for pulling up fifty weeds, 50p for washing the car or van, and so on. It would be more now of course.

Paul didn't want to do anything on the chart that needed doing.

'So, what do you want to do?' I asked him.

'I'm going to sweep the yard,' he said.

Behind our large Victorian semi, we had a garden that went back a long way, and at the side we had a sizeable, blue-bricked yard, where the kids used to ride their bikes or roller-skate, or whatever.

'OK, Paul. So what exactly are you going to do?'

'I'm going to sweep the yard and get rid of the leaves.'

'And the path?'

'Yes, and I'll sweep that as well.'

'Right then. You'll have to get the yard brush out of the shed and you'll need some old potato sacks from the back of the garage to sweep all the leaves and the rubbish into.'

'OK.' He looked a bit uncertain. 'How much will you pay?'

'Well, let's see how well you do it, but it's going to be quite hard work, so if you do a brilliant job of it, I could give you two pounds. How does that sound?'

'Good,' he said, with a smile. Two pounds went a long way in the 1970s.

I watched him from the kitchen window, as he got the brush and started at the far end of the yard, sweeping away energetically. There were mounds of leaves in some places, and with his rough and ready sweeping, they were going all over the place. I had to smile. It was typical of Paul. With his ginger hair and fair skin, he was going red in the face from all the effort. I saw him make a big pile of all the leaves he'd swept up so far.

Then I had to go and do something else, so I didn't see him doing any of the rest of the work.

After a couple of hours, he came back in to find me, his face covered in specks that had blown off the leaves, and a smear across his forehead, from the dirt.

'I've swept it all up.'

'That was quick.'

'It's bootiful.' He beamed with pride.

'Bootiful, eh?' We laughed, remembering how we all used to say that when we had Baby Boots staying with us.

'Come and see,' he said.

I called the others to join us, picked up toddler Lulu and we all trooped outside to inspect his handiwork.

'Oh, this is lovely,' I said. 'Well done.'

'Fab,' said Sheena, echoing an old 1960s expression that Mike and I often used.

'Mega fab,' chorused Ronnie and AJ.

'It looks much better,' agreed Mandy.

Daisy didn't look so sure, as she inspected her brother's handiwork. 'It's quite good . . . but you've missed a bit here,' she said, pointing at the paving behind one of the sheds.

'Oh,' said Paul. 'I forgot about that bit.'

'Never mind,' I reassured him. 'You've made a grand job of it – a good morning's work.' I gave him his two pounds and thought nothing more about it until a couple of days later, when Ed, who was doing some maintenance work on our house, came to tell me how he was getting on.

'You ain't half going to have a lot of damp there, love,' he said, in the tone builders usually use when they're about to tell you some extra work is needed that's going to cost an arm and a leg.

'What do you mean?' I asked.

'You're going to have a lot of damp,' he repeated.

'Sorry, Ed, you've lost me. What are you talking about?'

'Well, look out here.' He led the way outside the house and pointed at our coal-chute. We had this metal coal-chute contraption that you could open out and the coal would go down into the cellar, for the servants to collect and lay the fires with . . . some hope! We only had one servant, and that was me. But that's what they used the coal-chute for in Victorian times.

'I was just cleaning up this chute,' he explained, lifting his cap and scratching his head. 'And I found all this mess. Look.'

So I looked. What a mess it was. It was jammed with leaves, balls, skipping ropes, even a roller-skate – everything, all down the coal-chute. And because there was no window in the cellar, this was the only way for the air to get in. But now it was completely blocked. I was horrified.

'I think we'd better go down and look in the cellar,' suggested Ed.

So we went back into the house and unlocked the door to the cellar. We hardly ever used it so the stone staircase down and the wooden underside of the stairs above were covered in dust, cobwebs and grime. Here was another job for a couple of the children to do, I thought, if they were really keen to increase their pocket-money.

With the dim light on, we could just about see that the whole floor of that section of the cellar was filled with a huge mound of the rubbish that had come down the chute, before it became jammed. The smell was horrible, all musty and mouldy.

'Well,' I said to Paul later. 'That wasn't very good. Not at all bootiful down the coal chute and in the cellar,' I said. Come and see what you've done.' He reluctantly followed me down the stone stairs.

'Sorry,' he said when he saw the state of everything. 'I didn't think anyone would notice.' He looked so crestfallen and was so honest in accepting the blame that I almost felt sorry for him.

But I had to be firm. 'You're not going to have any more money from me if you're going to cut corners like that. A job has to be completed properly. This was the lazy way. If you agree to do the job a certain way, that's what you should do, right to the end.'

He tucked his head down and said nothing.

'You should have got those potato sacks, like we said. And you should have picked out the skates and ropes and balls before you bagged up the leaves and the real rubbish and put them at the bottom of the garden to compost for next year.'

'But that would have taken too long,' he muttered, in protest.

As I went in to prepare lunch, he stomped off down the garden. I looked out at him and I could tell he was having a big temper tantrum, probably calling me all sorts of names. It made me laugh, the way his thinking went . . . oh dear!

23

Mystery Illness

For a couple of weeks, twelve-year-old Daisy had not been well. At that time, if a foster child was ill, the doctor would come out to visit them at home. It was the same for all foster children, in our local authority at least. So we had called the doctor out a couple of times, but she could find nothing wrong with Daisy.

The symptoms were fairly minor at first – general fatigue, lack of energy and appetite. She was so lethargic she couldn't read more than a couple of pages at a time. Finally even that became too much and she developed a raging temperature, so we called the doctor out a third time. I think doctors, sometimes, seem to lack interest when you tell them the petty symptoms of something like flu or a stomach upset. But the minute I mentioned Daisy's high temperature, the doctor's voice suddenly sounded more alert.

'I'll be there in ten minutes, Mrs Merry.'

When she arrived, she took Daisy's temperature, which she agreed was unusually high. She asked a few questions and took her pulse.

'I'm concerned about Daisy's high fever,' she said. 'Do your best to keep her cool. Keep a wet flannel and some cold water to cool her forehead, and take her blankets off. Just a sheet or a light cover will help her temperature come down during the day, and just one blanket at night. If her temperature goes any higher, or if she's no better tomorrow, be sure to call me.'

I stripped Daisy's bed down to one thin cover and we put a folded flannel soaked in cold water across her forehead. I asked Sheena to pop up and see Daisy every now and then to re-wet the flannel and to keep her company when Daisy was up to it. I also went up to check on her at regular intervals.

That night, she slept fitfully, moving about quite a bit. I sat with her till late into the night, then Mike came up and took my place for a couple of hours, for me to get some sleep. Then I came back. In the early hours before dawn, she seemed a little calmer, but her temperature had barely dropped at all. *What could be wrong with her?* I wondered. Why doesn't she seem to get any better?

Mike took over from me again for an hour, while I got the children's breakfasts. When I came back up again, she was sitting up.

'You look better, Daise,' I said, cheerfully. 'It's good to see you sitting up.'

'It's only because I felt so dizzy lying down, so I sat up. But now I feel even dizzier.'

'I think you'd better lie down again,' I said, helping her with the pillows.

'Why do I feel so tired? My head is thumping and I'm so hot. Why won't this go away?'

I popped the thermometer under her tongue for a couple of minutes, then checked it. 'About the same. At least it hasn't gone up. Let's see how you get on today.'

Daisy had started the day quite lucid, but gradually drifted downhill, and by the afternoon, she was delirious. I rang the doctor and John, her social worker. They both came straight away.

'Daisy's temperature has risen again,' said the doctor, with an anxious expression. 'She has a dangerously high fever and we must find out what is causing it. I will arrange for her to go into hospital for observation and tests. They should also be able to regulate her temperature.'

'And I'll need to give Daisy's father a call to get his permission,' said John. 'It's just a formality.' He paused. 'Where's the nearest phone?'

'In our bedroom, straight across the landing.'

So John dialled Rocky's Swindon number and the doctor stood by, in case Rocky wanted to talk to her. Meanwile, I sat with Daisy, who was in and out of her delirium. All I could hear was this faint, one-sided conversation, so I turned my head away from Daisy, to listen through the open doorway.

'Hello, Rocky,' said John. 'Sorry to disturb you, but Daisy has a dangerously high fever and we don't know what's causing it. The doctor needs to admit her to the hospital for tests and observation, so can we have your permission . . . Oh! He's hung up.'

'Oh dear. I wanted to explain . . .' said the doctor

'I don't think he wanted to know.'

'But you got his permission?' she asked.

'No, I'm afraid not.'

There was some whispering between them, and a couple of minutes later, they both came back into the room. I was sitting by Daisy's bed, holding her hand. As she lay still, with her eyes closed, they must have assumed Daisy wasn't conscious enough to hear.

'I told Rocky how ill Daisy is and asked his permission for the doctor to have her admitted to the hospital . . .'

'What did he say?' I asked.

'He just said, "No, I'm working," and put the phone down.' John shrugged, with a look of disbelief. 'He couldn't have been clearer. No means no, I'm afraid, unless she becomes so dangerously ill that it can be classified as an emergency.' John obviously knew the Social Services rules very well – too well, in my opinion.

I was appalled – what a callous response to his only daughter's need.

I turned to the doctor. 'So what happens now?'

'I'm afraid she will have to stay here, with your loving care,' she smiled with sympathy. But her eyes betrayed her anxiety.

'I've got six other children to look after,' I said, feeling slightly panicked.

John reassured me as much as he could. 'I'll arrange for a support worker with nursing training to come in and relieve you for some of the day, but I'm afraid it might not be possible to cover the nights as well.'

'OK,' I said, thinking how we could manage. 'I'll get Mike to take the next day or two off work, so that we can take half the night each. In fact, I could move Sheena out temporarily into Tracey's old room, then one of us can sleep in here as well, if necessary.'

'That sounds like a good arrangement for the time being. Hopefully it will not be for long.' John looked at the doctor.

'Yes.' She seemed to have come to a decision. She took a hypodermic syringe out of her doctor's bag. 'I'm going to give Daisy a penicillin injection. It should act quite quickly to reduce her temperature for now.' She paused and looked at Daisy for a moment, with a puzzled expression. 'But I'm still very concerned about what is causing her to be so feverish that her own body can't fight it off.'

I nodded.

'I'll come back tomorrow morning,' she said, a little more brightly. 'Let's see how she is then.'

They both left and Mike sorted out all the kids, who knew their routines and were very cooperative because they were worried that Daisy was so ill.

Meanwhile, after John and the doctor had gone, Daisy regained consciousness for a few minutes.

'Hello, Daise,' I said with a sympathetic smile. 'How are you feeling?'

She looked at me with tears in her eyes. 'I heard,' she said, with quivering lips. 'I heard what Dad said.' Now the tears came. 'Doesn't he care that I'm not well?' she sobbed. 'It's like he's abandoned me again.'

I stroked and cuddled her, trying my best to soothe her, but she was inconsolable. Absolutely heartbroken . . . until she finally fell into a restless sleep.

After lights out, Paul got out of bed, crept along the landing and appeared in his pyjamas in the doorway of Daisy's room.

'Hello Pauly,' I said with a gentle voice. 'Come closer and see Daisy. She's sleeping at the moment. Sleeping will help her get better.'

This normally tough lad came to his sister's bedside and leant into me for comfort. I put my arm round him.

'Will she be all right?' he asked, with anxiety all over his face.

'I think so,' I said, optimistically. 'I will be sitting up with her to make sure she has the best care and she should be OK. The doctor gave her an injection and that has taken her temperature down a bit. Tomorrow morning the doctor will come back to see how she is – hopefully much better by then, if her temperature stays down.'

He nodded, and reached his hand out, laying it close to his sister's. For a moment, I thought he was going to rest it on hers, but at the last minute he obviously remembered that he was a boy with an image that he wanted to keep, even in front of me.

As I lay in Sheena's bed through that night, tired but too anxious to sleep, I kept thinking about Rocky's response. I couldn't believe that any father would say no to his daughter going into hospital if she needed to. He obviously put his work, or perhaps his wages, above his kids. But all he would have had to say was yes. It doesn't take any longer to say yes. He had often let the children down, through all the time they'd been with us . . . but never as badly as this. I used to think he must care about them, in his own way. But maybe I was wrong. Why did he have to be so heartless?

The penicillin injection did have a miraculous effect. Daisy's temperature continued to go down and by the morning she was well enough to sit up and read. However, it took a good two or three weeks before she was fully well again, and we never did discover the cause of Daisy's mystery illness.

But it wasn't just Daisy's physical health that had suffered. There was another recovery she was unable to make – from her father's callous response. She was tearful throughout most of her recuperation, and beyond. I think it had dawned on her that the only parent she knew was not reliable in any situation, even when she needed him most, just to say yes. She found it difficult to accept that he had refused to come to her aid that night, denying her the hospital treatment she needed.

'Has Daddy rung you to see how I am?' she asked me, almost every day. Her hopes dashed every time I had to shake my head. I wasn't sure she would ever come to terms with that sense of rejection.

24

The Awful Smell

'We've got an autistic teenaged boy who needs a good home,' said the voice on the phone.

'Why is that? Anything you can tell me about him?'

'Not much. His name is Kevin, he's thirteen, and his single mother can't cope with him as well as his three younger siblings.'

I had a quick think. We had quite a stable group of children now, all of them with us a long time, except for baby Lulu, who was now a toddler. Hmm. An autistic teenager – how hard could that be? 'Yes, all right. We'll have him.'

The following day, Kevin's social worker brought him to us in her little sports car. The boy was cajoled out of the car and slouched over to the front door. I welcomed him with my usual smile, but he kept his eyes down and didn't make a sound. He reminded me of a frightened animal, like calves at a cattle auction. He did not want to be here, in a new place, meeting new people, especially so many of us.

'Off you all go,' I said to the children, who had gathered in the hall. 'You can meet Kevin later. He needs some time to settle in with us first.'

We went through to the kitchen and I made us some tea. 'What would you like to drink, Kevin?' I asked him.

He mumbled something, but I didn't catch it.

'I think he said he'd like a Coke, if you have one, Trisha.'

'Yes, I think I might just have one, hidden at the back of the fridge. Ah, here it is.' I passed the can to him and he immediately pulled the tag and took a long gulp of the black liquid. For the first time, he held up his head as he was drinking and I could see his face. He was quite a good-looking lad, with straight dark hair and angular features. But his skin looked sallow, as if he hadn't been outside much.

I passed round some home-made cookies and went through the paperwork with Kevin's social worker, while Kevin himself looked around the kitchen. Suddenly he spotted a photo of an aeroplane that Mike brought home once from his engineering works.

Kevin took another cookie and went over to have a closer look at the picture.

'Do you know what kind of plane it is?' I asked.

He reeled off the answer in so much detail that I was none the wiser, and still can't remember it now. He used a string of letters and numbers in his answer, then started to recite all the features of this particular model. I was astonished.

'You obviously know your aeroplanes, Kevin,' I said, in genuine admiration.

'Yes, I'm an expert on planes. It's my obsession.'

'You'll have to have a chat with my husband Mike later, when he comes home. He designed a part of that plane.'

For the first time, I saw a hint of a smile on this boy's wan face.

Over the next few days, Kevin rarely looked anything but frightened, scared by there being so many people in our house, the sounds, smells, textures and colours of our daily lives, the different routines, the challenge of everything. I could see that he didn't like anything new, yet everything was new. For that reason, although I realised it was wrong, I didn't start him at his new school that first week.

I didn't know a lot about autism, so at the weekend, when Mike was home, I dashed down to the library and borrowed a book about it, and all the different related syndromes. It was quite an eye-opener, and I recognised several of the signs in Kevin. I began to look at him in a different light, like a research project. But to me, first and foremost, he was always a boy who needed our help and our love, even if he didn't know how to return it.

One of the things I found out on that first day was that he didn't like more than one thing on a plate at a time, and while everyone else had all their meal on one plate, he had his on three or four, so I sat him at the end of the table, to have enough space to spread his plates around him. His favourite foods were beans, toast (but not together), plain bread, ginger biscuits, bananas and bacon. He also tolerated simple breakfast cereal, but nothing mixed. The others thought it strange at first, but soon got used to it. Just like the unusual way he did some things, always in a particular order.

Whenever there were more than two or three people in a room (with the exception of meal-times) he ran off to hide. To start with, I thought this was very strange. He seemed like quite an intelligent lad, to have learnt so much about aeroplanes, and yet his favourite hiding place was to furl himself into the full-length curtains in the lounge. As long as he couldn't see anybody else, he seemed to think they couldn't see him. Sometimes he would stay there for ages. Other times he would curl up on the floor behind an armchair, or even squeeze himself into a cupboard.

Although our house wasn't the best place for him in many ways, he gradually began to settle. What helped a lot was his obsession with aeroplanes. Mike would bring home brochures, books and magazines from work and the two of them would tuck themselves away in the sitting room to look through them all and discuss the finer features of this or that wing mechanism or undercarriage, comparing engine sizes and other numbers that went way above my head. In fact, Kevin turned out to be a whizz at numbers. It was amazing the mental calculations he could do.

'How do you do that, Kevin?' I asked him once.

'I don't know,' he answered. 'I just see the patterns in my head.'

But for all his sophisticated thinking and advanced knowledge, Kevin was hopeless at putting his clothes away or finding the key to his locker at school. The number of new keys we had to pay for . . . In the end, they had to get the lock removed from one of the lockers so that he could always open it.

I didn't realise at first, until I saw the tell-tale sign of blood on his white school shirt, that he was self-harming. When I phoned and spoke to his social worker about it, she obviously already knew.

'Oh, he used to do that at his mum's as well,' she said. 'I expect it might stop once he is feeling more settled and used to everything.'

'But I've been reading up about autism,' I said. 'And sometimes an autistic child will never settle among a lot of people, in a busy house, with all the noise and movement that disturbs him so much.'

'I'll come round tomorrow after school and have a chat with him. Say about five? Will that be all right?'

So that's what she did. I had told Kevin before he went to bed, when he got up, when he got back from school and just before she came, so her visit didn't take him by surprise. I had already discovered he hated changes, and surprises scared him witless.

'Do you think your talk with Kevin was helpful?' I asked her afterwards as we sat down at the kitchen table.

'Yes, I hope so,' she said. 'He says he likes you and Mike. He especially likes it that Mike knows a lot about aeroplanes too, and even designs parts for them. That has made a big difference in helping him to settle here. But he's still very anxious. I think he always will be, Trisha. Wherever he goes and whatever he does. It's all part of his autism. He did say that he is sometimes scared because he doesn't understand when you are cross with him.'

'But I haven't been cross with him.'

'Well, I think he probably finds facial expressions and different tones of voice confusing, like many autistic children.'

'Oh yes. I read that in the book I borrowed from the library. I will try to keep my face straighter for him . . . if I can! I'm afraid I'm one of those people whose arms and face are all over the shop. My voice too, I expect. I'll try harder.'

'I asked him about the self-harming, and he says that it's not so much here, because he can get away from you all and hide if he wants to, but at school he can't, so when he gets anxious in the classroom, he gets to bursting point, he says, and has to cut his arm with his compass to relieve his tension.'

'Oh, I see. Do you think I should maybe talk to someone at school about it?'

'Yes, as long as they don't let on to him that you told them. I wouldn't like there to be any backlash for you. You're both doing such a good job with him.'

'Thank you. He's a good kid, but we're still feeling our way with him.'

'Well, you're doing more than most people would, reading up on autism, talking with him about his favourite subject. Kevin wouldn't say so, but I think he's fallen on his feet here, with both of you.'

I did feel relieved to hear that he felt it was OK being here with us. I arranged a meeting with his form-tutor at the secondary school and told her some of the things about autism that affected Kevin. I explained confidentially about the self-harming too, although, since that chat with his social worker, he seemed to have less blood on his shirt than previously, so I felt it might at least be under control.

'That's good,' said the young male teacher. 'He's a bright boy, gifted in both maths and technology, so he's doing well academically. He doesn't seem to have made any particular friends, but from what you say that may be the way he likes it.'

'Phew,' I said to Mike that evening. 'It was a good meeting with his form-tutor and I think that at last we are getting somewhere with Kevin.'

I should have known I was talking too soon. All the kids were at school, and a support worker had come for the day to play with Lulu, feed her and take her out to the park. So, after my usual visit to the sex-film children's house, where progress was very slow indeed, but just about perceptible, I came home again to start my spring cleaning. I always did the kids' bedrooms first, while they were out. I started with Kevin's room, as I had barely been in there since he arrived. He had put up a big sign on the door that said 'Keep Out!', so I usually did, but not on this day.

I had the shock of my life when I opened the door and the awful smell assaulted me. I knew straight away that it could be only one thing. A quick search took me to the place at the back of his wardrobe where he had hidden a pile of plastic carrier bags. I didn't even have to look inside them. I estimated there must be at least three weeks' worth of pooh in those bags – just the length of time he had been with us. I removed and disposed of them, then threw open his windows to air his room thoroughly.

I didn't know whether to have a talk with Kevin about it or not. I had never heard of anything like this before and I realised it was a delicate subject to discuss with a thirteen-year-old autistic boy who had only been with us such a short time. I ought to have had a child psychologist to talk to about it, but Social Services didn't run to that.

So, in the end, what I decided was to wait till all the children went to bed. Kevin was on his own in Tracey's old room at the end of the corridor, so I went and knocked on his door, then opened it before he'd had a chance to tell me not to come in. He looked surprised, sitting up in bed and reading through a new aeroplane magazine Mike had brought home for him that day.

I sat on the edge of his bed. 'I just came for a little chat, Kevin,' I began. 'I was cleaning out your room today, so I got rid of those old bags in the bottom of your wardrobe,' I said.

He never normally made eye-contact, so I was amazed that he did at that moment. He looked right into my eyes, as if searching my soul. It was a strange experience. After a long pause he shrugged and said 'OK,' then went back to reading his magazine.

I had intended to say more, but I wimped out. And anyway I rather got the feeling, in that long gaze, that it wouldn't happen again. I hoped I was right.

25

Porch-Boy

Early one morning I went downstairs as usual to stoke up our kitchen range. The next job was always to get the milk in. With so many children, we always had a lot of milk, so there was always a crate to carry in. This particular morning, I unbolted the front door, but as soon as I started to open it, I could feel there was something heavy against it.

I leant all my weight on the inside of the door, but I couldn't push it closed, so I gingerly opened it a little more. As I did so, what I thought must be a sack of something fell half onto the front doormat. But it wasn't a sack . . . it was a body – a male body, I guessed from the shortness of his dishevelled hair, his head on the mat and his feet on the tiled floor of our porch, with its front open to the elements.

Was this a tramp? His whole body was curled into a foetal position, with a thick, hooded coat over the top of him. As this body started to move, I realised it was a boy – a teenager by the look of him.

I suppose I should have pushed him out and closed the door, but that didn't occur to me. I leant down and touched his shoulder. 'Are you all right? You must be cold, lying there in this weather. Come on, sweetheart, you'd better come into the warm.'

He gradually uncurled and raised himself up, pulling the coat round his shivering body. As he did so, I stepped past him to pick up the milk crate. That was when I saw one of the bottles was nearly empty, so he must have helped himself to a pint of milk.

'Well, at least you've got some nourishment inside you,' I said as I turned to take in the crate.

'Let me carry that for you,' said the gruff voice from inside the coat, reaching his arms out to take it from me. Because it was still dark, I didn't get a chance to see his face until we both got inside the well-lit hallway. Here was a thin, very pale young lad with sandy hair and hollow cheeks.

'Come and sit by the range where it's warm,' I said, leading him through to the kitchen. He put down the milk crate and I set out a chair in front of the Aga, opening the bottom oven to warm his legs.

'Thanks,' he said as he drew his chair closer to the range.

I put away the milk bottles and switched the kettle on, then sat with him for a few minutes.

'I've got to go up and see to the rest of the family shortly,' I told him. 'I'm a foster-mum, with seven children here at the moment.'

'Yes, I know. That's why I came.'

'We haven't met, have we?'

'No, but I've heard about you. People say you're the best

foster-mum . . . and I've lived in so many awful children's homes and a few foster-homes too, and had to run away each time.'

'Oh, how awful. But I still don't understand . . . Were you sleeping in our porch all night?' I watched his pale face and his darting eyes.

'Yes, well, I was trying to, but I kept dropping off, then waking up again, shivering with the cold. All I want is a place to stay where people don't hurt me or go on at me because I can't do things.'

'Is that why you've run away from places?'

'Yes, I suppose so. Nobody has ever cared whether I stayed or went. Sometimes it was getting dangerous, other times they were just shouting at me all the time.' He gave a deep yawn. 'I'm so tired,' he said. 'But I had to wait till you found me. You were my last chance.'

'Right, I expect you're hungry, so I'm going to make you a quick fry-up and then off to bed with you my lad. You need a good sleep in a warm bed. I'll still be here when you wake up, and we can talk more then.'

He wolfed down everything on his plate and then I took him upstairs to the room where we kept the cots. Our youngest, Lulu, was nearly three and in a bed now, sharing Mandy's room, so the cots room was empty, apart from a fold-up single bed.

'What's your name?' I asked him as we went up the stairs.

'Luke.'

'And how old are you, Luke?'

'Fifteen.'

'Where should you have been last night? Will they be worried about you? They might report you missing.'

'Nowhere. I've got nobody at all. I've been on the streets for a few weeks, sleeping rough, under a bridge, or sometimes in a shelter.' He yawned again and I noticed his eyes were closing.

I showed him the bathroom and toilet, found him a spare toothbrush, then quickly got some sheets out to make up his bed. When he came back down the landing, I called him into the room and closed the curtains. 'Sleep well,' I said, as he shed his big coat and took off his shabby trainers. 'Come downstairs and find me when you wake up again. Then I'll cook you a proper meal.'

He climbed, fully clothed, between the sheets and was asleep in moments.

It was more than an hour later before I told Mike.

'WHAT?' he said in astonishment. 'You let in a homeless man, sleeping in our porch? You fed him and put him to bed upstairs in our house, among our children, not to mention all our belongings? Are you mad?'

'I didn't think of it like that. He's just a boy who needs a home, some feeding up and a lot of love. He came here because he had nowhere else to go, and somebody told him we would care.'

'Oh, right.' Mike calmed down, as I knew he would. 'That's different.' I knew he would have done exactly the same thing if he had been the one to find him. We're both suckers for any waifs and strays that need us.

'His name is Luke and he's fifteen. He's been sleeping rough for weeks, he told me. He was so desperately tired that I don't suppose he'll be down for hours.'

'Well, don't let him leave the house without checking his pockets first!' said Mike, with a twinkle in his eye. Then he went off to work, dropping Lulu off at the nursery, and the others all went to school.

The first thing I had to do was to call Social Services and ask for their advice about what I should do with Luke. I didn't want to break the law or keep him with us when he was supposed to be somewhere else. But I didn't get the response I expected.

'A fifteen-year-old called Luke?' asked the voice at the other end of the phone. 'Do you know his surname and his date of birth?'

'No, I'm afraid not. I forgot to ask him before he fell asleep. Do you have a missing boy on your list called Luke?'

'Not that I know of, Mrs Merry,' she said, snootily. 'We have more than fifteen hundred children currently in this region. Among those we probably have at least ten or twelve boys called Luke. As far as I can see, we have no missing Lukes at the moment.'

'Right.' I paused. 'Should I ring the police then?'

'Well, there wouldn't be any point, unless you know his surname.'

So that was that. I did think the police might have had a different view, but she was right: I should have asked for his full name. So I decided to wait until he woke up. I spent the rest of the morning finding a stand-in carer for the sex-film children's house, and someone to repair their cooker. I didn't hear a sound from Luke all day.

My friend Val kindly collected Lulu from nursery for me, and Mike took a late lunch-hour to collect all the others and bring them back, so that I could stay at home and 'protect our valuables', as he put it. I went up and woke Luke before the rabble arrived.

'Come on, sunshine,' I said to him, gently shaking his shoulder, 'time to get up.' I opened the curtains and sat on the end of his bed, while he gradually roused himself and stretched. He looked around the room with a puzzled expression before he spotted me.

'Did you wonder where you were?' I asked him with a warm smile.

'Yes,' he answered, rubbing his eyes. 'I thought I was in a hostel, but the cots confused me.'

'I'm not surprised,' I laughed. 'This is normally the babies' room, but we don't have any babies at the moment. We'll have to dismantle the cots and bring a proper bed in for you if you want to stay.'

'Can I?' he asked.

'Well, yes,' I said. 'As long as you're sure you're not meant to be anywhere else?'

'No.' He shook his head sadly. 'I don't think I'm on anybody's radar now.'

'And the other condition is that you have a lovely hot bath and wash your hair and then, when you're all clean and sweet-smelling . . .' I grinned. '. . . you can put on these clean clothes I've borrowed for you. The top is

Mike's – he's my husband. And the underwear and trousers belong to Kevin, our teenager, who's about the same size as you. So off you go.'

'OK. A bath will be great. I can wash the streets off my skin and out of my hair.' He gave a half-smile. 'Thank you for taking me in.'

'Well, as I remember it, you fell in when I opened the door!'

'Did I? I'm sorry.' He looked rueful and I laughed.

I gave him the clean clothes and he started to strip in the room, standing right next to me, stopping only at his tattered underpants. 'Just come down and join us for a cooked tea when you're ready,' I said, standing up.

'OK. Thanks.' He picked up the clean clothes and turned to go out of the room. That's when the shockwaves hit me. The whole of Luke's back and shoulders were covered with marks and scars. There wasn't even the smallest area that was unscathed. All of his skin was puckered, with rough, raised nicks, tracks and patches, mauve and purple, with some dark red wheals in between.

As he reached the door, Luke must have suddenly realised. He turned back to look at me and searched my face for a reaction, so I had to keep my expression as normal as I could. I knew that if I showed my shock and my feelings at what had been done to him, he might think I was judging him, instead of whoever did all that damage.

After about ten seconds, Luke turned again and went off to the bathroom. Now I could react. I blinked away tears. I couldn't imagine how this damage had been done, and was desperate to know, but at the same time, I just wanted to hug him and show him that I cared very much, and wanted to protect him from any more harm.

Luke must have been very tired and half-starved, because the next couple of days, he just slept and ate, slept and ate. We hardly talked at all. I thought it would be better to wait until he felt stronger.

I popped out and bought him some underwear and a couple of tops as well as some trousers and pyjamas. He must have got up while I was out, because someone had left the milk and a cereal packet out on the worktop, and it could only have been him. Remembering what Mike had said about protecting our valuables, I did pop up and check my jewellery box, but everything was still there. I breathed a big sigh of relief and I mentally congratulated Luke.

Later that day, I called Social Services again, with Luke's surname and his date of birth. Of course, I couldn't be sure he'd given me the right details, but it was worth a try. They checked their list again and said they didn't know of him. In fact, they didn't seem at all interested. I suppose he was only a few months off his sixteenth birthday and there was no evidence to show that he had come from this area.

'But don't you think you should take him onto your list?' I persevered. 'He is under sixteen, homeless and has no idea where his mother is. He's apparently been in a number of foster placements and children's homes.

He wouldn't tell me exactly where, but in the south-west.'

'I see,' said the snooty voice. 'I'll pass on this information to our supervisor. Thank you for letting us know.'

About half an hour later, the phone rang and it was a senior social worker, who said he was too busy to come out that day, but could he speak to Luke on the phone? This was a very unusual request. It had never happened to us before; but then I'd never found a boy sleeping in our porch before either.

I called Luke and he shambled down the stairs, bleary-eyed.

'I've only just woken up,' he protested.

'Can you come to the phone please, sweetheart,' I said, holding it out towards him. 'The senior social worker wants a word with you.'

'I don't speak to social workers,' he mumbled.

'Well, please do it just this once, for my sake.'

He hesitated, then took the receiver from me. He listened and said 'yes' and 'no'. Then he suddenly became more animated. 'But I don't want to leave here. It's the first time I've been in a proper home with a proper family that love each other. Please don't take me away. If you try, I'll just run away and come back here.' There was a pause while he listened again. 'Yes, I definitely want you to register me as a foster child at this address . . . until I turn sixteen.' He handed the receiver back to me.

'Mrs Merry. Luke clearly wants to stay with you. How do you feel about him being officially placed in your care?'

'I would be very happy to keep him on with us.'

'All right,' he confirmed. 'I'll get the paperwork done and one of our team will come round with it and meet Luke in a couple of days' time.'

26

Scarpered

'Somebody has drawn a picture in MY sketchbook,' wailed Daisy when she got home from school on Luke's second day with us. She brought it over to show me. 'I left it on the table this morning, and now look what somebody has done.'

I looked at this creative, fantastical sci-fi image, beautifully drawn, in an almost comic-book style.

'Wow! That's very different, isn't it?' I tilted it this way and that. 'I rather like it. What do you think, Daise?'

She looked at it again. 'Mmm,' she seemed to be warming to it. 'It's OK, I suppose. It's a good drawing,' she said, grudgingly, then carefully tore the page out of her pad and gave it to me.

We showed it to Mike later. 'You're the expert,' I said. 'What do you think of it?'

'Well, whoever did it – they've certainly got talent.'

The next time I had the chance to talk to Luke on his own, I asked him straight out. 'Did you do this drawing, Luke?'

He looked at it briefly. 'Yes.'

'Mike is a design engineer and he says it's very good. I like it too. Can I put it up on display in the kitchen?'

'OK,' he shrugged. 'If you want to.'

'Mike reckons you've got talent and he'd like to see more of your drawings. So I've brought you some spare drawing paper I found in the playroom cupboard and some different kinds of pencils and pens.'

His eyes lit up. 'Thank you.' It was the first time I'd seen him with a proper smile.

So he now had something of his own to work on when the others weren't around. But the only real interaction he had with the kids in those first few days was, surprisingly, with Kevin, who didn't like being with people. Somehow these two clicked. Perhaps it was their ages, at thirteen and fifteen; but also because they didn't seem to make any demands on each other, which suited them both.

'Why are Kevin and Luke always in their rooms?' asked Paul one Saturday. 'Shall I ask them if they want to come and play football with us?'

'That would be a great idea in a week or two, when Luke feels more settled, but he needs to be able to just do things in his own way at the moment.'

Daisy, who was usually so self-contained, but felt a bit mean that she'd been cross with Luke about drawing in her book, offered to take both Kevin and Luke some drinks and snacks upstairs, when everyone else was helping themselves in the garden.

'That's very thoughtful of you, Daise. But I think Kevin is reading the new book Mike bought for him, and Luke is busy drawing a whole comic strip, so they probably don't want to be interrupted. I expect they'll come down for something when they're hungry.'

Kevin had been with us for about three or four months by this stage and we had found him a place at a special school for autistic children, where he seemed quite happy, at last. So he was the first to leave in the mornings, on the bus they provided, and the last to get home after school.

About a week after Luke arrived, when everyone else was in school or nursery, I sat him down with me in the kitchen.

'I think it's time we had a chat,' I began. 'First of all, I know you said you were sleeping rough, which must have been awful, but what made you come to our door?'

'One of my mates told me that the local authority were on the lookout for someone, and I thought it might be me.'

'I see. So you were worried they would catch you?'

'Yes. One of the boys had been talking to a man who had been with you – one of your foster-children, years ago, and he said you were the best, and you didn't judge people. So you were my last hope.' He paused. 'And that guy was right, wasn't he?'

'Yes, and I'm pleased he sent you here. But who was this man?'

'I don't know his name.'

'Well I'm glad you managed to find us. We love having you here.'

'Thanks. But I probably won't stay long.'

'No. You'll be sixteen soon, won't you?'

'Yes, just before Christmas.'

'Well, now that you've been with us a week and have settled in, it's time we got you into a local school or college.'

He gulped, and his face immediately changed from relaxed to tense.

'I've rung the local secondary school and they have a place for you.'

'I don't do school,' he said, as if that was the end of it.

'I'm afraid the law says you have to attend school or college, at least until you turn sixteen.'

'B***** the law!' he exclaimed. 'They've not caught up with me yet.'

'What do you mean?'

'Well, I've hardly ever been to school. My mum never bothered to take me to start with, although some of her boyfriends took me just to get me out of the house, but I always ran away and hid when I was little. Then I was put in care, so I lived in a lot of different places. Children's homes are very dodgy – training grounds for criminals and paedos more like. The foster-homes I went to weren't much better. None of them cared about me.'

'It must have been terrible for you.' I genuinely sympathised with this lad, who seemed harmless enough and just needed to be loved and valued as a person. Not just a number in the social care system.

'Where do you come from, originally?' I asked.

'Like I told you the first day – the west country,' he said vaguely. 'A long way from here.'

I could tell he didn't want me to know the exact place, so I changed the subject back to his education. 'Didn't any of these homes send you to school?'

'Yes, they all did.' He paused to push his over-long fringe back out of his eyes. 'But I never stayed after registration.'

'Didn't you like school?'

'Nope. I didn't like them and they didn't like me. I could never learn. I'm just thick.'

'Who told you that?'

'Teachers, other children, carers, everybody really. Plus I could see it for myself. I've always had good ideas. I always wanted to learn, but nobody could find a way to teach me, so I never bothered after that. What was the point? I always bunked off. So it's my fault that I can't read or write.'

'No, I'm sure it's not your fault. Maybe you're dyslexic, like me.'

His expression changed. 'I've never heard of that.'

'You seem quite bright to me. But your teachers should have tried to find the right way of teaching you – different ways that could help you to learn.'

'I thought there was only one way, and it was no use to me.'

'No, there are lots of different things they could have tried.'

He looked surprised. 'Well, they didn't.'

I thought for a moment, while I made us a coffee and brought it to the table. 'I'm going to make a couple of phone calls to see if I can arrange an alternative solution.'

'It won't work.' He was adamant.

So, I changed the subject again. 'Tell me about your back,' I said, with my most sympathetic expression. 'Is it painful?'

'No, not now,' he said. 'A bit itchy sometimes, with being so messed up and tight, but most of that was a long time ago.'

'What happened?'

'It was when I was a littl'un, still living with my mum. There was just her and me . . . and all her boyfriends. She mostly had different ones every day. They had sex on the sofa, so that she could keep an eye on me, she said. But I hated it. I thought they were attacking her. Sometimes they did and she would have cuts and bruises to show for it. One guy even broke her arm. He was the one who came most often. If I ever made a sound, or tried to stop him attacking her, she used to get him to attack me instead. It seemed to excite him to hurt people. To start with, he took off his belt, with its big buckle, and beat me with that, mostly across my back. But then my mum got a cat-o-nine-tails from somewhere.'

'That sounds terrible,' I gasped.

'Yes, it was. She used to get this man to use it on me. He would thrash me again and again with it, while he and my mum laughed at my screams. In the end, I tried not to scream so much, so that he would stop hurting me.'

'Didn't anyone hear your screams?'

'I don't know.' I could see that Luke was quite distressed now, going back over these painful memories

I leant across and put my arm round his shoulder. I was pleased he let me.

'How old were you?' I asked.

'Oh, about three or four I suppose.'

'It's hard to believe that anyone can be so cruel, especially your own mother.'

'Well, they were.' He was quiet for a moment. 'Looking back, I think she must have been on drugs most of the time, and she used to drink a lot of booze as well. Anyway, Social Services must have had a tip-off in the end, because they came to get me. I never saw her again after that.'

The next day, a Friday, I went up to wake Luke. I used to let him lie in a bit, so it was after everyone else had gone out. I called him from the stairs, but there was no grunt of reply, like he usually gave. So I went to his room, which we'd done up specially for him . . . and he was gone. He must have sneaked out overnight.

'Luke's scarpered,' I told Mike when I phoned him at work. 'What do you think I should do?'

'Did he leave a note?'

'No,' I paused. 'Remember? He can't write.'

'Oh, of course. Well, he's fifteen. Maybe there's a reason. He might be back later. Let's wait till I get home and see if anything happens.'

'Mrs Merry?' the male voice on the phone asked that evening.

'Yes.'

'This is the Ashbridge police station. We have your young man here.'

'Oh . . . do you mean Luke?'

'I do indeed. He has got himself into a bit of trouble today, ramming a shopping trolley into the Co-op's plate-glass window and smashing it.'

'On no!' I exclaimed 'I'm sorry.'

'What I need to ask you is, are you willing to be his responsible adult?'

'Er, yes,' I said, and then, 'What does that mean?'

'Well, we've charged him, so now we need to interview him. But as he's under eighteen, we can't interview him without a responsible adult present. We have specially trained interviewers to work with young people. If you could come down here to the police station and attend his interview with us and sign the forms, that would move things along.'

'Will he have to stay there?'

'Only till you get here and the interview has been completed. Once you've signed for him, you should be able to take him home on bail.'

'Oh good.'

'But, depending on the interview and any previous dealings he may have had with the police, he may have to appear in court. Do you know whether he has ever been cautioned or charged with anything before?'

'No, I'm afraid I don't. We're foster-carers, and he's not been with us long.'

So I left Mike to manage all the children's bedtime routines, much easier now that most of them were old enough to sort themselves out, and down I went to the police station. The interview was quite straightforward, as Luke admitted what he'd done from the beginning.

'Well done, Luke, for owning up,' I said in the car as I drove us both home. 'You don't have to tell me why you did it . . .'

'That's OK. I don't really know why. My head just went wild, with everything raging inside it. I was confused and . . . I think it was going over all that stuff about my mum and her boyfriends. I can't cope with all that.'

'I understand, Luke. We don't ever need to talk about that again, unless you want to. Let's get home and have something good to eat. What do you fancy?'

'Sausages and mash?' he asked hopefully.

'I'm pretty sure I've got some lovely sausages in the fridge, so sausages and mash it will be. And this time, make sure you don't scarper overnight!'

Luke's youth-court case came up quite soon after the event. Mike went to support him and spoke at the hearing.

'I told them he's a good lad really, but he'd had a bad day, affected by having to go over bad memories of his past. And that it wouldn't happen again. So they took a while, in their side room, to make their minds up. But finally, as it was his first offence, they let him off with a caution.'

'Thank goodness for that,' I said fervently. 'Let's hope it's his last offence, too.'

27

A Man on a Mission

Social Services rang up one November day to tell me that Daisy and Paul's long-time social worker John had been taken off the case.

'But why?' I asked. 'He's been with them ever since they came, ten years ago.' No answer. 'It's such a shame.' I went on. 'He's been really good with them all these years. He can't be old enough to retire . . . Is he moving to another job?'

I was fuming. I've met a lot of mediocre social workers as a foster mum, but John was one of the best. We may not have seen him that often, but when we needed him, he had come to our aid out of hours at a moment's notice, like the time when Daisy had been so ill. Not many would do that, in their free time, referring us instead to the duty social worker. John really cared. I was furious that we had lost him now, without even knowing why.

'So do Daisy and Paul have a new social worker now?'

'Yes. His name is Bernard Brown. He'll give you a ring in a day or two.'

So that was it. I will have to break it to the kids, I thought. But maybe I'll wait till he's made contact and I can find out what he's like. In the meantime I decided to do a bit of sleuthing.

I started with John himself, which was more than likely against the rules, but nothing ventured . . . He couldn't say much, of course, just that it was a reorganisation, which sounded like a recipe for chaos to me as it's the kids who always lose out. I asked John what he knew about the new man, Bernard Brown. That's how I found out that he had been a bus driver for years, before switching careers, so he was a newly trained social worker – a rookie. Just our luck!

'What's happened about Luke's education?' asked Mike one evening. 'Shouldn't he have started at the high school by now?'

'Officially, yes. But I came up with another plan. I spoke to a senior social worker about him being so dyslexic that he couldn't read or write yet, and the fact that he's hardly had any formal education, and is adamant that school isn't for him.'

'So what did they say?'

'Well, that's where I gave them the solution. They discussed it with the education department and, amazingly they agreed! They'll give him his own home-learning tutor two days a week, as long as I supervise the work he's set on the days in between.'

'Well done,' said Mike.

'And,' I said, 'what's great is that they have someone in mind that they think will be just right for him.'

* * *

The following Monday the tutor arrived, as agreed. I don't know quite what I was expecting, but it wasn't what I saw. In fact, we heard it first, sounding like a fire-breathing dragon pulling up outside our house. I opened the door to a bearded, tattooed, leather-jacketed 'Hells Angels' type on a monster of a motorbike, gleaming proudly in the sunlight.

'Hi,' he said as he took off his helmet, to reveal his bald patch and his long pony-tail. 'I'm Guy. I guess you're Trisha?'

'That's right.'

'Hey Luke, my man,' he said with a grin and a strange hand-greeting that I'd never seen before, but Luke seemed to know what to do. 'How are you doing?'

'Good,' the boy replied, in an American accent.

They came in and I sat them down at our dining room table. 'Will you be all right in here for working?' I asked. 'I'll shut the door and put up a "do not disturb" sign, in case anyone comes.'

Luke looked a bit uncertain, but Guy took charge. 'We're not stopping,' said Guy. 'I've got a busy day planned.'

'Oh?'

'Yes.' He turned to Luke. 'Man, how do you fancy putting on my spare helmet and jacket and going out for a burn, to the hills?'

Luke nodded enthusiastically.

'Aren't you the tutor?' I asked, uncertainly, thinking I'd let in some anarchist Luke must have met on the streets.

'No worries, Trisha,' Guy reassured me. 'We're going to do all this week's history, geography, English and maths today, so let's get going, Luke. Are you up for it?'

'Yes,' replied Luke, with a bemused expression. I could tell this was not at all what he had expected either.

'Well, I did suggest he needed a new way of teaching and learning!' I told Mike over supper.

'What do they say? Beware what you ask for . . .' We laughed. 'How did they get on? Did they show you anything when they got back?'

'Yes. I have to confess, I was amazed at how much Luke had achieved. Probably more in one day than in any of his previous schooling! He got it all out of his backpack to show me. Apparently they'd gone on a breezy ride to the Malvern Hills. They sat on the top of the highest hill with a compass and worked out the different counties and geographical features, then Luke drew his own map, with things labelled. Guy must have helped him with that. Then Luke drew in Caractacus fighting the Romans on the map, and marked the civil war battles too. They followed a stream down to the valley to see what fish and wildlife they could find and sketched them. And then there was maths, like the distances on the map . . . I think they had a great time, and it was all about learning.'

'This Guy sounds like everybody's ideal teacher,' said Mike with a grin.

'Yes, and he's got loads of great ideas for other educational outings and subjects too! I've never seen Luke look so enthusiastic or so healthy after all that fresh air!'

* * *

In between worrying about Daisy and Paul's new social worker's inexperience, and supervising Luke's independent assignments, I also had developments to take care of at the sex-film children's house.

It was three years now since we had set up the wrap-around package for them, with all the amazing helpers and professionals who supported them. All five were making small steps of progress. However, the two youngest ones seemed better able to change some of their behaviours and instincts than the older ones.

'I think it's time to consider placing these younger two in a family setting now,' said the senior social worker as he sat with me and a psychotherapist one morning, down at the council offices. 'Duane is five and Sindy is six now, and they've both made a good start with their reading, writing and arithmetic.'

'Yes,' agreed the psychotherapist. 'It has taken a lot of specialist input and care, but I think they may now be ready to join the outside world, living with a caring family, going to school and making friends of their own.'

'That would be great,' I said. 'If you're sure they're ready, and that they can avoid the sexualised advances they made the day I first met them when mixing with other children and unknown male adults.'

The senior social worker turned to the psychotherapist. 'Would you like to respond?'

'Yes.' She turned to me. 'It's a chicken and egg situation, in a way,' she began. 'I believe they have left a lot of their early programming behind and that they're young enough to become normalised now. However, until we take this step, we won't know for certain that it will work.'

'Yes.' The social worker nodded, and looked straight at me. 'That's where you come in, Trisha.'

'What do you mean?'

'Well, I know you have some spare spaces, you and Mike, and I wonder whether you would now reconsider and take them in. They already know you, and you are the best, most experienced foster-carers we have . . .' She tailed off when she saw the expression on my face.

'You've caught me completely off-guard,' I spluttered. 'I wasn't expecting that.'

'Will you think about it?' he asked.

'Hmm . . . I'll have a chat with Mike this evening and see what he thinks,' I said.

What they didn't know was that Mike and I had recently decided not to take in any more children and to gradually run down the numbers, as they grew up or left, so that we could prepare for our retirement. Still, I explained it all to Mike as soon as we were on our own.

'Well,' he began. 'I know we agreed not to take on any more foster-children. But we do already have their younger sister, Lulu, so we would have to wait for her to grow up, anyway . . .'

So, we surprised ourselves by agreeing. First thing the next morning I called the senior social worker and told him we would take on both Sindy and Duane, on the understanding that it would be for a probationary period to start with. 'We have to give them the chance they need and the love they deserve,' I told him. 'As well as the time to renew their sibling bond with our Lulu.'

So I went to collect them a couple of hours later and they seemed to take to Lulu immediately. In fact, all our kids just accepted them straight away. But the next few days would tell, especially going to school for the first time.

A couple of days later, the overdue call from Daisy and Paul's new social worker, Bernard, finally came. He started by introducing himself and checking our contact details and the children's names and dates of birth.

'I believe their father visits them?'

'Yes, but very infrequently. He hasn't been for more than a couple of years now. And the one time we needed to contact him, to ask his permission for Daisy to have tests in hospital, he refused and put the phone down.'

'Yes, I can see that John has documented that.'

'And the doctor who was with John was anxious to go ahead, but Rocky took no notice.' I paused to let that sink in. 'Daisy felt very let down by her father, when she most needed him. She still does.'

'Yes. I can understand that.' Bernard seemed impatient. 'But what about the mother? I can't see anything here about her, other than her name and a contact number.'

'Well, that's more than we have. According to Rocky, she walked out on him and the kids just after Paul was born. She just abandoned them. I don't know if that's true, but neither of the children could remember her and they have never mentioned her at all.'

'I do believe that mothers should not be sidelined like this, Mrs Merry.'

'Trisha,' I said, indignant at his tone. 'I hope you're not accusing us of sidelining her? We've never heard from her, or anything about her. You may have a telephone number, but nobody gave it to us, and she certainly has never attempted to make any contact with us, nor even sent as much as a birthday card to either of her children. So I don't think sidelining is the right word.'

'I see. Well, I'm sorry if I have offended you, Trisha. I didn't mean to do that. I suspect the Social Services Department may have been guilty of not following through on the contact side. There's no record that anybody here has ever made contact with her. And all the paperwork was signed by the children's father, alone.'

'Yes, I was there when he signed the papers.'

'I do apologise, as it seems I haven't made a good start in my relationship with you as the children's foster-mother. I do recognise the great importance of your role in acting as their mother . . . while they are with you.' He was saying some of the right words, but I had an uncomfortable feeling about the way this conversation was going.

'Are you hoping to come round and meet the children?' I asked. 'I think it would be helpful for you to get to know them, and us too.'

'If you wish.' I didn't like the way he said that, as if meeting the children didn't really matter.

We arranged for him to come on the following Monday, 2 December, in the late afternoon.

Bernard came as agreed and spent the first half hour, sitting on the playroom sofa, chatting with each of the children in turn. I assumed he would be asking them about their schools, their friends and hobbies. Maybe he would ask them about living as part of our family, and about us too. He was a social worker. I trusted him. Perhaps that was my first mistake.

Next, it was my turn. 'Mrs Merry—'

'Trisha,' I interrupted him.

'Yes, Trisha, I've had a good chat with both Daisy and Paul, and they would like to see their mother.'

'What?' I spluttered in astonishment. How had that come about? They hadn't mentioned her once in ten years, so why would they say that to a stranger on his first visit? 'Did you actually hear them say that?' I asked, in a cool voice.

'Yes.'

'On their own initiative?'

'Well, no . . . but they seemed OK to talk about her.'

'But they don't know anything at all about her.'

'No, but I wanted to know whether they'd like to see her.'

'That's outrageous,' I protested. 'You are raising their awareness of their mother, giving them the hope that she might want to see them, when, as the last ten years have shown, she clearly has no wish at all to see them.' I paused to take a big breath and lower my shoulders. 'What do you think that will do to them?'

'But, have you considered her point of view?'

'No, because it's the kids I care about. I would never do or say anything that might lead to their disappointment and any further feeling of betrayal. Have you ever seen a child waiting all day for their parent to show up, then go to bed in tears because they hadn't? Daisy and Paul's mother abandoned them once. Why wouldn't she do it again? If she cared, she could have contacted them at any time before now. But she hasn't.'

'Don't you think that everyone needs the chance to at least meet their own mother?' he insisted.

I didn't answer that rhetorical question. I do believe in rights for all, of course, but he seemed to have this all skewed in his mind. What was he thinking of? I feared where this could lead and needed to say so. But, as I suspected, he had his own agenda.

'Well, I think that the children's mother should be part of their picture of who they are,' he continued. 'So, although the number I was given was wrong, I did manage to track down Daisy and Paul's mother, and I had a chat with her. As a result of that conversation, she has agreed to come and visit the children. Isn't that marvellous?'

Another question to which I could not give a polite answer. I was livid, but I had to try not to show it too obviously. I composed myself as best I could.

'I can only answer that with another question,' I replied.

'Yes, of course.'

'Did you ask her to come and see them, or did she ask to visit them?'

'Well . . . that's a good question.'

'Yes, I know. But I want to hear the answer.'

'Well, I think you know it already. I phoned their mother, had a chat with her and then asked her if she'd like to visit them.'

'And did she answer you straight away?'

'Er, no. She wanted to think about it. She rang me back the following day and agreed to come.'

'Why? What for?'

'Because she's their mother. Don't you think that's enough?'

'What I think is that you're setting the children up to be knocked down – very badly. I hope I'm wrong, but—'

'That's not the point,' he interrupted, clearly annoyed with my concerns.

'Then what is?'

He said nothing.

'Do we have a date?'

'Wednesday at noon. Will that be all right for you?'

I felt like snapping at him: *It will have to be, won't it?* But I didn't. I said 'Yes. Though it means they will have to miss school. At least I'll have the time in between now and then to prepare the children gently for her visit.'

'Thank you, Mrs Merry.'

'Goodbye, Mr Brown.' I shut the front door as soon as he had passed through and stood with my back to it, leaning against it.

How dare he get us into this mess? It would be fine, better than fine, if their birth mother genuinely wanted to get to know her children. I'd be delighted for that to happen, as long as she turned up and it wasn't a one-day wonder. If they really did develop a positive relationship, I'd be very happy for them and do all I could to support it. But I feared what it would do to Daisy and Paul if she let them down in any way, let alone abandoning them again. It would be so much worse this time.

Bit by bit, that evening and over the following day, I created opportunities to talk with them about their mother.

But I must say, they seemed remarkably matter-of-fact about it, both of them. The message I was getting from them was: *We've got a mother, but we don't remember her. We don't know what she looks like, or anything about her life. But she's a stranger, so we're not really interested.* That's how they seemed to be taking the conversation.

However, I hadn't yet broken the news to them that their mother was coming to see them the next day. I would have to do that after school tonight. I wondered how they would react.

28

Cold Comfort

Daisy and Paul had a similar reaction to mine.

'Why does she want to come?'

'To see you. I know you don't remember your mother, but she remembers you. When she last saw you, Pauly, you were probably a newborn baby, or not much bigger than that. And Daise, you were one year old – a toddler. You had probably just learnt to walk, but you couldn't talk yet, except gibberish, which only you understood.'

Paul giggled at the thought of himself as a tiny baby.

'Did I used to suck my thumb then?' asked Daisy, as she tried to imagine herself at that age. 'Maybe I didn't have this haircut yet?' she asked. It was still a sore point with her, and she blamed her mother for all the years of having to put up with it, and all the horrid things other children said about it. But she was not a child who held a grudge, so I hoped she wouldn't take it out on her mother. 'I expect that, when she sees you now, Daise, she might let you change it, if you ask her. I hope so.'

'Why hasn't she come before?' asked Daisy.

'I don't know, sweetheart. Perhaps she didn't want to

disturb your life here with us. The main thing is that she's coming here to meet you both now.'

'Will she bring us a present?' asked Paul, with a cheeky grin.

'Not if you ask for it!' I said. 'Let's wait and see.'

'What will we do when she gets here?' asked Daisy.

'Say hello and get to know each other. Maybe chat a bit. Then take her up to see your bedrooms, if you like.'

'Can I go outside and show her tricks on my bike?' asked Paul.

'Yes, of course, if it's not too cold and wet. Or she could watch you from the kitchen window if the weather's bad.'

'She won't want to take us away, will she?' asked Daisy, with an anxious expression.

'No. She's just coming to visit. She certainly can't just take you away tomorrow or anything like that. So you don't need to worry.'

'Oh good,' she sighed. 'I don't want to leave you and Mike. And I don't want to leave my school, and I've just started going to Guides, so I don't want to leave that either.'

'She's just coming to see you,' I said, putting my arm round her shoulders to reassure her. 'Then you'll know what she looks like, and you can tell her the things you like doing.'

Daisy chose what she wanted to wear and spent some time in front of the mirror, experimenting whether to do up her cardigan or not. Whereas Paul said, 'I'm not bothered – you choose.' So I picked out an emerald green jumper and the new pair of navy cord trousers I'd bought him the previous week. I had to remind him to change into them, just in time.

At exactly midday, Bernard drove up outside the house. The children were both with me when I opened the front door, and in came this carefully made-up, slim young woman with perfect skin and beautiful, long auburn hair, right down to her waist. Daisy couldn't take her eyes off it. This was just what she had always wanted, but could never have.

Seeing the way Daisy looked at her mother's hair, it was one of the few times in my life when I would have liked to be quite spiteful. I wanted to say to her, 'Oh, you've got long hair. What is it about your daughter that you don't want her to have the same?' But of course, I didn't.

She was superbly turned out, and such a contrast to Rocky. I couldn't imagine how they ever got together. He was rough and ready, while she was neat and tidy; he was brash, while she was demure. His clothes looked as if he'd worn them all week, and it wasn't just his clothes that were grubby, but she was the opposite – everything clean and ironed, prim and proper. To my mind, they didn't fit at all as a couple.

Bernard did the introductions, and when I shook hands with Pamela, it was like holding a dead fish.

I was intrigued to see whether the children, meeting their mother, might feel some slight sense of recognition from their infancy, especially Daisy; so I watched their faces and body-language, but it was no different from when they met any stranger. Daisy stood back, like an observer, while Paul was offhand and uninterested.

We all went into the sitting room and plonked ourselves on the chairs . . . except for Pamela. The temperature in our house dropped for me when I watched the careful way she sat down. As she lowered herself into her seat, she paid more attention to smoothing all the pleats in her skirt than she did to the children she hadn't seen for eleven years. She looked all around the room, and out of the window, but she barely gave them a glance.

Nobody spoke for a few awkward seconds, until I started a conversation with her.

'Did you have far to come, Pamela?'

'It wasn't too bad,' she replied, giving nothing away. Her accent had a west-country lilt, but her coarse voice took me by surprise. In fact, although she seemed prim and proper on the surface, and clearly tried to come across as genteel, I felt there was a rough rigidity about her, a lack of empathy perhaps. But that was probably just my imagination. I tried to stop judging her.

I could see, gazing sideways at Paul, that he looked expectant. I tried to shake my head at him without her noticing. But it didn't work. He couldn't contain himself.

'Did you bring us any presents?' It was the first thing he said to her, and she didn't look pleased.

'No, I'm afraid I didn't. Why? Is it your birthday or something?'

'Don't you know when my birthday is?'

'No . . . oh, wait a minute.' She was trying to dredge it out of her memory. 'Your birthday is in the summer, isn't it? And Daisy's too?'

'Yes, that's right,' her daughter said.

'Daisy,' I prompted her. 'Do you want to tell your mum about your school?' Fortunately, that was an easy subject for Daisy to talk about in detail, as she always enjoyed school. But I noticed she kept it short today.

'And what about you, Paul?' I asked.

'I don't really like school,' he told her. 'Except for PE and break-times.'

Their mother's eyes looked glazed, as if she was only half-listening.

Then Bernard tried to engage them in another conversation, about their hobbies, then their favourite foods

'That reminds me,' I stood up. 'I must get the lunch ready for all the children. It will be mainly sandwiches today, plus bits and bobs.'

'Can you do bacon sandwiches?' asked Paul. 'They're my favourite.'

'Yes, that's OK,' I said.

'Can I come and help you?' he seemed unusually eager. He never usually wanted to help with anything, unless he was being paid. But he wasn't a boy who enjoyed conversation, so any excuse to escape polite talk with adults.

'No thanks, Paul. Not this time. You stay here with your mother.' I turned to Pamela and Bernard. 'You can all come through in about ten minutes and join us in the kitchen for a help-yourself lunch . . . bacon sandwiches included.'

That casual lunch helped to break the ice, but Pamela remained detached and the atmosphere was still rather strained.

After they'd finished eating, Bernard went off to respond to a call, and I sent Daisy and Paul upstairs with their mother to show her their bedrooms.

Thank goodness, they managed to stay up there for at least thirty minutes, as they showed her where they slept and all their things. Daisy showed her the special homework she'd been doing about the Fire of London, with her careful drawings. Then Paul went to get his rather battered model of a Viking longboat.

When I'd finished clearing all the lunch things away, I went upstairs to join Daisy, Paul and Pamela. They were sat in silence on the bed in Daisy's room, while their mother flicked idly through one of Daisy's school books. She put it down when I arrived.

'What about showing your mum your new shoes, Daisy? She might like to look at your clothes as well.' I smiled to encourage Pamela, with no obvious effect. I don't normally use the word disdain, but it was the perfect word to describe her expression.

After a few minutes of that, with Daisy telling her mother where she had bought or worn each outfit, and Pamela never once responding with a positive comment, I felt really impatient with this impassive woman. Did she have any feelings? Most people would have said, 'Oh, that's a pretty dress', or 'It looks like pink is your favourite colour', or whatever. But Pamela made no effort to make her daughter feel good – or feel anything.

It was all so uncomfortable, so forced. I felt . . . *Arrrghgh!* It was like trying to unscrew a very tight lid.

'Paul is very clever on his bike,' I said. 'I think he wants to show you some of the tricks he can do.'

Paul beamed. 'I can do wheelies,' he said. It was the first moment he had looked animated since his mother had arrived.

'Really? I don't think so . . . it's rather cold outside.'

Paul's face fell. How could this woman be so indifferent to her children's needs?

'We don't have to go outside, Pamela. Come on, we can watch from the kitchen window.' I didn't give her any choice.

Paul put on a good show for her. Daisy stood with her mother and me to watch his antics. He fell off at one point, and I took in a sharp breath, but she showed no concern. He finished his demonstration, put the bike away and came in.

'Well done, Paul,' I said with enthusiasm and gave him a cuddle. I gave Pamela a look to urge her to say something too.

'Yes, well done,' she repeated half-heartedly.

Thinking back, I may have judged her too harshly, because it was a difficult situation for her, meeting her children for the first time in all those years, coming into an alien environment, in a huge house, full of children, with what probably seemed a chaotic lifestyle. I don't think chaos was in her vocabulary. It must have been daunting for her. I just wish she could have summoned up the slightest hint of enthusiasm.

It had been a long afternoon, with a strained atmosphere, so I think the kids were as relieved as I was when Bernard came back, looked at his watch and declared that it was time to go home.

'Give your mum a hug,' I said, and she stood back slightly as they came to her, Daisy first, then Paul. She leant down a little so that they could each give her a hug, but not close enough for their faces to come into contact.

I opened the hall door, shook hands and off they both went. I closed the door with relief. *Phew!* I thought. *Thank goodness that's over with.*

When Mike came back from work, he asked how her visit had gone.

'It was hard work,' I groaned. 'Like stirring treacle.'

'Oh, bad as that?' he laughed. 'What was she like with the kids?'

'Cold comfort – detached and undemonstrative. I was quite worried. I don't think she has a motherly bone in her body. It was almost as if she was here under duress, perhaps because Bernard had talked her into coming, against her better judgement.'

'That's probably it,' he said.

'Why did they have to give Daisy and Paul a rookie social worker, on a mission to reunite mothers with children, regardless of the damage that might cause?'

'How do you think the children felt about her?'

'They did try to engage her, but there was no bonding. They seemed as relieved as I was when she went. But it could have been different if she'd made an effort. Her heart just wasn't in it.' I paused. 'I'll be very surprised if we ever hear from her again.'

29

The Bombshell

We were well into December now and the excitement mounted day by day. The house was filled with tinsel, wrapping-paper, decorations and lights. We hung a holly wreath on the front door and mistletoe just inside. Most of the children gathered round the kitchen table to make paper chains, which we festooned around each room. Then Mike got Luke and Kevin to help him carry in the enormous Christmas tree and stand it in the hall. All the others helped to decorate the tree and, by the time we'd finished, it looked good enough for Buckingham Palace, apart from the wonky star on the top!

Luke was a changed lad, since Guy had taken him on. He loved all their outings and was learning amazingly fast, almost without realising it. He could now write a few lines about whatever he had been to see. He could do some simple calculations and he was always telling us new things he'd learnt.

'Did you know, the tallest mountain in England is Scafell Pike, and it's 3,209 feet high? It's in the Lake District,' he said proudly. 'Guy says we might go for a trip up there to see it in the spring.'

'Where are you going this week?' asked Mike.

'To the Potteries. Have you heard of Josiah Wedgewood? We're going to find out about him and we're going to find out where clay comes from. We're going to look round one of the factories and see where they make the pots and plates and things. Guy says I might get a chance to decorate one of them.'

'I bet you'll make a good job of that,' said Mike. 'You ought to do something creative when you've finished growing up.'

It was heartwarming to see that pale, cold boy whom I'd found huddled homeless in our porch that morning now healthy and full of enthusiasm for life.

'I want to be an aircraft engineer or designer,' said Kevin, his eyes down as if he was staring at something on the floor. 'Mike said he'd take me into work with him one day in the holidays, so I can see what they do.'

'Come on, Kevin,' said Luke. 'Let's go and have a game of chess.'

So off they went. It was strange how these two teenagers, with their different problems, had palled up, even though they hardly ever spoke to each other once they were concentrating on something. Kevin had stopped self-harming – a great step forward for him. Luke could now read and write some of the simple captions in comic strips, so he too could see his progress. For the first time in his life, nobody was calling him thick, and he was learning something new every day.

All through teatime, the younger ones were talking about what they wanted to do when they left school. Sheena wanted to be a model, Ronnie wanted to work in a supermarket and AJ was keen on becoming a builder, Daisy wanted to be a librarian and read all the books in the library, while Paul wanted to become a fireman. I think he still remembered that time when the firemen came into our house and one of them let Paul try on his helmet. Mandy wanted to be a scientist. Sindy, Duane and Lulu didn't know yet. My wish for them was simply that they grew up as normal, socialised individuals, leaving their abusive past behind them.

Daisy and Paul's former social worker, John, called in the following day to visit Luke, who had just been put on his caseload. When he'd finished talking to Luke, he joined me for a cup of tea in the kitchen.

'How did Daisy and Paul's mother's visit go?' he asked.

'Ooh . . . It was hard, John. I've never had anything like that happen before. Bernard said their mother wanted to come and see them, but she was cool and detached all day long. They tried to engage with her. But it was as if she was only here under sufferance.'

John listened intently, but said nothing. I was frustrated by his lack of response at first . . . until I realised how much his silence told me.

A few days later, just when I thought that was the end of it, Bernard phoned.

'Pamela wants to come on Saturday and take the children out for a couple of hours.'

'Right,' I gulped. I'd have to prepare them and boost them up again . . . if I could. 'Saturday the fourteenth? I asked, looking at the calendar by the phone.

'Yes, that's right.'

'Will she come back here afterwards as well?'

'No, she says she'll come and collect them at ten o'clock and she's only got about two hours, so it won't be like last time. She'll just take them into town, bring them back again and then she'll leave.'

I waited till after tea, before sitting Daisy and Paul down with me and telling them what Bernard had said on the phone. They both listened without saying a word, then looked at each other and turned back to me.

'We don't want to go,' said Daisy, coolly and clearly, as if they'd discussed what they would do in just such an eventuality. Could they have done? Would they? I have to say I was surprised by this united stand. Daisy and Paul were as unlike as it is possible for a brother and sister to be. But either it was telepathy or they really had discussed it.

'It'll only be for two hours.' I tried to encourage them to go, as I knew I must.

'But I don't want to go out with her,' protested Paul with a defiant pout.

'We can see her here, can't we?' asked Daisy, the peacemaker.

'Yes, of course you can,' I said. 'But she told Bernard that she wanted to take you both into town.'

'Yes, but we don't want to go to town with her,' repeated Daisy, patient but firm.'I'm not going,' insisted Paul. 'And that's that.'

I did my best to change their minds at breakfast the next morning, but they were adamant.

Pamela arrived at ten o'clock, as agreed.

'Are they ready to go?' she asked, when I showed her in.

'Let me give them a call,' I said, shouting their names. We had an uncomfortable couple of minutes, waiting in the hallway, talking about the weather.

Finally they both arrived from different directions at once. Paul looked rather dishevelled, but not too bad, while Daisy was her usual neat self, uncannily like her mother, I realised.

'Are you ready to go out?' asked Pamela ' Do you have coats to put on?' She looked impatient.

Daisy and Paul looked at me . . . and I remained silent.

Paul took the plunge. 'I don't want to go!'

'Oh,' said his mother. 'But I wanted to take you into town.'

'Please could we stay here instead?' asked Daisy.

'Oh . . . well . . . Are you sure?'

'Yes,' they said in unison, and nodded.

'All right then.' She looked slightly adrift for a moment. Then turned to look at me. 'Will that by acceptable to you, Mrs Merry?' I think she was hoping I would persuade them to go, but I didn't.

'Yes, that's fine with me. You can stay as long as you like. Join us for lunch again.'

'Oh no, I'm afraid I couldn't possibly do that.' She paused. 'My husband is collecting me at twelve for another appointment.'

So, I thought, *her children are just an appointment, are they?*

'I'd like to have a talk with Daisy and Paul. On our own,' she said.

'Why don't you all go and have a chat in the sitting room?' I suggested. 'And close the door.'

'I've got to go,' said Pamela, at the end of the two hours. 'Thank you.'

'I'm sorry they didn't want to go into town with you.' I apologised with a smile.

She just shrugged.

As on her first visit, the moment we closed the front door behind her as she left, both the kids relaxed. You could feel the tension leave them.

I finished my baking and Paul went off to join Ronnie and AJ in the garage, where they were constructing something, while Daisy went up to her bedroom to carry on reading her latest library book, *Little Women*. She had quite old-fashioned tastes in reading.

I suspect she needed to immerse herself in the escapism of nineteenth-century America, after what might have seemed an uncomfortable visit; or maybe I was wrong and the visit had gone much better than last time. I hoped it had, but I couldn't see it.

The following Monday, Bernard Brown called again.

'Pamela has applied to have the children.' This was Bernard's opening sentence. A complete bombshell. It blew me off my feet. 'We're making arrangements to view her house,' he said. 'Just to put you in the picture . . .' I noted the irony, since social workers were not usually keen to put us in the picture.

'She's recently married again,' he continued.

'Really?' I said, remembering that she'd mentioned a husband when she'd been here on Saturday.

'Yes, a few months ago.'

Well, the rules in those days were different – much more lax. Now, if a parent is in a new relationship, they can't have their kids back at the same time. Social Services would want the marriage or partnership to settle down and stabilise for long enough, before sending the children into this new family situation.

But the thing that really bugged me was why did she want to have her kids, after all those years of ignoring them? I couldn't manage to fathom it out then, and I still can't. Was it her, or her new husband . . . or was it Bernard's intervention? And, more importantly, was it in the best interests of the children? It was a very uncomfortable feeling – a mixture of anxiety and fear for their future. And, of course, great sadness that we would be losing them after more than ten years.

'All being well with the house visit,' continued Bernard, 'we will put things in motion for her to have her children back as soon as possible.'

I didn't like the sound of that. It seemed unduly rushed. 'How soon?' I asked. 'Weeks? Months?'

'Days, I expect. Hopefully in time for them to be together for Christmas.' He sounded pleased at the prospect.

It turned me cold. Nowadays, a move to an estranged parent would have a staged lead-in period – time for familiarisation. These children had never even met their mother's husband or visited her house. They barely knew her, nor she them. The acceleration of the process, especially at this time of year, seemed cruel to me.

Two days later, on the evening of the last day of term, the final decision came through.

'Pamela and her husband will pick up the children on Saturday morning,' said Bernard.

'What, this Saturday?'

'Yes.'

'Saturday the twenty-fourth? Christmas Eve?'

'That's right.'

'But that's only three days away . . . not even that. Not much time to break the news and get them ready, emotionally, is it?'

'I'm sure they'll be so pleased when they know they're going back to live with their mum, that you won't need to worry about that,' he said.

'Hmm.' I paused to gather my thoughts and tried not to say anything inflammatory. 'You don't know the children as well as I do.'

I didn't want to tell them just before bedtime, so on the Thursday morning I sent all the others off – the little ones to the park with Mike and the older ones to their own activities, and I sat with Daisy and Paul in the kitchen. They looked apprehensive.

'Have we done something wrong?' asked Paul, who was often in trouble for one thing or another. But it didn't usually involve Daisy as well.

'No, nothing wrong today . . . well, not yet!' I smiled.

'What is it then?' Daisy asked anxiously.

'I had a phone call from Bernard yesterday evening. He said that your mother wants you to go and live with her and her new husband.'

Both their mouths dropped open. I had braced myself for protests, but their immediate reactions were silence.

'I didn't know she had a husband,' gasped Daisy.

'Does that mean he will have to be our new dad?' asked Paul.

'But we've already got a dad,' Daisy pointed out. 'We can't have two dads.'

I explained that he would be their stepdad and he may be very nice, but he wouldn't replace their real dad.

'I don't want to live with them,' said Paul, looking scared and vulnerable.

'I'm afraid it isn't up to us, sweetheart. She is your mum.'

'But you're our mum,' said Daisy, in a sad voice. 'She might be our mother, but she's not our mum.'

I nodded. 'Yes, I understand what you mean,' I agreed. 'But I hope you will give her a fair chance to become your mum. It won't be immediate. Just give her time.'

'Do we have to go?' asked Paul, his shoulders hunched.

'Yes. She is your mother, Pauly, so she has the right to take you back to live with her.'

'But don't we have rights too? We hardly know her,' added Daisy.

'I know,' I agreed. 'But, like I said Daise, give her time.' I really felt for her, for both of them.

'Can I take my bike?' asked Paul – the typical boy, and always the pragmatic one. 'I'm not going to go unless I can take my bike.'

'I don't see why not.'

'Well, I don't want to go, but I don't mind as long as I can take my bike.'

'We haven't even been to her house,' moaned Daisy. 'Or met her husband.' She paused. 'When do we have to go?'

This was the news I dreaded telling them. 'Bernard has arranged it for the day after tomorrow, so that you can spend Christmas with your mother,'

'The day after tomorrow?' asked Paul, in disbelief. 'Father Christmas won't know where we are. We won't get our presents.'

'We've always had Christmas here,' said Daisy. 'You'll have to tell them we can't go until after Christmas.' She wasn't normally an assertive child, so I was surprised at the strength of this plea.

'I'm afraid I have no say, Daise. It's already been decided. Your mother wants you to be at her house for Christmas, and Social Services have agreed.'

I suspected it was the other way around, but I couldn't say so. They had more than enough to take on board as it was. No matter how good or bad the decision, this would be the most important change in their lives. A new start . . . and hopefully a good one. I had a disturbing feeling that it might not be, but we all had to hope.

30

Clinging On

The last couple of days in the run-up to Christmas were always jolly, but also frantic. Now we had the added complication of getting Daisy and Paul ready to leave us within forty-eight hours. Surely there couldn't be a worse day to leave a secure and loving foster placement than Christmas Eve.

So, the first thing was writing letters to Father Christmas, to let him know their new address, which Bernard had given me when I explained what I wanted it for. Even Paul was keen to sit at the kitchen table and write his letter to Father Christmas, while most of the rest of the gang were outside playing on the new rope swings we'd set up for them.

Next on the list that Thursday morning was bringing their memory-boxes up to date. We usually kept them in the kids' bedrooms, so that they could add to them when they wanted to, and go through them whenever they felt like reminiscing – Daisy more than Paul on both counts.

'Go up to your rooms and get out your memory boxes, and have a look through all your things, in case there is anything else you want to put in,' I suggested, 'while I go and find all the old photos of our outings, to see what else we can add.'

I got the old albums and boxes of photos and laid them out on the kitchen table, picking out ones we had copies of that they could take. When Daisy and Paul came back, we spent the next couple of hours chatting about all the happy memories they had, and laughing at some of the funny photos we'd taken over the years, mostly of the children, some of Mike and hardly any of me – I hate having my photo taken. We chose some of the duplicates we had, or the ones we had negatives for, to add to their memory boxes.

They had rummaged in their bedrooms and brought down some of their precious things that would fit in. Paul brought down his little 'Ted', that we had bought him when he first came to us, at one year old. The other thing he wanted to include was his times-tables book. This was a notebook we had given him in which he had written down every one of the times-tables, to help him learn them. It had taken him hours and hours to do. And, as he had never yet learnt them all, he used it all the time as a crib at school. It was the only sit-down thing I can ever remember him willingly working at. He slipped this precious notebook into his memory box, and laid Ted down on top of it.

Daisy delved through her memory box to check that her beloved plaits were in there, as well as that first square of knitting she had done with me. Then she added the first book she could remember reading, and had kept in her night-table drawer ever since. Next she put in some of her favourite drawings and colourings she had done over the years. Finally, as if it were some kind of a religious ceremony, Daisy added the French-knitting cotton reel on which she'd been working to make as long a piece as she could, which she coiled round the reel. So far it was about two yards long of multi-coloured wool and she was very proud of it.

'Two more sleeps,' said Daisy with a gloomy expression that night when she got into bed and I tucked her in. It was what we always said to the little ones, coming up to an important day. We were doing it for Christmas Day of course, but I knew Daisy had a more important day on her mind. 'Mum,' she called me back as I left the room. 'Are you sure we can't postpone going to our mother's until after Christmas? Can you try again?' she pleaded.

'OK,' I agreed. 'I'll call Bernard, or the duty-worker, but I think the answer will be no.' Sadly, I was right about that. I'm sure Daisy knew, but she was clutching at any last vestige of hope.

On Friday morning, Mike took the rest of the children out to a Christmas Fair, while I took Daisy and Paul to choose a new backpack each to carry their personal bits and pieces in, and the things that wouldn't fit into their memory boxes. I'd seen a huge stall at the market that had all kinds of really trendy backpacks, so that's where we went.

This guy had everything. Paul picked up a cheap plastic backpack, so I tried to draw his attention to the other, much more exciting ones that were also better made.

'What about this army camouflage one, Paul? Or look at the Spiderman one.'

'I want this one,' he said, holding up the plastic backpack in baby-blue.

'It you want a plain colour one, there's a black backpack, or a navy blue one. They're both in strong canvas and really smart, aren't they?' But he still held on to the tacky, plastic powder-blue one.

I decided that perhaps, if I left him alone, he might change his mind. So I switched to Daisy, who was looking quite systematically at all of them, running her eyes down the racks and along the rows.

'Look, here's a Wonder Woman one,' I said. 'Or Aristocats. You went to see that film with Mike, didn't you? Or you can choose geometrical patterns, or here's a pretty pink one.'

She picked one up from the middle, with wild flowers and butterflies on a cream background. 'I'd like this back-pack, please.'

'Yes, that's a good choice, Daise.'

Back to Paul again. 'Let's put this one aside,' I suggested. 'Have a last look at all the others, in case you want to change your mind.'

'No, no, no. I don't,' he said, picking up his pale-blue choice. 'I want this one, please.'

So, defeated, I bought them both the ones they'd chosen and we took them back home.

'Now, fill up your backpacks with what you want to take, especially the bits and pieces you have by the side of your bed. Don't worry about your clothes because we'll pack those in a case later on, ready to take tomorrow. While you put in what you want upstairs, I'll fish out all your old school reports and certificates to put in your backpacks.'

'Take a cardboard box each.' I pointed to where I'd put them on the kitchen table. 'Go and pick all your toys and anything large you want to take and pack them in there. I've got a large bin-bag each for you to take with you the Christmas presents that have your name on, from under the tree in the hall.'

Both the children looked relieved and excited that they could take their gifts with them to open on Christmas Day. They did the usual thing of trying to guess what was in each wrapping-paper, then put them in their sacks. Finally, that evening, we took the empty suitcases into each of their bedrooms, took their clothes out of the wardrobes and their chests of drawers and packed them ready to take.

Paul went straight off to sleep, as usual, but when I went in to check on Daisy, she was lying on her back, staring at the ceiling, with tears trickling down the sides of her cheeks and onto her pillow.

I sat down on the edge of her bed. 'What's the matter, sweetheart?'

She turned her head a little towards me. 'This is my home, and I don't want to leave it. You're my mum and Mike's my dad. I don't want to leave you.' She gulped. 'But what can I do?' She paused. 'Why do we have to go and live with strangers?'

'But your mother isn't a stranger,' I said. 'You just didn't remember her, but she remembers you.'

'That's not what I mean,' she sobbed.

'Yes, I know.' I sat and held her hand, stroking her hair as she gradually fell asleep. It did seem unfair to take children away from all they had ever known, to an unknown place with a person they felt they'd only just met, and a man they didn't know at all. They should have had the chance of a staged familiarisation process, like foster-children do now. I just hoped they wouldn't make a fuss the next morning, when it was time to go. But I couldn't blame them if they did.

Well, you should have seen Pamela's face when she saw all the things they wanted to take. I thought she was going to faint. She didn't introduce her husband, so we never even knew his name. He seemed a quiet soul – the type who might say or do anything to keep the peace. I wondered if he had any idea what he was taking on.

All of our kids had come out to say goodbye. Sheena and Ronnie had been with Daisy and Paul since the day they arrived, and they were devastated to be losing them so suddenly, and at Christmas too. All the others were almost as upset. Even Edie and Frank had come round to join the farewells.

'We're both so fond of them,' said Edie, with her hankie at the ready. 'We're going to miss them terribly.'

'I didn't know we were going to have an audience,' seethed Pamela, as she started to organise the packing of the car. 'What are we going to do with all this?' she asked, with a hint of panic in her voice. I don't know whether she thought they would come with nothing.

They didn't have a very big car, so they had to put the cases in, take them out again and put them in a different way round, squashing in the bin-bags of gifts and the cardboard boxes of toys and games. The children put their precious memory boxes and backpacks into the back seat for them to hold.

'Say goodbye,' said their mother. 'Quickly now.' She was obviously impatient to leave. Perhaps she hoped that if she hurried them, it would minimise the distress . . . but that didn't work at all. Quite the opposite.

Daisy and Paul came across to Mike and me, and we all hugged. Then suddenly, they panicked. They both clung on to us tightly.

'Come on,' said their mother with a shrill voice. 'We have to go.'

'No,' wailed Paul. 'I don't want to go. I want to stay here.'

'I don't want to go either,' said Daisy, the tears welling up again. Another few seconds and she was sobbing. 'I can't . . . I have to stay here . . . Mum and Dad . . . Father Christmas . . .'

'Oh, this is getting ridiculous,' snarled Pamela, cold as ice. 'We're your mum and dad now.' She looked straight at me. 'It's all your fault, Mrs Merry. You've put them up to this.'

She walked across and started trying to pull Paul away. I feared he was going to kick her; I'm sure he thought about it, but fortunately didn't do it. Then, when he adamantly refused to let go of me, she switched her attention to Daisy.

'Come on, love,' she said, with the conviction of an amoeba, but the intentions of a crafty fox, luring her prey. If I hadn't already taken a dim view of her, I would have done then. She was what my grandmother used to call 'a piece of work'.

'Look, Daisy,' I intervened. 'I know you don't want to leave, but your mother is waiting to take you to start your new life. You're going to be living with your real mother at last. Go with her, sweetheart. You and Paul will have each other for company.'

'But . . .' her bottom lip quivered as her eyes gazed into mine.

'Much as I would love to, we're not allowed to keep you here. So off you go, both of you. Your mother is your family now.' I hugged and kissed them both, one last, lingering time, as they took in what I had said.

Despite Daisy's misgivings, she put on a brave face and reluctantly agreed. 'Come on, Paul,' she said, with unexpected maturity. 'Let's do this together. We have to do it. Let's give it a go.'

'OK,' sniffed Paul. They crossed the gravel together, with tears still running down their faces, and climbed into the little car. As it pulled away, they looked back and waved out of the rear window. They were crying, most of our other kids standing with us were crying and so were we. It was horrendous.

I knew that would probably be the last time I would ever see either of them.

It didn't matter how many times I had said goodbye to foster children, it never became any easier. My own tears flowed as we waved them off, until they disappeared from our sight at the end of the road.

As I turned to go back into the house, I caught sight of Paul's bike, propped up against the hedge, next to where their car had been parked.

'Oh no . . .' I said.

'What?' asked Mike.

'Paul said he wouldn't go unless he could take his bike . . . and they've left it behind!'

31

Setting Fire to the Past

Every day I wondered how Daisy and Paul were getting on in their new home and all I could do was hope it was all going well for them.

One morning, seven years later, there was a knock at our front door. I opened it wide to find a tall young man in army uniform, standing on the doorstep. He took his cap off and I noticed the ginger hair. Did I know him? He looked familiar, but for some reason, I couldn't immediately place him. As our eyes met, he gave me a wide grin.

'Hello, Mum!'

For half a second, confusion; but then something clicked in my brain. Of course . . . I stepped forward and we had a great hug, right there on the doorstep.

'Hello, Pauly.'

'Can I come in?'

'Yes, of course. How wonderful to see you. Come and tell me where you've been, what you've been doing . . . everything.'

'I'm glad I've found you at last. I feel as if I've been looking for you ever since we left. Do you remember that day?'

'Remember it? I'll never forget it. We were all in tears for most of the day after you and Daisy had gone. We've missed you ever since. Come into the kitchen and I'll make us a mug of coffee.'

As we went through the house, he was looking around at everything, as if breathing it all in. 'It's great to be back here again. And virtually nothing has changed.'

'Well, it has had all new paint and a few other bits and pieces,' I pointed out with a laugh. 'But yes, most of it looks just the same.'

He looked out of the window, down the garden. 'You've still got the tyres! Do you remember that time when I got stuck inside one of them? I think that's my earliest memory.'

'Yes, we searched for you everywhere, until I saw that tyre moving about, as you struggled inside it.' I laughed. 'That was so funny!'

We sat down in the sitting room with our coffee mugs and biscuits.

'Are any of the kids still here?'

'No, they've all moved on now, apart from Mandy who has gone to live with her disabled father, but still comes to see us at weekends, and we often talk about the old days, when you and Daisy were part of the family. We laugh a lot about some of the escapades you got up to, Pauly!'

'Yes, I was a bit of a daredevil in those days, wasn't I?' He paused and seemed to almost choke up, then controlled it. 'Those were my happy, carefree years, those years I was with you and Mike. You were always kind and loving, no matter what. But you could be quite strict with me sometimes.'

'Well, you needed it!'

'Yes, but you were always fair with it. I can see that now.' He paused. 'And Mike was always the fun person – who took us on all those great outings and made sure we had all the sweets and things you wouldn't let us have at home!'

'Did he now?' I asked with a quizzical grin.

'You knew. I'm sure you knew all along,' he said with a smile.

'Well . . . maybe.'

Paul looked at some of the photos I had up on the notice board in our kitchen – photos of most of the foster children we'd had.

'There's Mandy,' he said, pointing at her photo. 'Do you remember when we lost her on holiday in Bournemouth, and Gilroy said she had fallen off the cliff?'

'Yes, he tried to convince me she had drowned. I almost believed him!' We laughed together. 'Well, that little girl is fifteen now, doing her GCSEs and almost certainly staying on till the sixth form.'

'She was always the clever one, wasn't she?'

'Yes, she wants to go to Cambridge University – I reckon she could do it too.'

'Daisy was quite good at things at school when we were with you, wasn't she?'

'Yes. She was always the studious type, and worked hard at everything.'

'It's a shame she didn't have the chance to continue.'

I was about to ask what he meant, but Paul swiftly changed the subject.

'What happened to that funny family?'

'Who do you mean?'

'Lulu I remember – she was the youngest. Then, just before we left, you took in her brother and sister. What were their names?'

'Duane and Sindy.'

'Where are they now?'

'Well, their parents were sent to prison for what they did to those children.'

Paul looked curious, but I didn't stop to let him ask.

'Their father is still in prison, but their mother came out last year, and she now has all her family back with her, in the house the council provided for the children to be looked after in. So she has a lot of support and supervision. It's all going quite well.'

I made us some coffee and we went to sit outside on the patio, next to the hole in the hedge. 'Edie and Frank are still next door,' I said. 'But Frank recently had a heart attack and Edie is becoming quite frail now.'

'I remember them too.' He paused. 'I've been looking for you for a long time, but I've moved around so much I didn't remember your address. I only knew the town and the park. So I thought, if I get here on the train and find the right park, maybe I'll remember the way home.'

'And did you?'

'Yes, well, I described the park to a porter on the platform and he told me which way to go, so that was the easy bit. But I stood there, hoping it would all come back to me, and it didn't. Well, not exactly. Then I just had a feeling that took me across the street and down a turning. I didn't know if it was the right road or not. I could see it was a long road, and I thought it looked right, so then the only clue I had was this picture I've held in my head of your green front door, with the black lion knocker and the black studs.'

'Oh Paul . . . it's seven years since you left – did you ever think that we might have repainted the door in another colour, or maybe replaced it, or even moved away altogether?' I laughed.

'No.' He laughed with me. 'I know it sounds daft, but I never thought about that. I suppose I so much wanted you to be still here, and everything the same, that I just assumed it would be. I kept looking at both sides as I walked along, just looking at the front doors . . . until I came to yours, and I knew.'

'I'm so glad you did, Pauly. It's great to see you, all grown up, tall, handsome and in uniform. I bet you have all the girls after you!'

'Well, not all of them.' He grinned. 'But I guess the uniform helps. I had to wear it today because I have to catch the train back to barracks in Wiltshire, to be posted abroad for a couple of years.'

'Oh no, where are you going?'

'Germany. I'll have to catch the one o'clock train. I'll be in a lot of trouble if I don't!'

'That soon? And you've only just found us, after all these years!'

'Is Mike here?'

'No, I'm afraid not. He'll be very disappointed to have missed you.'

'Tell him I miss our Sunday morning outings and the ice creams he was always buying us. Perhaps next time I come home, we can get together for a pint . . . and maybe an ice cream too?'

'Yes. I'm sure he'd love that. He often talks about the old days, when you and Daisy were here. How is Daisy? Is she still living with your mother? I bet she grew her hair as soon as she could!'

His face clouded over. 'I've heard she's OK, living in Reading I think. But I'm not really in contact with Daisy these days. We were separated you know, just a couple of weeks after we left you. And things went badly wrong for both of us.'

'No!' I was appalled. It sounded like my worst fears . . . 'What happened?'

'Well, it's a long story, moving about so much, but I'll tell you the main points and hopefully we can meet up again when I come home on leave and talk some more.'

'Yes, of course. So what happened after you left us?'

'Oh Mum, it was awful. Pamela – I'm not going to call her our mother. She could never be that to me . . .' He paused. 'Pamela and her husband drove us quite a long way to their house. I don't even remember where it was now. We had to be quiet all the way in the car and then we had to take our shoes off to go in. She told her husband to leave everything in the back of the car, so that's where it all stayed. She told us to leave our memory boxes and backpacks in the car too, and locked it so that we couldn't get at them.'

'What was it like in the house?'

'Awful. Oh, it was a nice enough house. But we couldn't do anything right. Everything was neat and tidy, and as clean as new. She told us not to touch anything and to sit still. Well, as you can probably remember, I never was any good at sitting still! So I was in trouble from the start.'

'Oh dear.'

'She gave us a little lecture about it being her house and we had to obey her rules. I can't remember any of them now, apart from silence unless she spoke to us.'

'Really?' I almost burst with the effort of containing my indignation.

'It wasn't so bad for Daisy, because she asked if she could just get a book out of the car to read, and Pamela agreed. Daisy brought in a colouring book and some crayons for me too, so I did that for a bit. But you know what I'm like . . .'

'Yes, I certainly do!' I laughed.

'Well, I was in deep trouble from about half an hour after we arrived. In trouble for fidgeting, for making noises, for creasing the cushion, for leaving a fingerprint on the coffee table, for eating my tiny sandwich too greedily, although we'd had nothing to eat for hours. You name it and I was in trouble for it.'

'I remember you were a real stoic, putting up with things and not complaining. But that must have been very hard for you.'

'Too hard,' he said, sadly. 'Much too hard . . . What time is it?' he asked suddenly.

'It's fine,' I said. 'It's half past ten, and it only takes about twelve minutes to walk to the station from here. Or I could even drive you down there.'

'Oh good. Well, that night, Pamela refused to get any of our things out of the car except our suitcases. So we could put on our clean pyjamas that you had ironed in the kitchen. I remember picking mine up and sniffing them. They smelt of home.'

'So you couldn't even have your Ted?'

'No. He had to stay in the car overnight, along with everything else. I don't know about Daisy, because we were in separate bedrooms, but it took me ages to get to sleep.

'The next morning it was Christmas Day, but nobody wished us Happy Christmas. We had to have one piece of toast each for breakfast with a glass of milk. No cereals and no seconds. After breakfast . . .' He stopped and seemed to gasp for breath. 'Oh, Mum, it was terrible.'

'Why? What happened?'

'She told her husband to put all our things from the car out in the yard at the side of their house. Then she made us go out and watch, while she put a metal dustbin in the middle, then started throwing all our belongings into it, one at a time. First went our new backpacks. Do you remember the one I made you buy for me?'

'Yes, I do,' I made a face. 'It was baby-blue plastic – the cheapest-looking one on the stall, and you insisted on having that one.'

'Yes,' He smiled ruefully. 'I remember you pointing out all these other, much better ones. But I was feeling obstinate that day. I don't know why I stuck to that one. I wouldn't have chosen it if I'd been staying on with you. But for some reason . . . it was like a voice inside me, telling me to choose a horrid, cheap backpack to take to Pamela's.' He paused again. 'Do you think there's something psychological in that?'

'Yes, it probably was. I always wondered about that!'

'Well, Pamela picked up my backpack by one corner, as if she was holding a dead rat's tail, then held it over the dustbin and let it drop to the bottom with a thump. Then she did the same to Daisy's backpack, which she loved. I remember poor Daisy's face. I knew what she was thinking, because I was thinking the same.'

'Didn't Pamela empty all your lovely things out first?'

'No, they all went into the bin. Then the sack with our Christmas presents in it, from you and Dad and Gramps – I think that was your father, wasn't it? All unopened.'

'Oh no!'

'Then she took our memory boxes that had all our photos and special things in them, and tossed them, one after the other, onto the top of the pile in the bin.'

'Couldn't you go back later and get out your most precious things?'

'No, because of what happened next.'

'What?' I dreaded what he was going to say, and I was right.

'She put a couple of firelighters in among our belongings and lit them with a match.'

'No!'

'That's what I shouted, again and again. "No! No!" I even tried to go and pull out my memory box, but it was too late. It was already on fire and the fierce blaze made it too hot for me to reach. So all we could do was to watch all our memories going up in flames. All our past happiness burnt to ashes.'

'And what was Pamela doing?'

'Smiling!' He spat out the word. 'She was enjoying our misery. It was like she wanted to get rid of our past, and everything that was important to us.'

There was a look of utter desperation on Paul's face as he sat silently remembering. I didn't want to interrupt, so I just reached across and put my hand on his.

'We were in floods of tears, Daisy and me,' he said. 'I lost everything that day. My Ted, my times-table book, my special pen, all my school reports, my photos of all of you, my everything. And it was the same for Daisy. I think one of the things she was most upset about was that French knitting snake that had taken her so long to do; just gone in a few seconds, eaten by the fire. We lost all our happiness that day, and we never got it back again . . . until maybe now. Now that I've found you. We can keep in touch now, can't we? Now that I'm grown up?'

'Of course. You won't stop me now! I'm thrilled that you found your way back here in the end. I can't wait to tell Mike. He'll be just as excited as I am that you came, and just as appalled about Pamela burning all your things.'

'I'll never forget that, as long as I live.'

I had an idea. 'Tell you what. Next time you come, when you're on leave, why don't we put together a new memory box for you?'

'Really? Can we? But how? Everything was burnt.'

'Well, it won't have all your treasures in it of course, but I can get copies made of the photos of outings we went on and all that. And I'll have a look around and see what else I can find to put in.'

'That would be brilliant,' he said, his face lighting up at the thought.

I looked at my watch. 'You've got half an hour before you need to go to the station. Would you like me to rustle you up a sandwich?'

'Yes please. Have you got any—'

'Bacon?' I interrupted.

He laughed. 'Yes please. A Trisha Merry bacon sandwich – Yum!'

'Yes, I remember. They were always your favourite.'

I made the sandwiches and a mug each of tea. 'Shall we go and sit in the garden to eat these?' I suggested.

He nodded, already taking a bite out of his first half. 'I used to love this garden,' he said, with a wistful smile. Then suddenly he thought of something. 'Have you still got my bike? The one she made me leave behind?'

'Yes, I think we might have, tucked away at the back of the garage. We kept if for you, just in case you ever came back for it.'

'Well, I'm here now! But it will probably be too small for me . . .'

'Definitely!' We laughed. 'I'll keep it till next time you come.'

'Thanks.'

'So, what happened after your things were burnt?' I asked as we sipped our tea.

'Well, Christmas came and went, without our presents from you of course. No tree, no party lunch, no carols or charades – no fun.'

'Didn't Pamela give you a present?'

'Just one book each. Daisy's was too young for her, and she had read it about two years before. Mine was a picture book for five-year-olds.' He shrugged. 'And nothing from Father Christmas.

'Oh no! I gave him your letters when he came.'

'Thanks. Maybe she wouldn't let him in!' We laughed again.

'So what happened after Christmas?'

'It was very boring, and I got told off every time I moved or made a noise. I remember we started at a new school, but she must have been talking with Social Services, because there was a social worker at the house when we got home on the first day.'

'To meet you?'

'No, to take me away. I didn't even have time to say goodbye to Daisy or take anything with me. He just whisked me into his car and took me straight to a children's home. He said my mother couldn't handle me any longer, so I would stay there.' He paused, his whole body caved in on himself. 'It was awful,' he said in a low voice. 'How could she do that to me? She didn't even get to know me – just rejected and abandoned me again on the first day she could.'

'Did you tell the social worker about having lived with us for ten years?'

'Yes, but he said it was a different area and he couldn't transfer me back to you. Anyway, he said, if I was too difficult for my own mother to handle, at eleven years old, a home was the only place that would take me.' Paul tried to choke back the tears. 'He didn't even try to understand.'

'Come on, Pauly,' I said. 'Time for a big hug before you go and catch your train.' We stood there, in the garden of his childhood, making up for lost years with a long, loving hug.

'Sorry I have to go,' said Paul, drawing away at last. 'But I don't want to be court-martialled!' He smiled. 'No, don't worry. That wouldn't really happen, but I don't want to get in any trouble.'

We quickly exchanged contact details and went out through the hall, where I looked at the clock and realised there wasn't much time left.

'Let me drive you,' I urged him.

'No thanks. It'll be all right. Remember, I'm a fast runner.'

'Yes, I do remember. But you've only got six minutes.'

'I'll make it easily. I've got my ticket. Byeee.' And he was gone, sprinting up the length of our road.

As I watched him disappear from sight, I went back inside and pushed the front door shut behind me. Mulling over the awful revelations of what happened after he was taken from us, I realised there must have been so much more that he didn't tell me. And it was all caused by a meddling, 'do-gooding' rookie social worker.

32

A New Memory Box

Over the next couple of years, while he was in Germany, Paul and I wrote to each other fairly regularly – one flimsy page of airmail letter at a time. And we rang each other when we could. Mostly, we couldn't talk for long, but once, when he was home on leave, he rang me from a private phone.

'Hello, Mum!' He always started the conversation that way, since he'd arrived on my doorstep that day. It was a running joke with us now. 'How's things?'

'Not bad,' I said. 'We're all fine. What about you? What have you been doing? And where are you phoning from?'

'Chester' he said. 'I've got a new girlfriend. She's gorgeous.'

'Oh yes?' I laughed.

'Yes, and she's funny, kind, everything that's good. I know you would love her, Mum.'

'You've fallen on your feet, then? Or has she knocked you off your feet?' I teased him. He had always been easy to tease, and usually enjoyed it.

'Yes to both,' he agreed. 'She lives in Chester, with her family. That's why I'm here.'

We carried on chatting. He told me about his latest escapades on his army base in Germany, and the exercises they'd been on. Then I told him what had happened to a few of the other foster children he remembered from his time with us.

'I'm sure you'll remember Ronnie?'

'Of course. He was my mate.'

'Well he did surprisingly well at school and went on to join the police.'

'What about Gilroy?'

'He absconded from the psychiatric unit and went off the rails I'm afraid, to a life of crime. I've often seen his name in the local papers, for a string of minor convictions, but he's now in prison, serving quite a long sentence I believe, so he won't be out for years.'

'Anyone else?'

'We lost touch with Sheena, I'm afraid, although I did meet someone who knew her father. Sheena went to her mother, but they moved away suddenly, so her father is desperate to find her. I hope he does, because I have some photos I'd like to pass on to her.' I paused. 'I've not been in touch with AJ. He left when he was sixteen and disappeared from the area. Do you remember Kevin, who loved aeroplanes?'

'Yes, he was always looking at aeroplane magazines with Dad.'

'That's right. Well, when he was meant to leave us at sixteen, Dad got him an apprenticeship at a factory, making parts for military planes. He stayed on for another year with us. He never liked change or new people much. But he always got along OK with Luke.'

'The boy in the porch?'

'Yes. Well, Luke did so well with his reading and writing, and he did such talented drawings, that he got a place at the art-college in Birmingham. When he left there, he got a job designing the graphics for those new electronic, hand-held games.'

'Wow. I bet that was his dream job?'

'He loves it, and Kevin has moved in with him. It's great for them both.'

'Sounds it.' He paused and changed track. 'Do you know what I wish?'

'No, what?'

'I wish you could have adopted us. Our lives could have been so different, so happy.'

'I don't think I ever told you this, but we did try to adopt you. We started the adoption process, but our local authority were against multiple adoptions when you were little, so they wouldn't let us adopt you both, and we couldn't choose one of you above the other. That wouldn't have been fair. And anyway, your dad might not have agreed.'

'No, he didn't even agree to let Daisy go into hospital that time when she was ill. We had a miserable life with him.'

'Really?' I felt so sorry things hadn't worked out for them.

'I've got a lot more I can tell you when we meet,' he said.

'OK.' Then I suddenly thought. 'Are you in a phone box?' I was aware that we'd been talking for quite a while.

'No, it's all right. My girlfriend's parents invited me to come and stay when I came back on leave and they said I could call you. They're lovely people – very kind. Will you be in tomorrow? I've got a free day. I could get a train down to Birmingham and then on to visit you. Would that be OK?'

'Yes, of course,' I agreed. 'I'd love to see you. We could start on that new memory box for you if you like. I've found some things to put in it.'

'Yes please. That would be cool. I'll try and be with you by about midday, or possibly sooner. I'll look up the trains and let you know.'

The following day, I drove to Ashbridge station and picked him up from his train, then back to our house.

I made us some coffee and we caught up on news.

'So, tell me about your girlfriend.'

'She's a lovely girl, Mum – very pretty, and intelligent too. I'm sure you would like her. I'd like you to meet her one of these days. But she had to work today. And anyway, I wanted to tell you about her first. Maybe I could bring her next time I come?'

'I'll look forward to meeting her,' I said, with a smile.

Gradually, the conversation turned back to when Paul and Daisy left us. 'I've been wondering what happened to you after Pamela sent you to that children's home,' I said. 'What was it like? Did you settle there all right?'

'No. It was awful, but I wasn't there for long.'

'Why? What happened?'

'Well, I'm not quite sure how it happened, but Dad – Rocky – do you remember him?'

'Yes, of course.'

'Well, I hadn't seen him for years, I don't think, but then he turned up at the home, out of the blue, really angry.'

'With you?'

'No, not at all. Well, not then anyway. I assumed he was angry with Pamela.'

'Right?'

'Well, apparently, Rocky had been told we'd been moved to Pamela's, so he rung her. He was furious that she'd already sent me away, after just two weeks. So he guessed which school Daisy went to, drove there as the kids came out and picked her up.'

'So he abducted her from the school?'

'Kidnapped her, yes.'

I suddenly recalled that awful day when a man phoned me to say Daisy had been abducted from school when she was about five. What a trauma that was.

'Next, Rocky turned up outside the children's home with Daisy. Boy, was I glad to see them! I had been worried about her, coping on her own at Pamela's. Rocky asked them at the home if he could take me out, so off we went . . . and I never went back, thank goodness.'

'So where did he take you?'

'To our grandma's. Apparently, she looked after us for a couple of months when we were babies, but neither of us remembered, and we hadn't seen her since. She was quite old, but seemed pleased to see us. That was a change for the better. We stayed there, in hiding. We didn't go to school for about four or five months. Rocky turned up every now and then, and his sister came to stay there to help Grandma, so it was quite good for a while. We even saw that boy, Carl, but he just ignored us.'

'So what did you do at your grandma's, if you didn't go to school?'

'We watched television a lot. And there were some fields and a bit of woodland behind her house, so we ran wild there, well I did anyway, while Daisy sat under a tree and read, or drew something.'

'Typical!'

'Anyway, the police got involved and Social Services tracked us down in the end, so we both had to go to new children's homes. None of them had more than one space, so we were separated again. And a few months later I was moved to a new one, so Daisy didn't know where I was, and I lost her address in my move.'

'So neither of you went back to Pamela?'

'No. She didn't want us.'

'And where was Rocky during all this time?'

'Oh, moving about I think. You know what he was like. He still is as far as I know, but we fell out about three years ago, after he took me away from my third children's home and down to Canvey Island in Essex for a bit, sharing a room with him above a pub. Then we collected Daisy from her children's home and went on to a tiny flat in Clacton.

That's when we really got on each other's nerves and he started knocking me about. He got really violent. Well, I wasn't going to stick around for any more of that, so I went and joined the army cadets and slept rough until I could join the proper army.'

'What about Daisy?'

'I don't know, but I had my suspicions. I could see the signs.'

'What do you mean?'

'I think she stayed on with Dad for a bit, but I'm pretty sure he abused her a lot.'

'Sexually?'

'Yes. She was very unhappy and depressed. She stopped eating, and I think she started self-harming too, just before I left. I lost contact with her after that.'

'Oh dear, you have had a hard time of it, the two of you. What an awful shame you were taken away from us.'

'Yes, I've often thought that about you, and about what our lives would have been like if we could have stayed on with you and Dad.'

'Well, it's all in the past now. But maybe we can make things better in the future? Let's start by having something to eat. How about . . .'

'Bacon sandwiches? Yes, please.'

After lunch I brought down all the things I'd been collecting and a new box to put them in. 'Let's do you a new memory box, Pauly.'

'OK. Do you know, you're the only person who has ever called me that. I've missed it.'

We sat down at the kitchen table and started looking through all the photos I'd found.

He pointed at a boy in a group photo. 'Who was that little boy with the elephant?' He asked. 'You know, the one we took to the zoo to see the real elephants. Didn't he run away or something?'

'Yes, that was Alfie. He wasn't expecting real elephants to be so big. Mike had to run off and find him. That was a funny day.'

'Most days were funny days, as far as I can remember,' said Paul with a wide grin.'

'Yes, you're probably right!'

Then I went to get a couple of things I had seen in town and bought especially to go in Paul's new memory box.

'Here's a present for you,' I said, giving him a bulging paper bag.

'What is it?' He looked intrigued.

'When I saw it I had to buy it for you. Go on, open it. I want to see what you think.' Slowly, Paul opened the bag and peeked inside. 'Oh,' he said, laughing, and pulled out a little teddy that looked very like his original Ted, only a bit smaller and a lot softer.

'Thank you, Mum.' He got up and came round to give me a hug. 'How did you find him? He's just like my Ted.'

'That's why I bought him.'

'That's brilliant.'

'I'm glad you like him.' Then I handed him the other present I'd bought for his memory box.

He slid in his hand and pulled out what was inside, then burst into laughter. ‘A times-tables book!’ he said.

‘To replace the one you made . . . that got burnt.’

’Yes! Thank you.’ He gave me a big bear-hug, then slipped the tables book into his box. ‘I still can’t remember all my tables!’ He grinned.

He chose some photos and we spent a happy afternoon, sharing memories, punctuated by laughter, until it was almost time for him to catch his train.

I got him a black carrier-bag, which looked quite macho, to put it all in. And he put his jacket on for the journey home.

‘There’s just one more thing I want you to see before you go,’ I said, opening the back door. ‘It will only take a minute. When you said you were coming today, I scrabbled about and found it to show you.’

Paul looked puzzled as we went out across the yard, then his face lit up when he saw it standing against the garage wall.

‘My bike!’

‘Yes, we kept it for you all these years.’

‘Thank you, Mum. That’s amazing. A shame it’s miles too small for me now, but wonderful to see you kept it and polished it up specially for me. I was so proud of that bike.’

Another hug and off we went to the station.

As I waved him off towards the platform, I wondered when I would see him again.

33

Finders Keepers?

After Paul left that day, I didn't see him for a long time, because he was moving around with the army. Then I had a brief phone call from him to tell me his baby boy had been born, he'd got married and he'd left the army. A few months later, he sent me a photo of his little boy and his wife.

Soon after that, we moved house, took on four more siblings to foster and I started up my fostering agency, so I was always busy. But I couldn't get him out of my mind. The only clue I had to where he might be living was that his wife came from Chester. But how could I track him down in a city like that? And where would I begin to look for him if he was anywhere else? I didn't even know whether his wife was the girlfriend he had told me about, or someone new.

'Why don't you get a private detective to search for him?' suggested Mike one evening.

So that's what I did. I gave this detective the only clues I had, which were Chester, Paul's name and details, a copy of the photo of his wife and son, the fact that he'd left the army, and I had an idea that he was working at a large factory somewhere in the Chester area, but I could have been wrong about that.

This private detective worked away at tracking down Paul for three whole weeks, without any leads at all. The only phone number I had for him had been disconnected, and he'd never given me his Chester address, so it was a complete dead end. Why couldn't we find him? Where had he gone?

It was very frustrating, but I had to give in for now.

Many years later, I was talking to my grown-up granddaughter Laura about some of the children I'd fostered, and I mentioned Daisy and Paul.

'Paul came to find me when he was eighteen and we kept in contact for a few years. He married and had a little boy, or the other way around. They moved and then we moved too and sadly we just lost touch. It was such a shame.'

'We could try to find him,' suggested Laura.

'I did try to find him. I even hired a private detective, but he couldn't track him down either.'

'Let's see if he's on Facebook,' she said, opening up her laptop on the kitchen table. 'What's his name?'

So I gave her his full name and she typed it in.

'Where do you think he might be living?'

'I don't know, but it could be Chester.'

She typed that in and scrutinised her screen. 'No, that's not come up.'

'Oh. I thought that, with such an unusual surname, he might be easy to find.'

'Well, it's drawn a blank for that name anywhere in the UK. Do you think he could be living abroad?'

'I don't know.'

She typed in variations of just initials or the full three names. 'Still nothing,' she said. 'I've tried it every way I can think of.'

'Oh well, let's leave it then. I can't think of any other clues.'

But later on that evening, I suddenly remembered the photo he'd sent me. I went straight up to my files and found it. I turned it over to see if anything was written on the back . . . and that's when my luck changed. I found his wife's name, Annalise. So I went to bed that night with her name on my mind: *Annalise* . . .

The following morning, when Laura was having her breakfast, I told her about the photo. 'And when I turned it over, the name Annalise stood out. That must be the name of his wife.'

'Well done, Nan,' said Laura. 'Let's give that a try. I'll just log in.' She reached her laptop down from the dresser and pressed the on switch. In only just over a minute we'd found the only Annalise with that surname on Facebook.

'But what if Paul's Annalise isn't on Facebook?' I asked. 'Like he obviously isn't?'

'Well,' said Laura. 'There's only one way to find out.'

'How?'

'You could send a message to this Annalise that's come up with the right surname.'

So that's what I did. I wrote:

I am trying to trace someone called Paul who has the same surname as you, and I wondered whether this Paul could be a relative of yours? If so, could you possibly send me his contact details, please, if he gives you his permission?

Then I went off to put on some washing, and Laura started to get on with the assignment she was doing for college.

Suddenly, Laura called me, and it sounded serious.

'What is it?' I rushed back to the kitchen.

'You've got a message, Nan,' she said, excitedly.

I sat down with her to read the message. But it wasn't really a reply, which was disappointing:

What do you want to know for?

'Oh,' I said. 'I've got to be careful here. Even if it is the right Paul, this could be his ex-wife, his daughter . . . it could be anybody.'

So I wrote:

Paul played a big part in my life at one time, and I just wanted to know if he is happy, and how his life has turned out.

We checked it every hour or so, but no answer came back.

Then Laura said: 'That's odd.'

I went back to sit next to her at the table. Another message had come through:

Do you have a contact number?

'Think hard about that one, Nan,' she said, going off to the cupboard to fetch the lead for her laptop, as the battery was getting low. By the time she came back I'd answered.

'Oh Nan!' said Laura. 'You didn't give her your personal phone number did you?'

As soon as I heard her tone of voice, like an adult telling off a silly child, I knew I mustn't have had my proper head on, to do a daft thing like that.

'Yes, I did,' I owned up.

'You shouldn't have done that, Nan,' she continued. 'Now you've got no way of blocking them. You won't even know who it is.'

Five minutes later, the phone went.

Without thinking, I picked it up . . . and was immediately glad I did.

'Hello, Mum. It's Paul. This is a strange coincidence. I've been looking for you, but I couldn't find anyone called Patricia Merry!'

'Didn't you think to look for me as Trisha?'

'I did, but I couldn't find you. '

Then I realised. 'How did you spell Trisha?'

'T-R-I-C-I-A, as in Patricia.'

'Ah, that's why. I spell it as T-R-I-S-H-A.'

'Well, no wonder I couldn't find you. To be honest, I just stopped looking, because I thought you were too old to be on Facebook!' He laughed, so I knew he was teasing, and I laughed with him.

'Well, I am now,' I said. 'Because my granddaughter got me going. She's the one who suggested we try to find you on Facebook, but we couldn't, so then we tried looking for Annalise. Do you have your own page?'

'No, Annie's the one who uses the computer most, her and the kids, so I leave it all to them. I'd rather be out running, or helping a mate with his building work, or tinkering with my motorbike in the garage.'

'So you haven't changed! You always were the action man.'

'That's me!' He paused and I could hear a voice in the background. 'I've got to go,' he said. 'But I'd love to bring the family up to see you. Would that be all right? I'll phone to arrange it nearer the time.'

About a month later, Paul called to suggest a date.

'That'll be perfect,' I said. 'We have so much to catch up on. Are you bringing Annalise and the children?' I had a feeling that he had more than one.

'Yes, a boy and two girls, all teenagers now, so they don't always want to go places with us; but they've heard me talk so much about you that they think of you and Dad as family too, so they all want to come that day. I reckon they're curious to meet you, to see if you really do have haloes floating above your heads!'

'Are you sure you rang the right number?' I said, laughing happily. 'Only fallen angels at this address.'

The morning they were coming, we were so, so nervous. Neither of us could understand why, because we were really looking forward to seeing them. It was a strange feeling, being happy and apprehensive at the same time.

My phone pinged, so I picked it up. 'Paul's just texted,' I called to Mike out of the kitchen window as he got some garden chairs out of the shed. 'They've just come off the motorway.'

'Oh good.' He looked at his watch. 'They won't be long now.'

Only fifteen minutes later, I heard the noise of Paul's car bumping and crunching up the long drive we shared with the farm.

'They're here,' I called out to Mike.

As I went out to welcome them, Paul came to a halt and the second he'd put the handbrake on he threw open his door, leapt out and ran towards me, then flung his arms around me in a great bear-hug that almost stifled me.

'Hello, Mum!' He drew back to look at me.

'You haven't changed at all, have you?' I laughed. His wife and children, left to their own devices, got out of their car and came over to join us.

'Hello, I'm Annalise,' said his pretty wife, with a beaming smile. 'I'm so glad to meet you at last. I've heard so much about you.'

'Don't believe all you hear!' I said.

Paul was right. She was a lovely girl, and the children were typical gangly teenagers, determined not to smile . . . but they couldn't help themselves in the end, as our rescue dogs rushed out to get in on the act.

We had a brilliant day with them all, reminiscing with Paul and making his wife and children laugh at some of his antics. And as I talked so easily with Annalise, I remembered back to when Paul had just met her and told me then how lovely she was. His judgement was spot on.

They stayed for hours, but the day seemed to pass in a flash and it was nearly time for them to go.

'I know you lost touch with Daisy a few years back,' I said to Paul. 'But have you made any efforts to find her since then?'

'Not really.' He shrugged his shoulders. 'I wouldn't know where to start.'

'I tried once, at the same time as I tried to find you,' I told him. 'But no luck. I guess she might have married and changed her name . . .'

'I don't know,' said Paul. 'I've not heard from her in years.' I saw the sadness in his eyes. But outwardly he hid it well. 'I honestly don't know what happened, or why she stopped all contact.'

'Please let me know if you do hear from her again one day.'

'Yes, of course I will.'

Annalise came to join us. 'I'm sorry to break up the conversation,' she apologised. 'But we really do have to go. We have two dogs and a cat at home, waiting to be fed.' She looked at Paul and he nodded. 'We've had a lovely day. Thank you so much for having us all. It was very kind of you.'

'It's been great getting to know you and we've enjoyed catching up with Paul's news.' I smiled.

'Come again soon, Paul,' added Mike. 'And we'll go for that pint.'

'What about the Sunday after next?' suggested Paul, looking at his wife to make sure. She nodded and turned to me. 'Can we come again then?'

'Yes, of course. That'll be lovely.'

And that's what they did, every other week for the next two years.

We're still waiting and hoping that one day we'll find Daisy. I'd like to be able to give her some photos and tell her how much I have missed her. I think Paul would love to be back in touch with her too. Then this family will be complete.

Acknowledgements

To my family who have followed my journey through this book, thank you for your endless patience and belief. You have travelled with me through laughter, tears, tantrums and giggles, for which I am eternally grateful.

To Jacquie, thank you for your empathy, humour, patience and friendship. I could not have done this without your belief in me. I have gained not only a new vocation; I have gained a friend for life.

To Clare Hulton, thank you for helping me achieve my second dream.

To Simon & Schuster, thank you for allowing me to share my story.

To all foster carers and adopters, never give up.

To all children in the care system, follow your dreams.